MW00575883

"A beautifully written, informative, sensitive, and powerful book on the hugely important, widespread, and complex area of trauma, adversity, and resilience. Not to be missed."

DR. KAREN TREISMAN
Clinical Psychologist, Trainer, and Author of several books including *A Therapeutic Treasure Box for Developmental Trauma.*

"Reading *Eyes are Never Quiet* is like eating dessert first! Those of us working in the ever-changing world of education can identify the gaps, but until now, have had few resources for implementing sustainable and systemic change. Lori Desautels, Ph.D., and Michael McKnight, co-authors of *Eyes are Never Quiet,* are **Neuro-Educational Thought Leaders,** providing a framework of actionable, evidence-based interventions for our most complicated students. Imagine a world where students and staff spend their school hours creating and deepening relationships and attachments to make space for learning to thrive. Dr. Lori and Michael share this brain-aligned, trauma-responsive framework promoting student-centered connections through intentional relationship building. This framework, focusing on the premise that 'brains in pain can't learn,' transforms a school community into one that is physically, emotionally, and psychologically safe."

ROBIN COGAN, MED, RN, NCSN
Nationally Certified School Nurse, Faculty, Rutgers-Camden School Nurse Certificate Program, Johnson & Johnson School Health Fellow

"Many children who live with complex trauma express their need for support and connection in ways that have the opposite effect. Working with emotionally challenged young people necessitates a dogged commitment to see beyond the surface behavior to the events that underlie it. In *Eyes Are Never Quiet*, Desautels and McKnight unravel the dynamics underlying defensive behavior and offer ways of helping young people understand how their brains react to stress and how to build resilience. The book also, and very importantly, highlights the importance of the role of the professional or caregiver who sits beside the child through good times and bad. The authors remind us of the power of relationship. We highly recommend *Eyes Are Never Quiet* to anyone who wants to make a difference in the lives of challenging young people."

FRANK A. FECSER, PH.D., MARY ELLEN W. FECSER, M.ED.

"Brain research and educational meta-analysis have brought important insight to our instructional practice. We are learning how stress and early negative childhood events can become obstacles to learning and often exacerbate undesirable classroom behaviors despite even the best efforts of the most effective teachers. With more and more students arriving at school each day suffering from the influences of childhood trauma, unready to learn but seemingly quite eager to misbehave, it takes both stamina and courage to teach in today's schools. However, the authors of this book provide hope to those teachers and administrators who sometimes are left feeling abandoned. They do so by sharing stories that highlight the research on resilience and neuroplasticity, evidencing that much can be done to help our students face and address these obstacles.

In *Eyes Are Never Quiet*, Desautels and McKnight share stories that revisit the impact that adverse childhood experiences have on cognition, but more importantly, they share stories that validate the promise of forging connections with every student, the value of learning more about resiliency and brain development, and the significance of helping every student deal with adversity, so that learning can actually occur. This book is a must read for anyone interested in educating **all** students, especially those who are the most reluctant to learn, the most unwilling to engage, and the most eager to act out. The ideas and the strategies provided in this book will prove to be invaluable!"

DR. JUDITH DESTEFANO-ANEN
Interim Executive County Superintendent, Cape May County, NJ

"In *Eyes Are Never Quiet* Desautels and McKnight help educators and parents see the intersection of Neuroscience, Pedagogy, and Psychology for the benefit of children who are suffering from exposure to trauma and 'toxic stress.' Their neuroeducational perspective will quickly become the seminal guide for educators seeking to move away from punitive reactions to what we know is pain-based behavior in children toward positive brain-aligned educational practices. These practices level the playing field for children affected by adverse childhood experiences so that they can achieve socially, emotionally, and academically."

JEFFERY G. WELLINGTON, M.A., NCSP, ED.S.
MARYLYNN STECHER, M.ED. LD/TC
Hamilton Township Public Schools, Mays Landing, NJ

"There is no better place to address the social and emotional well-being of our children and youth than our schools and this book so articulately and passionately outlines the science as to not only why but how. When we know better, we do better, and this book provides us with all we need to know to improve the social, emotional, and academic outcomes of not only our most vulnerable children, but all of our children and therefore, ultimately, our communities. This book, at its core, is nothing short of a call to action for every single one of us."

CHRISTY GAUSS, M.S.W.
School Mental Health Facilitator I, Indiana School Mental Health Initiative, Indiana Institute on Disability and Community at Indiana Univ.

"This book is truly a gift and essential reading for educators who work with children who experience trauma and diversity. For decades, I have been privileged to work with young children who have come to our school in great pain and experiencing ongoing toxic stress. Intuitively we, as educators, have understood that the child's behavior could not be labeled as 'bad, non-compliant, stubborn, mean or unkind.' We knew that something had happened to this child and believed in approaching the child with love and support.

The absolute 'miracle' of this book and the work of Dr. Desautels and Michael McKnight, is that we now have the research and the words to understand and express the truth behind the pain. In addition, we now have a clear understanding of how to help our children self-regulate, make connections, and ultimately learn. Our school culture has changed and we have witnessed the powerful resilience of our strong, competent and capable young children. I am so grateful!"

CONNIE SHERMAN
Executive Director, St. Mary's Child Center

"*Eyes are Never Quiet* goes right to the heart of the vital issues for the future of education. It is a compassionate and intelligent analysis of the intersection of neuroscience, pedagogy, and psychology that can serve as a guide for best practices in the classroom and beyond."

LOUIS COZOLINO, PH.D.
Author, *The Social Neuroscience of Education*

"*Eyes Are Never Quiet* paints a vivid portrayal of the effects of adverse childhood experiences and the effect on student learning through narrative depictions of real lift situations. Most, not all, educators have experienced positive, stable family engagement from a young age. Therefore, we need to better understand that those students who have not experienced the same family privilege may not be prepared to learn until we intervene and provide them with the love, support and resources so desperately needed to survive. We must develop the appropriate mindset to respond to youth who have experienced toxic trauma. Desautels and McKnight help educators understand the neuroscience that impedes brain development caused from severe stress. The good news is that the authors also help us recognize how we can help students by teaching them about their own neuroanatomy and how to self-regulate! This book is a must read for all educators and administrators. It will forever change how we think about student behaviors and discipline!"

DR. COLLEEN MORAN
Superintendent, North Montgomery Com School Corporation

"Knowledge of child development and brain development can unlock so much, especially when working with children dealing with trauma and adversity on a daily basis. True student learning cannot fully happen without quality relationships. In times of adversity, the very students who need these quality relationships appear to be pushing them away. This book helps us see past their hurt to gain an understanding of what they truly need; the strategies and resources provided here are invaluable. Thank you so much for providing these insights and strategies, backed by research that will change lives!"

DIANE PIKE
St. Mary's Child Center, Director of Outreach and Professional Dev.

"*Eyes Are Never Quiet* is a beautiful book that engages all of us in the latest research in trauma. As educators, we love our students and are constantly trying to understand them. The CDC's original study on ACEs was completed in 1995-1997. Enter Dr. Lori Desautels and Dr. Michael McKnight with a 21st century approach to the crises we see with today's children. They are practitioners who demonstrate in this book that educational neuroscience embraces attachment, engagement, and a deepened understanding of brain development as it relates to the teaching and learning process. People change people, not programs! They pave the way for educators to employ strategies to help our children thrive.

As educators, we are motivated and enthused because of this emerging research that aligns with engaging and connecting to students. We are excited to see how students respond with brain-aligned strategies that energize and rejuvenate learning. We are excited because students are responding in positive ways to the new understanding of how attachment and brain development are opening doors to academic achievement and positive emotion. There are many social and emotional mindfulness programs that are clearly enhancing social and emotional student well-being, but the core of all these programs is grounded in the brain science beneath them. It is time for the 21st century brains who walk through classroom doors with an exorbitant amount of emotional, social, and cognitive adversity to have teachers who are equipped. High achievement, academic success, and closing those learning gaps occur when we 'prime' the brain for regulation, connection, and purpose because many of our youth are coming from environments where emotional connection with a significant other and a sense of purpose have been lost, denied, or buried. *Eyes Are Never Quiet* is brilliant in opening the eyes to all who want to help children overcome trauma and have hope for a better tomorrow."

PEGGY BUFFINGTON, PH.D.
Superintendent, School City of Hobart, Indiana

"This book is a must read for anyone who works with children in today's world. Change is coming to all systems that address the needs of families and children; this book is extremely useful for anyone who wants to be a part of shaping the culture of education and social services for the future.

Too many of our young have been affected by the epidemic of drug addiction. Families are being destroyed by loss and heartbreak and in its wake this epidemic is leaving behind children without parents to lead them and causing toxic levels of stress and fear in our children and youth. Childhood trauma is our next epidemic.

We need to arm ourselves with the tools of resiliency to help our children grow beyond their trauma. This book provides beautifully written examples that highlight the complexity of the issues facing our youth. This book is an amazing tool for anyone who wants to live or work in a community that raises healthy and resilient children."

KATIE FALDETTA
Executive Director, Cape Assist, Wildwood, New Jersey,
www.capeassist.org

EYES ARE
NEVER QUIET

EYES ARE NEVER QUIET

Listening Beneath the Behaviors of
Our Most Troubled Students

Lori L. Desautels, Ph.D.
Michael McKnight, M.A.

Wyatt-MacKenzie Publishing
DEADWOOD, OREGON

NOTICE

There are many links contained within the book and resources, therefore we've made this a Kindle Matchbook — if you purchase the print edition at Amazon, you can download the Kindle edition for free and the links will be clickable!

Eyes Are Never Quiet
Listening Beneath the Behaviors of Our Most Troubled Students

Lori L. Desautels, Ph.D., Michael McKnight, M.A.

ISBN: 978-1-948-018-41-8
Library of Congress Control Number: 2018961503

©2019 Lori L. Desautels, Ph.D., Michael McKnight, M.A.

No part of this book may be reproduced in any manner whatsoever without written permission except in the case of brief quotations embodied in critical articles and reviews. Publisher and editor are not liable for any typographical errors, content mistakes, inaccuracies, or omissions related to the information in this book. Product trade names or trademarks mentioned throughout this publication remain property of their respective owners.

Wyatt-MacKenzie Publishing
DEADWOOD, OREGON

TABLE OF CONTENTS

RESOURCE SECTIONS

A PREFACE

From Cathy Pratt, Ph.D., BCBA-D
Director, Indiana Resource Center for Autism, Indiana School Mental Health Initiative, Indiana University

So, first of all, confessions. I have spent my entire career as a public educator and/or in supporting public educators. I am also a behaviorist who has been trained in the science of conducting functional behavioral assessments, and in designing behavior support plans that look at manipulating antecedents and consequences with precision and fidelity. I am invited into classrooms to look at student's behaviors. Often, there is the expectation that I will have a strategy or trick that will resolve the behavior problem quickly. This approach is difficult/impossible on many levels. First, it gives the impression that all behavior rests "inside the child" and does not consider the role of context. It perpetuates false belief that there is a group of children who are just inherently "bad." Second, it does not look at the entire child and their life in and outside of school. Finally, it does not consider what we, as educators, bring to the table (e.g., our own trauma, experiences, biases).

As this approach become less effective and as behaviors have become increasingly more challenging, conversation has turned to either "tightening the reigns" (e.g., zero tolerance, increased suspensions, longer expulsions) or to building in a stronger and systematic reinforcement system (e.g., tokens, etc.). Unfortunately, neither of these approaches acknowledges the shifting reality of our students. More students are living in poverty, experience violence in their lives, do not have a stable home life and are impacted by many other factors that lead to these children living in chronic stress. The result is that they come to school with brains that are not prepared to learn, and are unable to develop meaningful and positive relationships.

Thanks to the work of Lori Desautels and Michael McKnight, a revolution is moving across Indiana and elsewhere. This revolution requires a paradigm shift away from traditional disciplinary approaches to acknowledging the impact of stress on behavior. It dictates that we look at the whole child and their entire life, rather than making superficial judgements about behavior based on what we see in the classroom. It requires us to dig deeper into a child's world and recognize that for some of our students, school is the safest and most positive place in their lives. It requires us to move beyond academic learning only and to acknowledge the importance of social/emotional learning. It requires us to understand the impact of chronic and complex stress and the role of neuroplasticity.

We are at a crisis in American schools. Drugs use, bullying, suicide or suicide ideation, anxiety, and other factors signal the diminishing state of our schools. All this makes learning and teaching more difficult. The good news is that change is possible. This book provides recommendations for changing our approach and for creating the type of schools that match the needs of students today. Our students deserve and need a calm and safe environment in which to learn. They deserve our very best.

Lori and Michael ... thank you for leading the way.

FOREWORD ~ PART ONE

Written by Dr. Ena Shelly
Dean of the College of Education, Butler University

*"All you have to do is look into somebody's eyes and you see
their soul. And you see their history."*

KAREN BELL

This incredible text created by Lori and Michael gives
the reader the ability to hear children through the communication of what is seen in the child's eyes. It also gives the
readers the opportunity to look into our own eyes to examine our history, beliefs, and assumptions about behaviors we
see in children. In the 1970s I had the opportunity to hear Dr.
Marian Wright Edelman, founder of the Children's Defense
Fund, speak at a national conference. She had an image of a
beautiful young child with very sad eyes on the screen with
the words: "Look into my eyes and tell me it is ok to grow up
poor." That image and those words have been with me my
entire academic career in the ongoing quest to create better
childhoods for all children. More recently, Dr. Jill Bolte Taylor, author of the book *A Stroke of Insight*, described her experience of losing her ability to speak after a massive stroke but
how she understood language through the energy people
brought into her hospital room and what she saw in their
eyes. She wrote, "I am in here, come find me." How many of
our children feel that way and when we look into their eyes,
can we find them?

I had the good fortune of first meeting Dr. Lori Desautels when we both were speakers for TEDX Indianapolis in

2012. We immediately knew we were on the same page about our work with children and educators and subsequently met for coffee and conversation many times. Lori was at Marian University at this time and kindly offered a special registration rate to Butler University students to attend her applied education neuroscience conference. It was at the conference that I first became acquainted with Michael McKnight and the powerful work he was doing in his home state and in collaboration with Lori. When an opportunity of a faculty position became available in 2016, it was a privilege to have Lori join the Butler University College of Education team. Lori and Michael continue to share their work in symposiums at the university and in consultation and conferences across the country as well as internationally.

With Lori's leadership, a graduate certificate in applied education neuroscience is now offered in the College of Education to help meet the growing demand in schools and communities to have this knowledge. This book is for anyone working with children of any age who have experienced trauma, toxic stress, and pain in their lives. The authors delve deeply into the definitions of each of these and how the brain is impacted. By understanding how the brain is shaped by these factors, one can begin to better understand the subsequent behaviors and how to effectively apply brain-based strategies to assist the child. I truly believe this text should be required in every teacher education program as well as in service sectors that work with children and families.

May your eyes be opened to new ways of thinking and understanding by reading this outstanding text. I am profoundly grateful to Lori and Michael for sharing their wisdom as each of us works to make each child strong, healthy, and in control of their behavior.

FOREWORD ~ PART TWO

Written by Deb Lecklider, Ph.D.
Associate Dean and Professor, Butler University, College of Education

This book is about Hope. Hope for our children. Hope for our families. Hope for our schools. And, yes, hope for our future workforce and economy. Far too many children are in pain—more than I wanted to acknowledge. When I close my eyes and think about the millions of children who are troubled, traumatized, sad, fearful, and abused, I quickly open my eyes so the pain goes away. I wonder if this is what children do when they are in pain. I wonder how it is that in the richest country in the world we have so many children experiencing adversity and trauma. What is the connection between the brain and meeting these emotional challenges? Lori Desautels and Michael McKnight share important research, data, insights, solutions, and strategies by helping us understand what is behind the pain in *Eyes Are Never Quiet*. There is hope.

Michael and Lori bring us this hope by offering another book with a sense of urgency like no other. They share a brain-aligned framework of how neuroscience, pedagogy, and psychology will change the direction of these beautiful youth.

> *"Alone we can do so little; together we can do so much."*
> HELEN KELLER

When I first met Michael and Lori, I saw the passion in their eyes. I saw a desire to change the narrative—to help us understand how we can work together to help and support our most troubled youth. They have been on a tireless journey to help one child, then two, and as important, to help the caregivers, parents, teachers, and policymakers. Imagine a world, a nation, a state, a community, a school, and family all operating on the same premise—sitting beside our most troubled youth and   seeing the underlying issues and taking action by collaboratively training, mentoring, and educating all of us who want to help our children.

Hope. Our children need us. Our future depends on it.

PROLOGUE
Written by Michael McKnight

There is no greater challenge than teaching a troubled child.
If you're willing to be creative, to risk, to try and fail and try again,
working with a troubled child can teach you more,
and touch you more deeply than any other encounter.

LARRY TOBIN[1]

As I enter my 39th school year I recognize that the troubled young people I have had the privilege of working with over those years have changed me in many positive ways. I would not be the person I am today without the often confusing, sometime painful experiences of working with these young people. If we stay open-minded and follow their lead, they will change the way we see and perceive many things in our lives. No one can begin to work with these children and youth and not be impacted emotionally, not make mistakes, and not sometimes question ourselves deeply. There are very few certainties when working and teaching children who carry pain into our schools and classrooms. There are very few steadfast rules to follow. They will teach you about re-thinking the way you thought the world worked and will show you what the term "grit" is really all about. Grit is that combination of passion and purpose that allows people to make it through difficult times. These young people will take you on a journey through the ups and downs of their lives, and you will experience the highest of highs and the lowest of lows. You will have days of tears and frustration, and days of smiles and deep satisfaction with the progress you see these children make over time. There is nothing fast about this work; all healing takes time and can be viewed as an endurance event. Your ability to be able to accurately see what is underneath their troubling surface behavior is the source of your most effective interventions. Get to know their story: it will break your heart open and shift your thinking toward healing. Connection matters, and the path Lori and I have described in this work will lead you toward creating resilient and restorative environments where all our children can thrive.

INTRODUCTION
Eyes Are Never Quiet

*"Let us build communities and families in which our children and
youth, especially those who are most troubled, can belong.
Let us build a country in which our children and youth can
learn to care for and respect others."*

NELSON MANDELA[2]

Eyes can often tell our stories. Eyes reflect the pain, the joy, and the complexity of emotions we experience throughout our lifetimes. The eyes of our students are never quiet. If we listen through the stare, the glare, the glazed over anger, and dig into the roots of those reflective mirrors, we will learn deeply about our students and ourselves. This book is about children and youth who have experienced pain and adversity in many areas of their lives. It will focus on our most troubled and troubling young people. We will travel into their worlds to begin seeing what sits beneath their negative surface behaviors, while gaining an understanding of what drives the behaviors that are so difficult and challenging for the adults who work beside them.

Larry Tobin, author of *What Do You Do with a Child Like This? Inside the Lives of Troubled Children*, puts it like this: "Troubled kids are distinguished by their regrettable ability to elicit from others exactly the opposite of what they really need."[3] A growing body of research shows us that many of our society's most troubled children and youth have experienced significant adversity in their young lives. Our current educational systems, and the adults who are working to support and serve these young people within them, have not been prepared to enter their worlds and work successfully with them. The majority of the institutions that serve our most troubled young people continue to focus on managing their surface behaviors rather than fostering their healing and growth. Often our traditional school systems, distracted and discouraged by the troubled child's or youth's disruptive behavior, have dealt with these disruptions by labeling, medicating, excluding, punishing, or expelling them. We hope, with this book, to change this dynamic.

This book is for anyone sitting beside troubled young people who have experienced trauma, toxic levels of stress, and pain in their lives. The word pain is used intentionally. James P. Anglin coined the term "pain-based behavior" to describe behaviors that have roots in deep emotional pain. Children who carry extreme levels of emotional pain into our schools and classrooms struggle with emotions like fear, grief, sadness, anger, hopelessness, and rage. By causing a host of challenges—including "acting out" behaviors like fighting and disrupting class—these young people show us behaviorally the pain they are in. Pain-based behaviors, though, can also show up in the form of "acting in" behaviors like cutting, apathy, and depression. We see youth disrespecting teachers and other adults along with disengaging from school. Coupled with a multitude of other challenges, this creates frustration and hopelessness on several levels for all involved: educators, students, and parents.[4]

Adversity and trauma change our brains, perceptions, and behaviors in dramatic ways. Trauma lives in the nervous system and can reorganize how our brains respond to every day occurrences. Babies and young children are most susceptible to toxic levels of stress as their body's immune, perceptional, and nervous systems are underdeveloped and require nurturing experiences and healthy dyadic relationships to buffer life's adversities. Because babies' and children's nervous systems are immature, they cannot self-regulate on their own. The opportunities and experiences to regulate emotions quite possibly were left out of the developmental equation for many of our children and youth walking into our classrooms. When emotional regulation is NOT a part of the child's experiences, we can see reactive and negative behaviors because a sense of trust and safety has not been etched into the child's memory templates.

Most negative behaviors arise from a stress-response brain state and chronic levels of adversities, both of which create a brain that is wired to defend, protect, or shut down. Our brain in survival mode produces oppositional, defiant, aggressive, and withdrawn behaviors. These are brain issues, though, not behavioral ones. As we sit beside our students, we must understand that it will be a difficult and tenuous journey encountering this brain physiology. Recent research on neuroplasticity and the potential for resilience our brains naturally have, however, should remind us that this journey can indeed be a hopeful one with continued awareness and intention.

Emotions are contagious, and all the behaviors these young people employ can frustrate, irritate, annoy, and anger teachers trying to work with them. The negative behaviors demonstrated by young people in pain can also cause adults to be fearful, triggering our own adversities and insecurities. We fall back on simply trying to stop a behavior. We punish young people or we send them as far away as possible from our hub of comfort. Sometimes we send students to another program or school, while other times we suspend them, or even expel them to nowhere.

The central challenge educators and school systems face when working with these young people, though, is dealing with their primary pain without inflicting secondary pain through our use of punitive or controlling reactions.[5] Nevertheless, there is good news. The field of education and youth work is now beginning to integrate, and by doing so, is bringing together many fields of study that are emerging to guide our work. We can now draw on the strengths of neuroscience, pedagogy, and psychology to inform our efforts to change the outcomes for our most difficult and troubled young people.

MBE Science as a Multidisciplinary Field

Neuroscience
Brain and its Functioning

Pedagogy
Individual Education and Learning

Neuroeducation
Mind, Brain and Education Science

Psychology
Mind and Behavior

Source: Interpretation of Tokuhama-Espinosa's transdisciplinary field by Nakagawa (2008

The interdisciplinary brain-aligned framework acknowledges the lives, the pain, and the unrelenting efforts of parents who are raising our young people to the best of their abilities. Oftentimes, we do not understand the personal stories of many parents and caregivers. We do not see their traumas and adversities or understand their environments. We have to remember that, in our classrooms, every student is someone's whole world.

As we begin these journeys, know this: the resiliency research is very clear. We have the power and the opportunity to change the direction of the lives of the children and youth we serve. This book is designed to support you and all people who teach, parent, and sit beside our young people, helping them to begin to see and create a better world.

CHAPTER ONE

Awakening

"There is no such thing as a baby; there is a baby and someone."
DONALD WOODS WINNICOTT

Secure, trusting bonds with caring adults are critical to human beings during the unfolding of their innate potential. For our children to thrive, they need to be connected and cared for in an ongoing and persistent manner for years.[6]

When these connective relationships and care are impaired or absent from a child's life, the child communicates this mistrust and detachment through behaviors we often misunderstand. The most difficult children in our schools, classrooms, foster care placements, and juvenile facilities are children with broken connections. Dr. Sandra Bloom, the founder of the Sanctuary Model for the treatment of trauma-related emotional disorders, suggests reframing the question we typically ask when trying to understand our troubled students. Instead of asking ourselves, "What is wrong with these young people?" we need to rephrase our question and ask, "What happened to these young people?"

"There can be no keener revelation of a society's soul than the way in which it treats its children."
NELSON MANDELA

On the one hand, our children are not doing well. On the other, our children are rising to the occasion. We have an immediate paradox in this first chapter because, as we are writing parts of this story, on March 24, 2018, millions of our young people protested, marched, and spoke about the prolific gun violence that has created a nation in crisis. We will speak to this later in the chapter.

Even a cursory look at the state of children and youth in America can give any teacher, parent, or youth worker cause for concern. A recent report from the Children's Defense Fund, for example, sheds some light on the current ways many children are growing up in the richest country on earth. According to the report:

> Millions of America's children today are still suffering from hunger, homelessness and hopelessness. More than 13.2 million children are poor—nearly 1 in 5. About 70 percent of them are children of color who will be a majority of our children by 2020. More than 1.2 million homeless children are enrolled in public schools. About 14.8 million children struggle against hunger in food-insecure households. Despite great progress, 3.9 million children lack the health coverage they need to survive and thrive. Millions of young children need quality early childhood programs during their critical years of early brain development, yet only 5 percent of eligible infants and toddlers are enrolled in Early Head Start and only 54 percent of eligible 3- and 4-year-olds are served by Head Start. The majority of all public school fourth and eighth graders cannot read at grade level, including more than 75 percent of Black, Hispanic and American Indian/Alaska Native children. Every 47 seconds a child is abused or neglected and the number of children in foster care is increasing rapidly in some parts of our country as the opioid crisis spins out of control.[7]

The United States finds itself in the midst of this opioid crisis, a crisis stemming from drugs designed to reduce pain. These include both legal painkillers, like morphine prescribed by doctors for acute or chronic pain, as well as illegal drugs, such as heroin or illicitly-made fentanyl. To put the crisis into numerical terms, during 2016, there were more than 63,600 overdose deaths in the United States, including 42,249 that involved an opioid (66.4%). That's an average of 115 opioid overdose deaths each day.[8]

In November of 2016, I (Lori) traveled to Austin, Indiana, a town in the southern part of the state where the opioid epidemic had made national news in 2015. This small community recognized that their students, educators, and families were in a perpetual state of crisis and survival. The elementary, middle, and high schools were feeling the effects of a community ravaged by drugs and alcohol. The students' negative behaviors—their lack of engagement and motivation—were showing up day after day in the midst of this community crisis. In children, anger is fear's bodyguard. I will never forget the stories I heard during my visits to this school district in Indiana. Teachers, administrators, and counselors were making powerful connections and relationships with their students, but they observed unprecedented levels of stress and depression in children as young as five years old.

These toxic levels of stress in these students need to be understood in the context of how the body's stress response system works. Within this system, there are three broad categories of stress—not all of which, of course, are bad—that make up our stress response system: "positive stress," "tolerable stress," and "toxic stress."

Positive stress is a type of stress that helps us learn how to cope with the ups and downs of life, and is considered the first level of the stress response system. This type of stress is an important part of childhood development. When we feel threatened, the human body is designed to respond automatically by increasing our heart rate, increasing our respiration rates, increasing our blood pressure, and releasing stress hormones such as cortisol and adrenaline. When a child's stress system becomes activated within an environment of care, the physical effects of the stress response return the body back to its baseline state. Over time and with caring adults, co-regulation of a child's stress response in the child's life results in the healthy development of this stress response.

The next type of stress is tolerable stress. This is the second level of the human stress response system in which more severe difficulties or challenges activate the stress response. These can include a host of negative experiences people encounter that oftentimes feel momentous, such as a death in the family, a car accident, or any kind of emergency. This level of stress can also be supported and buffered by adults in the child's life.

The highest level of the human stress response system is toxic stress. This type of stress is triggered when a child is exposed to ongoing elevated levels of adversity, oftentimes unpredictable. This can include a wide variety of toxic experiences along a continuum. Chronic neglect, physical abuse, ongoing emotional abuse, exposure to violence in the community, social rejection and humiliation, and other negative experiences that increase chronic levels of anxiety occurring without the healthy co-regulation of an adult.

These are the indicators that influence the adverse childhood experiences mentioned in the studies earlier in this chapter. Prolonged and persistent mistreatment activates the stress response system and can impact neurological development. Without ongoing adult support, this level of stress impacts all facets of the young person's life, and can even reprogram a young person's development while transitioning into adulthood. These young people are in pain. They are emotionally and behaviorally in a persistent state of alarm. These are the children, youth, and parents we focus on throughout this book.[9]

When our stress response systems are constantly turned on with little to no time for repair and recovery, our brains and bodies are hijacked by a brain state that produces chronic amounts of cortisol and adrenaline which can shut off the areas of the brain responsible for learning, emotional regulation, attention, and working memory. Educators in the Indiana schools I visited were seeing the effects of a chronically activated stress response system daily, and students were expressing this anxiety, fear, and angst through negative behaviors. The students' behaviors, to the outside world, often looked apathetic, shut down, and unmotivated, but their brains' physiology told a different story. These students were frozen in trauma.

These school districts, moreover, observed patterns in children's behaviors, eventually recognizing that these negative behaviors would often escalate on Friday afternoons when students began to anticipate the weekend ahead. Oftentimes, for the students, these weekends were filled with unpredictability, as a child might not know where they would sleep, what they would eat, or who would be caring for them. The high school also reported greater absences on Mondays, learning that the students stayed home from school to make sure their caregivers came out of the alcohol and drug binges that had taken place over the weekend. These patterns that the school recognized were just that, patterns of continuity that were becoming unintentionally normalized, just as they were in many other communities around the country.

In the schools in Austin, Indiana, we worked with teachers and students, teaching them about their own neuroanatomy and how toxic stress impairs thoughts and feelings. We shared tools, practices, and strategies, all of which helped these students regulate their emotions and stress response systems with an adult who could stay connected through all conflicts. Although we have a long road to travel, this educational neuroscience work is continuing in Austin, and the students are learning how their brains have a super power: neuroplasticity! Put another way, these students are learning that their brains change structurally and functionally with every experience they encounter. To help create circuits of resiliency and well-being, we feel it is critical to reach students at a young age when the brain has its greatest plasticity and malleability.

Based on our work in this Indiana community, it is beneficial to read the words of an educator, Kelly Stagnolia, who not only teaches in the local schools, but also grew up in this small town when poverty and the opioid epidemic began to make their presence felt. In the piece below, which is titled "Coming Home," Kelly engages with her own adverse childhood experiences, explaining her decision to return to her hometown to teach at the local high school. According to Kelly:

> When everyone else was running away from Austin, I was coming home. My name is Kelly Stagnolia, and I decided to leave the comfort of a Four Star school to come home to the town that I grew up in the summer of 2015. Why? The answer runs much deeper than the question. In the spring of 2015, an HIV epidemic rocked my small Indiana town. The virus was being spread mainly through intravenous drug use. There were hundreds of cases confirmed in a matter of months. One of these cases affected me directly and intimately.
>
> It was very late spring night, when I heard a tender knock on my back door. I opened the door to

find my sister, frail and weak. I hadn't spoken to her in a couple of years. She was a very broken soul. My sister told me that the CDC (Center for Disease Control) would be testing her the following morning for HIV. She wanted to know if I would sit beside her the next morning for the test.

The sun was coming up as I drove down Rural Street to my sister's poverty ridden home. I entered to find my sister sitting on a worn and tattered brown couch. She greeted me with a hug and thanked me for being with her. A few minutes later, a white car pulled into the drive. Two well-groomed women appeared in the driveway. My sister seemed to have a bond with these women. We entertained small talk for a few minutes and then there was a palatable and uncomfortable quiet. Finally, one of the women, Jane, asked my sister, "Does she know?" At that point, my sister broke down and told me that she had already tested positive for HIV. The women were there to test the virus load in her blood.

My mind started spinning. How could this be? My heart felt shattered, but a voice deep within me whispered, "Love her, care, give hope, and do anything she needs." She needed me. My thoughts traveled back in time seeing my sister in earlier years. She was the one I looked up to for the latest fashion trend, and the sibling with spunk and humor. The one who welcomed me into her home my junior year of high school when mom and I had another fight. The sister who defied all odds by receiving her RN degree after dropping out of school her senior year. How could this be? My life changed that day. Could I change this? Now was the time to fight for my community and family.

When a chance to teach at Austin Elementary arose that summer, I decided to come and give hope to as many children as I could in this town just as my teachers in the Austin schools had once done for me. They gave me hope, an education that broke cycles, and the confidence I needed to climb many mountains alone.

I remember packing my former classroom with tears streaming down my face. My principal, superintendent, and curriculum director all pleaded with me to stay. I felt appreciated and loved at this school. Now, I was moving my resources, knowledge, and most important my soul back to a town that had not always been so good to me. I was afraid. Mostly afraid of breaking open wounds that ran deep in my soul. You see, I was a child who grew up in Austin with much adversity in my life. I have nine adverse experiences that have had a significant impact on my life as an adult. I was afraid of so many things. What would the parents say about their child bring taught by a daughter of Lonnie Johnson. My dad was well known in the community for committing the murder of two local men in the mid-80s. Would they remember that I was pregnant with my daughter when I graduated from Austin High School in 1996? Would they judge me to be like many of my family members who had stayed in Austin and made terrible decisions? What would my new students be like? I have always set high expectations for myself and my students, but would these kiddos be different? Would seeing and feeling the many adversities my new students carry in break open my old wounds?

It is now three years later and I have survived. I am a better person than the day I returned to the Austin schools. Teaching in Austin has taught me humility. I am a better teacher, wife, mother, and individual. The parents of my students at Austin elementary have been kind and compassionate. What I have learned is that these caregivers, whether they are sick, addicted, well-educated or rarely home, love their children. There is a deep rooted connection between broken parents and the children they are raising that I have experienced myself. In most cases, parents are doing the best they can. It just may not be what is best for their children. I instinctively knew I needed to build connections with these families inside and outside the classroom. I have sat on the couch with a grandmother who cried because her daughter was returning to jail for the third time, and she would be raising her two young children. I have taken food to a student's family that had nothing to eat. I have cried with parents at conferences as they expressed their gratitude for my simple gesture of seeing and noticing the strengths in their child. I have observed the worn sad faces of parents who love their children, but do not know how to help them or themselves. I have been forever changed by working in this community and seeing the pain that this epidemic has caused entire families.

The children I have taught are some of the sweetest, and most eager to learn children that I have ever taught and guided. They are arriving to school wanting to be loved and accepted, just as I did growing up. I've never received more letters of appreciation and love than I have the past three years. Their words mean something more to me. Their appreciation does something to my soul in healing my past. I'm planting seeds of knowledge, confidence, accountability, love, and structure that will go with them on their journey of life. That is the resiliency and the attachment that can trump the adversity in their lives.

We cannot teach these children in the same way. We have to educate them about their own neuro-anatomy and stress response systems. We cannot prevent the adversity each child experiences but we can provide the buffers needed to help them better handle these life experiences. If the adversity is never addressed, the learning will not take place. The way we engage, teach, and discipline these students makes all the difference. The truth is these students need hope.

I have held a child on the floor during a field trip, because the presenter turned out the lights, and it triggered something within her brain. I walked out of the auditorium and sat on the floor as she sobbed and told me "her story." I've seen a tough young man run back into my room, knocking me out of my chair in the tightest hug, while pleading with me to not let his mother take him home because his step-father is there. He said, "Please, just take me home, Mrs. Stagnolia," as if it were that easy. I've watched a child fall asleep in the office waiting on someone to pick him up and care for him for the night. I've released many trembling hands into the face of an addict and watched the parents yelling at them all the way to the car for walking too slowly. I understand these stories because I have lived them. For now, I will let each one of them know they are loved, they are deserving, and they are worthy of a different life. These students are some of my greatest mentors.

Across America

While Kelly's essay makes it clear that some of our communities are in a state of crisis, another way to get a sense of this is to glance at the raw statistics. For example, across the United States, every day:

2 mothers die from complications of childbirth.

4 children are killed by abuse or neglect.

7 children or teens commit suicide.

8 children or teens are killed with a gun.

167 children are arrested for violent crimes.

311 children are arrested for drug crimes.

566 babies are born to teen mothers.

589 public school students are corporally punished.

1,414 babies are born without health insurance.

1,759 babies are born into poverty.

1,854 children are confirmed as abused or neglected.

2,805 children are arrested.

2,857 high school students drop out.

4,388 babies are born to unmarried mothers.

12,816 public school students are suspended.[10]

Certainly, these statistics are alarming. But what do they have to do with teaching and learning? In 2006, the first significant and long-term research study concerning the effects of adverse childhood experiences on adult health outcomes was published by Dr. Vincent Felitti and Dr. Robert Anda (Adverse Childhood Experiences study; ACE). This landmark study was an in-depth analysis of over 17,000 adults. During the study, Dr. Felitti and his colleague documented the frequency of traumatic life experiences in the childhoods of over 17,000 adults enrolled in the Kaiser Permanente heath care system. Defying conventional belief, the study revealed a powerful relationship between our emotional experiences as children and our physical and mental health as adults.

The Adverse Childhood Experiences—or ACEs—that Felitti and Anda discovered in their study include the following: 1) emotional abuse; 2) physical abuse; 3) sexual abuse; 4) physical neglect; 5) emotional neglect; 6) substance abuse in the household; 7) mental illness in the household; 8) mother treated violently; 9) divorce or parental separation; and 10) a household member in jail. The tally of the number of adverse experiences in a person's life is that person's ACE score, meaning that the highest possible ACE score a person can receive is 10. After documenting the various traumatic life experiences in their study, Felitti and Anda then correlated the person's ACE score with health risk behaviors and outcomes. They discovered that ACEs were extremely common. Sictyseven percent of those who participated in the study, for instance, had at least 1 ACE, while 12.6 percent had four or more ACEs. This idea of a composite total ACE score is critical to our understanding of how adversity impacts children and youth. Put simply, the higher the ACE score the more likely the young person will experience emotional and mental challenges in their lives.

Since the original ACE study was conducted (2006), other similar studies have been carried out. In 2012, the Institute for Safe Families formed the ACE Task Force to study the prevalence and impact of ACEs in Philadelphia, an urban city with a socially and racially diverse population. Analysis of the Philadelphia Urban ACE Survey surveys that were completed by 1,784 adults showed a higher prevalence of ACEs than had been found in previous studies: 33.2 percent of Philadelphia adults experienced emotional abuse, for example, and 35 percent experienced physical abuse during their childhood. Approximately 35 percent of adults grew up in a household with a substance-abusing member; 24.1

percent lived in a household with someone who was mentally ill; and 12.9 percent lived in a household with someone who had served time in prison or was sentenced to serve time in prison.

The Philadelphia Urban ACE Survey also examined the stressors that exist in the communities where people live. The study found that 40.5 percent of Philadelphia adults witnessed violence while growing up, which includes seeing or hearing someone being beaten, stabbed, or shot. Over one-third (34.5 percent) of adults reported experiencing discrimination based on their race or ethnicity, while almost three in ten adults (27.3 percent) reported having felt unsafe in their neighborhoods or did not trust their neighbors during childhood. Overall, 37 percent of Philadelphia respondents reported four or more ACEs.[11] Clearly, then, large segments of Philadelphia's population are growing up in the face of tremendous adversity.

Wendy Ellis's and Bill Dietz's recent research exploring the community environments where our children and adolescents grow up has expanded the concept of adversity to help consider the effects of living in environments where ACEs are all too common. While it seems obvious that our children and youth experience adversity in their individual family situations, Ellis and Dietz argue that adversity can also manifest itself in our actual communities. In their framework, the symptoms of Adverse Community Environments include the following: poverty, discrimination, community disruption, violence, lack of opportunity or economic mobility and social capital, poor housing quality, and unaffordable housing.[12]

To thrive, children need to be raised in safe communities and environments. Each year, 19,000 children and adults are victims of homicide and more than 1,600 children die from abuse or neglect.[13] When children are abused or neglected, state agencies intervene and sometimes remove these children from their homes and place them in our foster care system. In 2015, an estimated 427,910 kids were in foster care in the United States.

Foster care children, it should be pointed out, are at an extreme risk for poor emotional, social, and physiological health outcomes and have high rates of Adverse Childhood Experiences (ACEs). Sixty-one percent of children in foster care were removed from their home due to abusive neglect, while 32 percent of children were removed from their homes due to parental drug abuse. Fourteen percent of children, moreover, were removed due to the inability of the caregiver to cope, and 12 percent of children were removed from their home due to physical abuse.[14] Early exposure to adversity, moreover, is an unfortunate reality for many youth involved with the criminal justice system. A 2014 study found that 97 percent of sampled youth in juvenile justice settings reported one or more ACE. Of these, 90 percent reported at least two ACEs, and nearly 75 percent reported at least three. More than 50 percent of these youth reported at least four ACEs, and nearly 33 percent reported five or more.[15]

Trauma, though, can come in other forms, too. Kenneth V. Hardy, a therapist and a professor at Drexel University, has written extensively on the hidden wounds of racial trauma. His work has deepened and expanded the understanding of trauma to include racial oppression. Hardy has brought attention to a far too often neglected topic of the hidden wounds of racial oppression. In his framework, Hardy identifies five hidden wounds of racial trauma, including: 1) internalized devaluation; 2) assaulted sense of self; 3) internalized voicelessness; 4) the wound of rage; and 5) the sense of being a nobody.

Internalized devaluation—Hardy's first wound of racial

trauma—comes from cultural messages that reinforce the message of being bad and unworthy. Hardy states that profoundly devalued youth become hyper-vigilant about gaining respect. Underneath all the surface behaviors these young people have connected to through their experiences, being respected becomes a counter balance to internalized devaluation.

The second wound of racial trauma, an assaulted sense of self, is interconnected with the sense of internalized devaluation. Repeated race-related cultural messages make it extremely hard for young people to know who they really are. Over time, these messages not only become internalized, but they also damage self-esteem in individuals.

Internalized voicelessness, according to Hardy, impairs the young person's ability to be assertive and an advocate for oneself. If a child is too loud, then the child is seen as aggressive, hostile, and dangerous. He or she then needs to control their sense of self-advocacy and anger.

This leads to the forth hidden wound of racial trauma, the wound of rage, which is complex. Rage can be seen through the trauma lens as the result of cumulative effects of devaluation and voicelessness. According to Hardy, it can appear as anger, explosiveness, sadness, and depression, all of which are associated with developmental trauma.

The last hidden wound of racial trauma is what Hardy terms "the case of a nobody." This wound is the wound of feeling less than human. It is the sense of true despair and hopelessness that comes from systematic devaluation. These wounds are not sequential, but interweave with each other in an ongoing manner in the lives of many children and youth of color.[16]

Taken together, then, the research and statistics are clear. Our most troubled children and youth have experienced high levels of stress, adversity, and trauma in their lives. Adversity—in line with the expanded concept mentioned above—can also include natural disasters, accidents, social rejection, and humiliation. For many of our students, educators, and parents, schools are areas filled with adversity, with negative experiences accumulating each year. Schools, in other words, are turned from places of learning into places of pain. This pain, though, lives beneath the behaviors we face daily in our schools. Without awareness and action, our biographies can turn into our biology.

What all these statistics show is clear: Our children are hurting. What these statistics do not show, however, is that our children are resilient. When one child, family, or community is struck with adversity, it can affect the entire system. Our nation is a collective system that is currently in a survival brain state, with gun violence on our streets and in our schools. This violence, however, has generated a community response unlike any we have seen in recent times: "March for Our Lives," a movement led by our nation's youth.

These young people are sharing their trauma and stories of loss and hope. As we listen to the speeches of our youth today, we hear similar calls for change. In addition to thoughts and prayers, we hear our youth plead for action. They share how they have learned how to duck bullets before learning to read. This movement transcends race, gender, politics, and ethnicity. These children and youth are asking for educational justice. They live in the here and now where zero tolerance policies, added security in schools, and armed teachers are not working. They are pleading for increased mental health services, restorative justice programs, and work-funded mental health resources and support. They are exhausted from the profiling and criminalizing of their black and brown brothers and sisters. Many of our young people have experienced the intimate loss of a loved one through gun violence. We must begin to awaken to the conditions that breed these adversities individually and collectively.

We have a great opportunity to do this in our school systems. Students spend, on average, approximately 1,000 hours a year in our schools. These can be places of connection and inspiration where students have the ability to thrive with healthy connections. They can be places of opportunities that shine a light on strengths and passions, and environments that feel safe and secure. We are far from there, but we are hopeful that together we can pave the way for these systemic changes. We have an opening to meet these emotional challenges with understanding, relationships, and hope.

What is Trauma?

Trauma arises from an inescapable stressful event that overwhelms an individual's coping mechanisms. An extreme traumatic event causes acute traumatic stress and can overwhelm a young person's ability to cope.[17] For the sake of clarity, this book discusses two types of trauma—acute trauma and complex trauma—that we find in the lives of the children and youth we work with and support.

Acute trauma results from a single incident that overwhelms the young person's ability to cope. These single incidents can include things like being a victim of a crime, being involved in a serious accident, or any other serious event that triggers a stress response. Put another way, acute trauma stems from an event.

Children and youth growing up in environments with toxic levels of stress often have complex trauma. Complex trauma is different than other types of trauma.[18] This trauma is associated with ongoing and persistent adversity in their lives. In Van der Kolk's words, complex trauma occurs when a young person experiences "multiple, chronic, and prolonged, developmentally adverse traumatic events, most often of an interpersonal nature...and with early life onset."[19] Children who have experienced complex trauma exhibit a more pronounced deficit in developmental brain-aligned stress response systems. In other words, this trauma compromises these young people's ability to self-regulate their behavior.

The most troubled children and youth in your classroom, school, juvenile justice programs, child welfare systems, or youth sports programs are children experiencing toxic levels of stress and trauma. Without intentional interventions by adults in their lives, the outcomes for our most traumatized children and youth are predictably poor.

Working together, though, we can change the predictable outcomes from one of despair to one of hope, resiliency, strength, and growth. This book is designed to provide people working with our society's most troubled young people the tools they need to do this critical work. This work begins with us. It begins with our brain states and how we address the adversity in our own lives. Following is a letter Lori sent to the Indiana Education Committee. At the time, the state of Indiana was debating on discipline policies throughout the state. Not only is it time we address the adversities our children and adolescents are bringing to schools, but it is also time to change the way we discipline children in pain.

Dear Education Committee:

Thank you for the opportunity to share this research, the experiences, and the core need of all educators who sit beside our students in our state's schools and districts.

In Indiana, one third to one fourth of our students bring significant adversity/trauma into the classroom.

These students are living in a survival brain state and their neuro-anatomy is in a state of dysregulation, which drives their behaviors and neurobiologically hijacks their ability to learn.

We have continued to address and purport that we are in the midst of a national educational crisis, in which our math, science, and reading scores continue to fall, and yet, this crisis is rooted in childhood adversity and trauma with poverty contributing to these statistics. We believe it is time to pause and ask critical questions: What happened to these children and youth? What are we doing? We are misunderstanding a critical component to all of this: To develop and strengthen cognition, we must begin at the students' level of brain development.

Trauma-Sensitive Schools must also address the emotional well-being of our educators who are sitting beside our students carrying in pain-based behaviors. Education is an organic process and the anxiety and adversity many of our state educators are facing as they sit beside students who are holding much adversity and trauma is critical to the shift in education policy. This bill must focus on the emotional and social well-being of our children, youth, educators, and all those who interface with Indiana children and youth.

A traumatized brain can be tired, hungry, worried, rejected, or detached, and these states are often accompanied by feelings of isolation, shame, worry, angst, and fear. Shame and fear in children can look violent and aggressive. The neurobiological changes caused by negative experiences trigger a fear response in the brain. When we feel distress, our brains and bodies are flooded with emotional messages that trigger the question, "Am I safe?" We react physiologically with an agitated limbic system that increases blood pressure, heart rate, and respiration as the levels of the hormones cortisol and adrenaline increase in our bodies. Chronic activation of the fear response can damage those parts of the brain responsible for cognition and learning.

When the brain has experienced significant adversity, it becomes fundamentally reorganized. Past experiences can live on in the body and may be experienced as flashbacks, memories, or repetitive thoughts about the painful event. Adversity and trauma live in the nervous system and don't go away just because the trauma is over.

Many children and adolescents come to school with a deep mistrust of adults because they've never formed healthy attachments. These young people have brains that are in a constant state of alarm. Attachment is the carrier of all development. These children we see every day. Below are three children I (Lori) met this school year who are experiencing toxic levels of stress and adversity. Their resiliency was remarkably significant in that they could get to school each morning and complete the day.

"T." is eight years old although his lexicon is that of a street-wise nineteen-year-old. He is angry all the time. He is volatile, aggressive, and defiant beyond words. He feels deeply and is known to protect his younger sister at all costs. A few years ago, T. watched his mother murder his father. His mother is incarcerated, and his father is dead. He lives with his grandmother. Last week, he walked into Room 9 telling his teacher that gunshots went through the screen of his window, just missing everyone in the living room. They are hoping to move. T. is on ADD medication, blood pressure medication, and medication for depression. Some mornings he walks into the classroom and just flops on the carpet and sleeps.

Quinn is seven years old. He cannot sit still for more than fifteen seconds. He is constantly hungry, trying to find crumbs on the classroom floor to eat. He will drink water out of anyone's bottle, and was bathed at school last year because he was so dirty arriving to school each morning. This is when the school found welts all over his little body. He flinches when an adult comes near him. He cries most of the time, with an empty, far away stare that I have rarely seen from another. His eyes and mind are not present during the school day as there is a state of disconnect that I am having trouble defining. When the classroom song comes on in the afternoon reminding students it is time to clean up and get ready to go home, Quinn panics. When he is walked to the bus, he waves at his teacher until he can no longer, then presses his face against the window of the bus and waves a little more. To see Quinn in class is confusing because he can start several fights each day with a look, a punch, mean words, or an act of aggression. He is not a soulless "bad" child. He is a child bathing in trauma.

Unfortunately, there are millions of stories that sound like the ones I just shared. We are living in a time of crisis. Our nation is experiencing a drug/opioid epidemic, significant national and state poverty, and fifteen million of our youth have been identified as having an emotional or mental disability. Only 25 percent of these youth are receiving assistance for these emotional disorders. The rest are left to cope on their own.

Children and adolescents who carry trauma and adversity into the classroom also bring "pain-based behaviors" with them. These behaviors are misunderstood and oftentimes dismissed as intentional acts of disobedience and defiance. When we use zero tolerance and punitive measures to correct these pain-based behaviors, we are elevating the child's stress response and creating increased fear, aggression, or dissociative behaviors where the child or adolescent simply shuts down. This can become a negative cycle, and we are missing the mark. I see this every day across Indiana and our nation. These students are starving for regulation and relationship.

The attachment and neuroscience research is clear: The practices of attachment, attunement, and regulation must be in place and active before learning and cognition can occur. Educational neuroscience offers a framework for exploring brain development, dampening down the stress response, and implementing strategies that engage and build brain architecture from the bottom up. It is in our schools that regulation and relationships can develop because educators spend time with students each day. But unless we are mentored and trained in the brain science of adversity and trauma, we will continue to cycle in negative patterns, escalating conflict and aggression along the way, while also elevating survival responses within the brain's architecture.

Respectfully,
Lori Desautels, Ph.D.
Assistant Professor, College of Education, Butler University

CHAPTER TWO

How Are You Doing?

"To put the world in order we must first put the nation in order;
to put the nation in order, we must first put the family in order;
to put the family in order; we must first cultivate our personal life;
we must first set our hearts right."

CONFUCIUS

Our Brain States

As I (Lori) think about Confucius' quote, I have never been more aware of how not only our own life adversities affect our emotional, physical, and mental health, but how the adversities and trauma of our children and others can create a secondary firestorm inside our own nervous systems. Secondary traumatic stress profoundly affects our experience of everyday life and relationships. When we are constantly attuning to negative emotion, co-regulating students who are agitated, buffering triggered children and adolescents, *and* resetting boundaries with challenging behaviors and emotions from others, we often carry these worries into our perceptions, thoughts, and feelings.

All this creates an emotional contagion of sorts, which is capable of slowly diminishing our sense of agency and purpose inside our own lives. We forget, moreover, that this emotional contagion is a part of our social survival as our brains are social organs sensing and detecting the range of emotions and sensations we intuit from others in all moments. We are neurobiologically wired for attachment and relationship, and we are constantly reading the non-verbal and verbal communication cues of others as we evaluate what feels safe, familiar, threatening, distressing, hopeless, or exhausting.

Time and time again, I have experienced this process as a mom and as a teacher. I have felt my own emotions escalate when I unintentionally entered into a conflict with a child or adolescent that has triggered me, activating my survival instincts in the brain's lower regions. Words are not effective when spoken from this survival response, and I have left school on those days feeling emotionally spent and hopeless. Every day, however, I am learning there is no easy way to "fix" students. The behaviors triggered by toxic stress and trauma are not remediated quickly. Young people that bring high levels of stress, adversity, and trauma often take three steps backwards for every one step forward. Staying connected and regulated through a conflict is at the core of educator and parent well-being.

For the past two years, I have been sitting beside educators in a variety of schools from around the country. "Exhaustion peppered with hopelessness," is an apt description of how those working with our students feel emotionally. To repeat a common refrain, it seems impossible to teach a student the mandated academic standards when the student's brain is wired for survival, meaning they are prepared to protect, defend, flee, and fight the minute they walk into the school. As we shared a few years ago in our first book, *Unwritten*, teaching is an organic process and schools are living systems. Our most troubled kids create "discipline" issues in our schools. Young people in pain often act out that pain in our schools. When we attempt to control these young people, what we get instead is an escalation of their inappropriate behaviors. This can quickly spiral out of control and the culture of the school becomes negative. In these environments, troubled students are punished at excessive rates and are often expelled to nowhere.

Stress is contagious. Toxic levels of it, when carried into our schools by students who have experienced high levels of adversity in their lives, can dramatically affect the entire culture of a school. Decades ago, Nicholas Long, the founder of the Life Space Crisis Intervention Institute and leader in the field of mental health and special education for over 50 years, made the connection between a troubled child's behavior and adults' reactions towards that behavior. According to Long, "kids in stress create in us their feelings, and if we are not trained to this process, we (the adult) will mirror their behaviors."[20] Long also argues that when a student is stressed, his or her emotions will also reflect in the adult. If the adult is not trained to accept their own counter-aggressive feelings, the adult will act on them, in effect mirroring the student's behavior. He offers several reasons that adults become counter aggressive with the young people they serve. These can include, for example, the adult being caught in the student's conflict cycle or the adult's reaction to being in a bad mood. Other reasons are the adult's perception of having their value system or beliefs violated by a student or even the adult's feeling of rejection and hopelessness.

When adults become counter aggressive with students who carry in traumatic levels of stress—no matter the reason— it destroys their ability to work effectively with these young people. Long also notes that it reinforces traumatized and troubled students' beliefs that all adults in their lives are rejecting and punitive. To combat this, Long suggests adults must be aware of this process. "Our ongoing professional struggle is to become more aware of how the seven underlying reasons for counter aggression affect us personally," Long writes. "As adults working with young people," he continues, "we need to be aware of our own triggers. As we gain more insight into our own behavior it opens up space for us to be able to consciously and intentionally choose how we react to the young people that we serve.[21]

Teachers, administrators, and all adults working with traumatized children and youth must become intentional in their actions if they are to be successful in helping to heal our most wounded young people. To do so, we must be extremely cautious not to treat children and youth who are pain with pain-based discipline techniques. As Bessel van der Kolk warns, "Faced with a range of challenging behaviors, caregivers have a tendency to deal with their frustration by retaliating in ways that often uncannily repeat the children's early trauma."[22] It is critically important for adults working with traumatized young people to remember that the motivation for change in our most troubled children and youth depends on the ability of the adult to communicate respectfully in times of crisis and extreme stress.

What can we do to elevate our own sense of purpose, connection, and well-being? This question is personal and needs to be answered by us all. Although this book cannot provide a recipe for well-being, this chapter offers some practices that will allow you to increase your effectiveness while working in high-stress environments.

Steps Along the Path

When thinking about our schools, I always return to Joseph Campbell's age-old story, "The Hero's Journey." Campbell was an American mythologist who studied myths from all over the world, and he created the famous "Hero's Journey," a monomyth that explains how each individual goes through continuous cycles of change and transformation. Nothing could be more fitting when we apply this monomyth to educators, students, and schools, because the learning process and the development of emotional connections are real-life cycles of continual challenges, births of new ideas, successes, and transformations.

As I reflect upon this past school year, and all the Hero Journeys I observed within my own life and those of the teachers I worked beside, a strong teaching practice always grabs my attention: modeling. I am learning that modeling our own Hero's Journey for our students provides not just a powerful tool for teaching, but also one for life. It offers opportunities for reflection, problem solving, hindsight, foresight, and cognitive flexibility for working with students whose struggles, celebrations, and identities are constantly developing. By being aware on our educational journey, we can begin to model empathy and understanding for one another. We can embrace all that we do, experiencing it as a heroic adventure with no predictable outcomes. Each moment, hour, day, week, and month, we enter into a cycle and travel toward change, challenges, and new beginnings. In the section below, we outline how the Hero's Journey applies to our teaching.

Status Quo

We begin with an embrace of our ordinary existence. Life feels neutral here. As teachers, each year we return to a classroom with students who will be learning with us for the next several months. We anticipate and encounter new students, schedules, back-to-school nights, upcoming assessments, grade-level and district meetings, and the list goes on. We are aware of our personal lives and the relationships and experiences that coexist with our professional responsibilities.

Call to Adventure

We meet our new students and begin to see novel behaviors, encounter unfamiliar and familiar words, and observe the mini-worlds that each student carries into our classrooms. We notice apathy, excitement, negativity, enthusiasm, and an array of cultures and belief systems. Questions arise:

- How can I meet the academic, social, and emotional needs of so many students?
- Where do I begin?
- What were the most significant challenges in years past, and how will those help me now?

Assistance

We realize that we need the help of someone who is possibly more experienced in navigating the ups and downs associated with this struggle that lies before us. In this part of the journey, we begin to seek the resources we will need to meet the challenges. Maybe we turn to a person and share our frustrations, hopes, and ideas. Maybe we reach out to parents in a way that emphasizes collaboration with a gentle underlying request: "I need your input." In this stage, we also ask ourselves:

- What are the realistic goals for this child or adolescent?
- How can I begin to create a safe environment and a connection with this individual so that mistakes and struggles are embraced?
- How can I begin to share and model my problem-solving resources so that my students feel and see my struggles and calls for assistance?

In this stage, I would suggest adopting a mentor, someone who can listen, validate, and help us walk through the inescapable confusion that occurs when humans interact with one another. This mentor could be another colleague or friend, but it must be a person who lifts us up and assists us in seeing the best parts of ourselves in the worst moments.

Of course, this relationship must have boundaries, with specific times set aside to lean into one another and build trust. These mentors can change partnerships periodically, but because there is repair and healing in simply having one's voice being heard, this practice is critical for educator and parent well-being.

Departure

It is time to step outside our comfort zone and try new ways of interacting with the situation or individual that has stimulated a particular change or challenge. In this stage, we cross the threshold of sameness by listening to learn rather than listening to respond. We have left the ordinary world.

Trials and Hard Work

Here, we begin to ask difficult questions that might propel deeper dives into reflection and observation, while simultaneously noticing how our own triggers can escalate the impending challenge or perceived crisis. These questions are for students, parents, teachers, and anyone who sits beside our young people.

- What do I need?
- What can my class do to assist me?
- What can my teachers do to assist me?
- How do I handle this negative situation?
- Who are my heroes? What character traits do I admire in these individuals?
- How will I know when I am on the right track?
- What are three positive emotions that I often feel? What are three negative emotions?
- What are my strengths?
- What are two or three challenges or obstacles that prevent me from reaching these small or large goals?

Approach and Crisis

Within this stage, we approach our worst fear. We sense that a change in relationship, instruction, dialogue, or physical movement is necessary. We begin to understand that the status quo can no longer be sustained. We enter into a type of crisis. One the one hand, we understand that crises induce movement and change, which brings with it intense difficulty. On the other, an opportunity, allowing us to learn and grow from our darkest hours, has presented itself. We face our vulnerabilities, triggers, worn-out belief systems, and long-held private logic. During these times of high stress, it is critical for us to provide emotional first aid to one another. Once we demonstrate that we can be with one another at our worst, we begin to build trust.

Treasures

We claim our treasures by acquiring a new perspective and a personal power that redefines our experiences and relationships. Rather than becoming caught up in an escalating conflict or weighed down by guilt and shame, we learn the skills that help us drain off hostility and frustration, and we look at our situation through a new lens. Here are questions to ask during this stage:

- What could be two or three new coping strategies?
- How could these new shifts fold into my everyday life?
- What old habits or practices can I begin to leave behind in gradual ways?
- How will I hold myself accountable for this new perspective, coping strategy, and self-care exercise?
- Are there two or three words I can begin saying to myself as a reminder I am in new territory and a new time?

Resolution

When we reach this stage, we begin seeing difficult behaviors as opportunities to teach young people (and ourselves) how to manage conflict and solve problems. We see our role as teacher expanding to include our ability to restore emotional equilibrium in our classrooms and schools, but more importantly within ourselves.

Status Quo

Now we have upgraded to a new level. We have embraced a perspective of growth and have learned, connected, and reshaped who we are constantly becoming. We begin anew. The school year is characterized with waves of calm, followed by the chaos of testing, unexpected changes in school schedules, holiday breaks, and personal adversities that can shake up our worlds. Educator stress at the end a semester or school year intermingles with student stress. For many educators, certain times of the year—the anticipation for the holidays or summer vacation, for example—brings significant stress. This time of year is so challenging because of testing requirements along with the constant requests to differentiate our instruction, incorporate school projects, conference with parents and students, keep engagement high, *and* attend to students' emotional needs. Simply put, it can feel overwhelming. Teachers walk into summer break with many of the same questions as our vulnerable students. We, too, ask ourselves:

- Will our students have enough to eat?
- Will there be anyone home at night to tuck them in?
- Will they hear kind words?
- Will they have any structured time or supervision?
- What will happen the day after they walk out of our classroom?

Five Strategies for Closure and Transition

Following are strategies for students and educators that can help lessen everyone's perceived stress while easing the transition to the unknown. These strategies are for all grade levels.

1. Symbolic Gifts

A talisman symbolizes ritual and ceremony, which our brains enjoy. Could we create a talisman for ourselves, a tangible reminder that we embrace in times of change and upheaval? This could be a painting, mantra, a love note to ourselves, an object we cherish, or words that soothe us from a favorite writer. Remembering our gifts and strengths with these items creates a connection. These symbolic gifts not only help us, but also demonstrate to our students what it means to self-reflect in a healthy manner. Using these tokens, talismans, or any other items that can be shared are a great resource for our students in transition. As they leave our classrooms, they still know that we will always be a part of their journey, even if we no longer see one another daily.

2. Photos and Affirmations

We all loved photo booths when we were young. Create an affirmation photo booth in the last weeks of class. Take a picture with you and your class. Then write a positive affirmation on a post-it note. Long after the school year is over, this photo can be embraced by all of those in it.

3. Planting and Nurturing

Metaphorically, a connected school always focuses on planting flowers instead of pulling weeds. During a transitional time in the school year, design a ritual seed-planting celebration. With paper cups, soil, and seeds, students can water, provide sunlight, and take care of their small plants all summer long knowing that they have been the caregivers in a project connecting the symbolism of the plant to their own lives. When we care for ourselves, we grow and flourish. When we care for another, he or she grows and flourishes. What types of planting or plants will enhance your repair and renewal?

4. Remember to Breathe

As we demonstrated in the previous chapter, calming the brain's stress response is critical to positive emotion, clarity of thought, and emotional regulation. When we use breathing or focused attention exercises to quiet the emotional center of our brains, we activate neural circuits in the brain that strengthen the flow of oxygen and glucose through the prefrontal cortex. Each day, invite students to join you in a guided or breathing-focused attention practice.

5. The Family Tree

A healthy, emotionally connected classroom mimics a family that embraces family privilege. During challenging times in your classroom, when we all are feeling the sting of being overwhelmed, we can create a family tree where branches symbolize students' and educators' strengths, contributions, and successes within the classroom. Small groups of students can represent larger branches, but all are connected. When the tree's leaves change colors or when its branches bud with new life, these events hold the stories of all students who have been a part of this tree of life. Whether we create this symbol with an actual tree or from art supplies, students should take part of their branch home. We should ask ourselves, what branches, leaves, or parts of this tree can we carry into our lives?[23] In addition to these strategies, Katherine Volk, Kathleen Guarino, Megan Edson Grandin, and Rose Clervil, from the National Center on Family Homelessness, have suggested other strategies to help us cope with everyday life. These are short strategies and are designed to be put into everyday practice to help us build joyful and pleasureful connections.[24] I have added a few of my own stress-reducing strategies for a swift release.

Here is the first strategy the authors offer. For two minutes, do one of the following:
1. Breathe.
2. Take five to ten deep breaths, tracing your hand with a pen until you feel the negative emotion lessen just a little.
3. Take a walk and notice three colors, sounds, and textures, spending two minutes focused on these experiences or sensations.
4. Run your hands under warm water, massaging them as you feel the warmth of the water coating and rinsing your hands free of tightness.
5. Laugh.
6. Doodle.
7. Compliment yourself.

Here are some other strategies that can be done in five to ten minutes.
1. Check in with your family or friends to see how they are doing, or to share a moment of encouragement. Nothing is more uplifting than when we serve each other, even in our moments of exasperation.
2. Exercise with the help of a YouTube video, or simply create a five-minute routine where you move your body through stretching, walking, or self-massage, focusing on your hands and neck.
3. By using your phone, record your frustrations, anger, and anxieties. When no one is around, and

your mind is full, have an honest talk with yourself. Share your feelings, the reasons, and the experiences from the angst and anxiety (even without recording). Having that conversation with ourselves can be beneficial in regulating our own stress response systems. As Dr. Dan Seigel makes clear, what is bearable is shareable, and what we can name, we can tame.[25]

4. Listen to music.
5. Enjoy a snack or a hot drink, like a cup of coffee or tea.

All of these strategies can be helpful in dealing with stress and adversity, particularly the types we described in the previous chapter in regard to the Adverse Childhood Experience study (ACE). These adversities affect all of us, and we can become emotionally triggered by past experiences. When students act out their pain, this mirrors our own life disruptions. By assessing our own ACE scores, however, we can have a better understanding of how adversity has affected our own lives. Knowing this score can be empowering and can start the process of healing between us and our students. Research shows that awareness can help our brains and bodies to repair and heal themselves, allowing for the release of past adversities and pain.

Many of our students attending our nation's schools have been given a classification of "emotionally disturbed," "developmentally disordered," or diagnosed with attention deficit disorder. Often, though, the root of these labels is a young life filled with violent, debilitating, and toxic disruptions. What science is now sharing is that once the traumatic event is over, the trauma continues to live in the nervous system of each individual. If there is not a caregiver that is perceived as safe to the child to buffer these adversities, the brain, in the regions where empathy, compassion, emotional regulation, and collaboration usually form, are actually not structurally or functionally present in brain architecture. This is also true for the caregivers or educators sitting beside our youth. The effects of these adversities may lay dormant in our bodies for ten, twenty, or thirty years and suddenly erupt, leaving us perplexed and anxious about our own emotional and physical health outcomes.

I want to close this chapter with a story that has touched me as a mom, an educator, and a friend. Our daughter, Sarah, is a first-year teacher in Columbus, Mississippi, in a self-contained classroom of seven boys who have received the classification of "emotionally disturbed." These five- to nine-year-old boys have all experienced significant violence, neglect, and abuse in their young lives. A more accurate classification of these resilient boys would be "developmental trauma disorder." Over the course of the school year, Sarah has become a steadfast and loving presence in her students' lives, providing the emotional, social, and cognitive experiences they require. During the last few months of the year, however, her own emotional reserves have been significantly depleted. We talk every weekday after school, and on one late afternoon, my words were not only inadequate, but seemed to trigger her own despair and exhaustion. I called Michael and asked him to reach out to her. Here is what he wrote to her:

Hi Sarah,

I am sitting thinking of your experiences so far this year!! No teacher, therapist program, or counselor preparation program can begin to get close to preparing anyone for the inside, up-close world of troubled kids. There is no cognitive explanation and certainly no way to prepare for this work. There is also no way to get around the intense emotional experiences you are currently experiencing. I wish there were.

These kids will show you pieces of yourself that you may never have experienced before. The intensity of the emotional experience will bring you to places that no one visits intentionally and often makes you feel really bad. No one talks about the feelings of hopelessness and despair that are part of working with these kids, and the absolute way that they fracture your self-confidence and your entire idea about yourself. No one speaks of the pain that pain-based behavior causes those who work with them.

You can now get a really clear sense of why most people want to stay as far away from these kinds of kids as possible, and why the vast majority of adults working around them want nothing to do with them. Why most principals do not go near them, and most schools would rather hire a new teacher (or three) every year and ignore the needs of the staff attempting to do what seems impossible. You now know why the vast majority of teachers leave this work...as quickly as possible.

There is a hidden secret to doing this work well, and it is a paradox. This work literally breaks you. It breaks you wide open. As I have gotten older, it is apparent to me that another thing most folks will not tell you is...that this is spiritual work. Real spiritual work is the work that breaks you. Most fear the breaking...but one cannot do the work with the kids you are working with without being broken. No one even got close to telling me this, and when I was your age it was beyond uncomfortable. It was painful. Pema Chodron puts it this way:

"To stay with that shakiness—to stay with a broken heart, with a rumbling stomach, with the feeling of hopelessness and wanting to get revenge-that is the path of true awakening. Sticking with that uncertainty, getting the knack of relaxing in the midst of chaos, learning not to panic-this is the spiritual path."

The threshold you have crossed this year is not experienced by many people. They have changed you, and you will never forget this year and these experiences...no one shares this with anyone, but this is the soil, the true dirt of growth. Know that the kids you are having this experience with are also being changed by experiencing you. Not your teaching, but YOUR personhood, your essence. It is an interaction that grows and heals both you and them.

You may never know this, Sarah, but you have provided these young people with a person that they will remember forever, and they have done the same for you! Both parties have been changed by the encounter...changed deeply and forever. You are on a real heroine's journey. It may not feel pleasant, but it will increasingly forge you into more of a person that you were born to become...

Be gentle with yourself.
Michael

Conclusion

Research in neuroscience has demonstrated how emotions and learning are intimately connected and processed in the brain. The story of the educator is about emotions and cognition. The message from social and affective neuroscience is clear: No longer can we focus solely on the level of the individual student to analyze effective strategies for classroom instruction, discipline, and behaviors. Teachers and students interact and learn from one another in ways that cannot be understood only by examining the cold cognitive aspects of academic skills. When we look inward and explore the adversities, obstacles, passions, and life processes of our own lives, we model this reflective ability for our students and their pain-filled life experiences. It is in this space of self-reflection that we might subtly alter how we present ourselves inside our classrooms, allowing us to return to the joy of teaching.[26]

To conclude, we would like to share a quote from author and international speaker, Sir Kenneth Robinson. According to Robinson:

> Imagination is the primary gift of human consciousness. In imagination, we can step out of the here and now. We can revisit and review the past. We can take another's view and this is the gift of empathy which is the beautiful gift of imagination. This imagination liberates us from our immediate circumstances and holds the constant possibility of transforming the present.[27]

May we all delve deep into the imagination of possibility, knowing that our emotional and mental brain states are never static, but have a fluidity of creative, dynamic, and diverse patterns of ideas, thoughts, and feelings. When nurtured, these can grow into the resilient capacity that is innately ours.

CHAPTER THREE

Brain Development through an Educator's Lens

Early Development

Much of the media continues to purport that the United States is in the midst of an educational crisis where our math, science, and reading scores continue to fall, the segregation of students by income as well as race continues to deepen, all while teacher effectiveness is still being measured by test scores. We have experienced the purported academic crisis through the significant increase of schools and districts around the country emphasizing and providing professional development on Science Technology Engineering and Math (STEM) curriculums. As a nation, we continue to implement hundreds of expensive school programs that, among other goals, promise to offer social and emotional well-being, improved cognition, enhanced social *and* emotional skills like coding for future jobs in technology. To put it simply, our youth are under more and more pressure to succeed in school and are tested and measured more than any previous generation. All these programs, expectations, and tests are contributing to a stressed and anxiety-prone generation of students.

It is time to pause and ask a critical question: What are we doing? With all the focus on the newest (and often most expensive) educational programs, we are forgetting that people change people, not programs. To develop and strengthen cognition in our young people, we must begin at a student's level of brain development. In this window in time, understanding brain development is critical in helping us teach to the neurodiversity of our students.

We continue to miss the mark with our students. We neglect the foundation, the very core of the challenges. We still overlook, and often dismiss out of hand, how adverse- and trauma-filled experiences are changing the way the brain develops structurally and functionally. Even the promise of trauma-informed programs, though, often only scratches the surface, expecting immediate results to complex problems. In other words, we keep looking for a "quick fix" solution where we can fix first and understand later. We see poor behavior choices, and we opt for compliance and obedience because, in the heated moments of conflict, even adults can fall back into a survival brain state where flight and fight overrule our cognitive and emotional strengths. We are quick to speak and slow to listen. We do not really "see" the young people seated before us. Rather than ask what is wrong with these kids, we need to ask instead: What happened to them? What is their story?

Admittedly, we do have a national crisis. Our crisis, however, is not centered on poor test scores. This crisis is rooted in childhood adversity and trauma. This crisis is severely affecting how our brains develop, how they get wired, and how they form neuronal circuits based on our experiences, relationships, and environments. As educators, we need to understand that many of our students who have experienced adversity and trauma sit in our schools and classrooms with a brain that is not functionally prepared to learn. No matter our fabulous lesson plans, curriculum designs, and enthusiasm for the academic content, we cannot change the brain states of our students by ignoring what student behaviors are communicating to us each day. Adverse childhood experiences (ACEs) change the architecture of the brain, triggering inflammation in both the brain and body. Early chronic stress can even reprogram how we will respond to stress and adversity in adulthood, affecting how we learn, relate to others, parent, and live life with all its many challenges.

Brain development is complex, and even today, we know very little about how individual regions of the brain work collectively through neuronal connections and projections. We do know, however, that human brains are not complete at birth, but, by design, continue to develop throughout a person's life. We also understand that the brain consists of a hierarchy of three primary systems: the brain stem, the limbic system, and the cerebral cortex. These are described below.

The Brain Stem

Linda Chapman describes the brain stem functions this way: "The brain stem contains vital areas of cardiopulmonary functions, primary visual and auditory centers, sensory and motor pathways, and areas of neurochemical production."[28] The limbic system is our emotional center and memory formation area. This area works for our survival and can initiate our instincts for fight or flight. The cerebral cortex is our left and right hemisphere, which processes our ability to pay attention, regulate, problem solve, create, perceive, and reason, among other cognitive functions. The brain is a social and historical organ and it implicitly remembers experiences innately creating a memory template that holds these early life events, emotions, and visual images.[29] The brain develops not only from back to front, but also from the inside out.

From utero through the first two years of life, the brain is in its greatest time of maturation. During this time, an infant's nervous system is also developing. Stimuli from the social environment enters the brain stem where attunement and attachment with a caregiver is critical for regulating the sensory and motor systems that are so important for emotional, social, and physiological well-being. According to Peter Levine, "The fetal period through the first two years of life creates the blueprint that influences every system in the body from immunity to the expression and regulation of emotion, to nervous system resilience, communication, intelligence, and self-regulatory mechanisms for such basics as body temperature and hormone production."[30]

The language of the brain stem is sensation, and if sensations such as discomfort, hunger, touch, and exaggerated emotional responses are not buffered or attuned to in those first few months or years of life, the child or adolescent may need to re-experience those critical earlier missed developmental steps and skills that occur in the brain stem, such as rhythm, movement, and sensory regulation. Rocking, balancing, fine motor activity, touch, and temperature regulation may need to be re-experienced later in life no matter the chronological age of the child or adolescent. These sensory and motor skills, which are developing in the brain stem, also lead to emotional regulation. Allan Schore argues this attachment process is integral for not only sensory and motor development, but also for developing connections with others, which he sees as the fundamental building block for emotional and behavior regulation needed for learning. If the sensory systems are not developing sufficiently, behavior, emotional regulation, and learning are negatively affected.[31] Before learning and cognition can be developed, children need patterned, repetitive, appropriate developmental experiences to assist them in meeting the needs of all lower brain regions.

Because the brain develops from the bottom up—from

the brain stem to the limbic system and then to the cortex—children and adolescents who have been affected by chronic adversity may enter our classrooms with varying levels of brain development. We have seen how many of our students come to school with high levels of adversity and trauma, and we are beginning to realize that their levels of brain development have also been compromised by these experiences. Right now, we have an opportunity to attend to the neurodiversity of our students. We need to meet them where they are in their development and prime their brains for cognition and healthy structures and functions for appropriate growth and well-being.

The Limbic System

After the brain stem has developed, the limbic system takes center stage. An emotional switchboard, the amygdala is buried deep in the brain's limbic system. It is in this area where our survival instincts and emotional messages are subconsciously prioritized and learned. We continually scan environments for feelings of connection and safety. Students in pain may look oppositional, defiant, aggressive, or aloof. Currently, we are learning that most negative behavior arises from a stress response. When we feel distress, our brains and bodies prioritize survival, and we concentrate on the emotional messages flooding our brains and bodies, all of which trigger the question, "Am I safe?" We react physiologically with an irritated limbic system that increases blood pressure, heart rate, and respiration. Chronic activation of the fear response produces high levels of cortisol, which can even damage brain cells responsible for cognition and learning.[32]

While the language of the brain stem is sensation, the language of the limbic system is feelings. When stressed students get angry or shut down, they do not hear our words.

In the heat of the moment, for example, explaining a disciplinary procedure to a student or making them reflect on their actions in the heat of the moment IS NOT a good time to ask students to reflect. In these moments, we need to remember that we are creatures who prioritize feelings over thought. We are neurobiologically wired to survive this way, and we do so by reading the feelings of others. In other words, we use nonverbal communication. Children and adolescents with histories of neglect, abuse, and violence are constantly concentrating on tones of voice, facial expressions, and movements of others, constantly staying alert for danger. Unfortunately, any information not associated with danger is ignored and dismissed.[33]

The Development of the Brain Hemispheres

The right-brain hemisphere develops earlier than the left-brain one. The right hemisphere contains implicit memory, emotions, and visual images. It is the seat of the development of our core identity. In contrast to the right side, the left-brain hemisphere begins to develop language in the second year of life. While both sides of the brain are critical for brain functionality, the integration of hemispheres is foundational for healthy development. When this does not occur, emotional and cognitive challenges can occur in the adolescent. Abused and neglected children, for instance, can have core identity challenges that affect the development of the right-brain hemisphere. Underdeveloped sensory and motor systems, furthermore, are unable to process, organize, or express incoming sensory information.[34]

Babies sleep long hours in the early days after birth as their sensory and nervous systems begin to develop. Infants can tolerate very little stimulation as they adjust to the outside world. In this stage of early development, the role of an attachment figure becomes significant in helping co-regulation develop. An infant's underdeveloped sensory and nervous systems require gentle stimulation and a gradual progression of co-regulation techniques such as holding, rocking, healthy eye contact, and soft talking. During these processes, the infant is invited to explore new people, sounds, places, and experiences. Without a secure and steadfast attachment figure introducing these new stimuli to the infant, the infant instead experiences negative arousal. If this negative arousal becomes prolonged and chronic, the infant's brain begins to wire in a disorganized way. This affects the development of a healthy brain and nervous system.[35]

In our roles as teachers, parents, counselors, or mental health providers, we can create and implement brain-aligned strategies that can help the integration of both the right- and left-brain hemispheres. In addition to helping to regulate sensory, motor, and control processing in these children, these strategies can also assist in developing healthy emotional responses. Brain-aligned strategies, however, are not programs we can buy, nor are they instructional practices that add more work to our days. Rather, these strategies are procedures, routines, structures, and transitions we can construct through morning meetings, bell work, and closing activities at the end of the day or class period. They can be implemented individually, in small groups, or for whole classrooms. These strategies can be found at the end of this chapter.

Below is a description of a child I met this year. This child, "S.," has experienced chronic, unpredictable adversity, which has not only affected the lower regions of his brain development, but also the development of his stress response system. He functions significantly below his respective grade level, and his ability to think clearly, problem solve, reason, create, and explore has been tremendously compromised.

S. is small for his eight years. His left arm is paralyzed as he holds it close to his stomach. He has become a genius at all tasks with the use of one hand and arm. He unzips his jacket with his teeth, dribbles a basketball with one hand in a spectacular way while dragging his left leg behind him because he runs and walks with a significant limp. His classification under IDEA law is Traumatic Brain Injury caused by physical abuse at the hands of his uncle. This occurred when he was sixteen months old. His conscious brain does not remember this, but his body does. He is easily frustrated, is difficult to understand, but S. loves to love. He craves attention. He held my hand most of the time in his class, and became visibly sad and frustrated when I needed to attend to another student. His cognitive capacity is severely limited, and he struggles to recognize numbers greater than twenty and only recognizes a few letters of the alphabet. He is on constant alert and defends against perceived threats, irritates others, and can instigate an altercation easily.

There are millions of stories like S.'s in this country. We now understand that high emotional states equate to low logical states, and dampened emotional states lead to higher logical cognition. We need to train our experienced, new, and pre-service educators in regulation and attachment strategies to help them teach this type of students. These students make up almost a third of all students in general education classrooms. When we add the number of students who are also under the negative effect of anxiety, this percentage becomes even larger. According to the National Institute of Mental Health, "In 2015, about 3 million teens ages

12 to 17 experienced at least one major depressive episode in the past year," and "More than 2 million [teens] report experiencing depression that impairs their daily function. About 30% of girls and 20% of boys–totaling 6.3 million teens have had an anxiety disorder...."[36]

As we described earlier in this chapter, when children or adolescents enter school with activated limbic and brain stem regions, their brains are not functioning in a way to allow for logical understanding, the use of words, or thought processes that enable improved choices to occur. They also cannot self-regulate or relate with empathy, social attunement, and logical thought processes. Attachment and neuroscience research clearly supports practices that promote positive relationships, connections, attunement, and co-regulation with adults. In order for the brain to focus and reason logically, the research makes clear that these processes must be emphasized at a young age.

Adolescent Brain Development

The first critical stage of brain development is during infancy. This stage was described in the first part of this chapter. The second greatest time of brain development, however, occurs during the early adolescent years. During this time, the brain reorganizes, and there is a proliferation of new neural synapses that are soon consolidated. This process produces a great deal of emotional instability as older neuronal connections lose out to new ones, in effect creating room for the new specialized skills a young person will need during this time of brain growth.

Inside Out, the 2015 Pixar film in which the emotions of the main character, Riley (Kaitlyn Dias), are personified on screen, has a great example of this process. There is not a more profound scene in the film than when Bing Bong,

Riley's imaginary friend (voiced by Richard Kind), dies. Just like in reality, when Riley approaches her twelfth birthday, her brain begins to develop, starting a process that leaves her imagination behind. In the real world, just like in Pixar, this is the time when childhoods begin to close, and children enter into adolescence.

Redefined Purpose and Identity

Inside Out embraces this developmental shift in a visual and meaningful way. Bing Bong represents Riley's innocence, imagination, creativity, and childlike joy. As Riley's brain begins to confront intense emotions, she revisits many of her childhood core memories, which start to enrich this new developing stage of life. As in reality, Riley begins her search for a new identity and social status just like other adolescents begin to navigate this critical time of development. Finding a new purpose—and discovering who we are becoming as human beings—characterizes the great neurobiological changes of adolescents.

Within this stage, an adolescent's job is to question authority and search for an identity. As young people grow into these new responsibilities during their personal development, teachers and administrators need to create classroom cultures and relationships that promote creativity, autonomy, and positive social interactions. It is our responsibility to help our young adults see a larger life picture filled with optimal choices and possibilities.

There are also significant changes happening in the brain during this stage, particularly the increase of the secretion and baseline levels of neurohormones. The adolescent brain contains lower levels of serotonin, which can decline in these years. Lowered serotonin levels can contribute to increased aggression along with higher levels of testosterone, which can also contribute to angry outbursts and impulsive behavior. The baseline for dopamine, our "feel-good" neurotransmitter, is also lower, meaning more dopamine is required during adolescence for a satisfying feeling to occur. Additionally, the frontal lobes of the brain are not fully developed in these years, in effect limiting brain function for problem solving, discernment, emotional regulation, and sustained attention.

When adversity and trauma are a chronic part of an adolescent's experiences, brain development can be compromised or become highly disorganized from these chronic life disruptions. As mentioned earlier, when children enter adolescence, they go through a natural period of developmental "pruning" of neurons. When we are very young, we have an overproduction of neurons and synaptic connections. Some of these die off naturally, allowing us to turn down the noise in the brain to increase new mastery skills that interest us. The brain, in other words, is becoming more specialized at the things we excel at and interest us. Young people who have experienced toxic levels of stress and adversity prior to adolescence, however, can experience this pruning early. Furthermore, during this sculpting process of neuronal connections in adolescence, these young people may experience excessive pruning and consolidation of neurons and pathways. With excess pruning in the integrated areas and circuitry between the hippocampi, corpus collosum, prefrontal cortex, and amygdala, these brain changes have profound effects on self-regulation, attention, thoughts, learning, and behaviors.[37]

Adolescent Brain and Trauma

"One of the greatest challenges and responsibilities as an educator in this time is teaching through the adversity and trauma our students bring into the classroom each day."

— NATALIE

Natalie is a fifteen-year-old student in eighth grade. She was retained in fifth grade (and perhaps one other time, but being new to her school, the staff is unsure of her exact past educational history). Natalie usually is in school only three days a week. She rarely completes any work and is quiet and withdrawn. Most days, she shuts out the world with her head on her desk, glancing at her phone, or scanning the hallway or classroom windows for any activity. The school knows she lives with an older sister and three younger brothers. Her parents' whereabouts are unknown, and it also seems like she is one of the primary caregivers in her family. She is a "young carer," that is, a child or adolescent who provides emotional and physical support and takes on household responsibilities while looking after his or her own needs.[38]

Trauma has many faces. Adverse experiences that lead to feelings of isolation, rejection, and mistrust can be sudden or subtle, but the neurobiological changes caused by negative experiences prompt our brain to create a fear response. During adolescence, this fear can look oppositional, depressed, moody, anxious, and sometimes can even turn violent and aggressive. Our repetitive reactions become hard-wired pathways in the emotional centers of the brain, shutting off the frontal lobes, which are the parts of the brain controlling decision-making, problem solving, and emotional regulation. Our ability to mindfully respond—rather than negatively react—is compromised.

Bessel van der Kolk and Bruce Perry are pioneers in the study of trauma. They have demonstrated how the onset of past trauma can be triggered by memories, flashbacks, visual images, the sound of a voice, or anything that is a reminder of the particular adversity. According to these scholars, the very event that has caused so much pain often becomes our source of meaning, identity, and a place of familiarity, no matter how dysfunctional it feels or looks. With the help of this research, we now realize that we must create an emotionally safe environment for students like Natalie, which will provide them the opportunity to feel connected and understood.

Stress Response Systems

In her book, *The Deepest Well*, Nadine Burke-Harris demonstrates that when our stress response systems are in good working order, they can save our lives; but if they are out of balance, they can also shorten our lives.[39] Our stress response systems, much like the brain, are at birth. Both of these systems develop throughout childhood and young adulthood. During these years, our brains and our bodies are constantly processing incoming information. One of the ways we process all the external and internal stimuli is through a system called the Hypothalamic Pituitary Axis (HPA). This system is deeply affected by early life experiences and genetics. The HPA is our longer acting stress response system and produces cortisol with the adrenal glands.[40] When activated by early chronic stress, the brain and body become flooded with inflammatory neurochemicals. Early childhood stress, moreover, can reprogram how we respond to stress for a lifetime. For the developing brain, being able to predict what comes next is crucial. When unpredictable experiences appear over and over again, the brain continues to be activated in this "fight or flight" stress response state, thus altering how we perceive our environments, relationships, and experiences. In addition to this, the HPA directly impacts our immune system, the body's operating system.

Epi-genetics

"I feel very strongly that I am under the influence of things or questions which were left incomplete and unanswered by my parents and grandparents and more distant. It often seems as if there was an impersonal karma within a family, which is passed from parents to children. It always seemed to me that I had to...compete, or perhaps continue, things which previous ages had left unfinished."
— CARL JUNG, *MEMORIES, DREAMS, REFLECTIONS*

Genes are not fixed, as environments and life experiences can trigger biochemical messages that can affect how the gene behaves. This process is defined as epi-genetics.[41] New research contends that human DNA is actually our recipe book—our genetic blueprint—and although this blueprint is fixed, experiences can change the way DNA is expressed and read. The epigenome is how genes express themselves based on signals from the environment. These environmental signals from inside or outside the organism can affect the way a gene is activated or inhibited. According to Rachel Yehuda, professor of psychiatry and neuroscience at Mount Sinai School of Medicine in New York, we are all born with an innate set of skills or functions for survival that allow us to adapt to stressful experiences.[42] These skill sets, however, are vulnerable to changes in our environments. The child of a parent who was always on alert from past negative experiences, for example, may inherit the impulse to startle easily or recoil in times of perceived danger or threat. Although these adaptive changes are protective, they can actually reset how the body responds to the perceived unfamiliar or unsafe environment, keeping the brain and body in a hyper-vigilant, hyper-aroused alarm state. These adaptive changes are caused by the chemical signals in the cells, what researchers refer to as "epigenetic tags." These signals can either activate or inhibit a specific gene. We now know that environments, events, perceptions, feelings, and thoughts can all affect how a gene will be positively or negatively affected. Our genome is the genetic material in our body, and although cells have the same genome, they have different epigenomes. Our epigenome is diverse and unique to us.

The history we share with our families begins much before our awareness. Rachel Yehuda studies generational adversity, epi-genetics, and trauma. She has studied the stress response systems of adult children of Holocaust survivors as well as the pregnant mothers who were in their second to third trimester when they experienced the 9/11 attacks in or near the World Trade Center. These women went on to develop PTSD. Although still controversial, her research is groundbreaking in its examination of the lowered cortisol levels of parents and their children affected by trauma. Traditionally, we think of high chronic stress being associated with higher levels of cortisol. While this is often true, in Yehuda's research she observed lower levels of cortisol in both mother and baby following birth, and this could originate from the stress response systems that have reprogramed how cortisol is produced based on the sixteen different genes that were altered and expressed differently in her studies.[43] When cortisol levels are compromised, so is our ability to regulate our emotions, create pauses, and implement behavioral choices that serve us well. Yehuda argues that children of mothers who have significant PTSD are three times more likely to be diagnosed with PTSD than children in the control groups. She also has found that children of the Holocaust survivors are three to four times more likely to struggle with anxiety and forms of depression.[44]

What can we take away from this? While many of our students and youth perhaps may not have been directly confronted with a traumatic event, according to this research, they can still experience the effects of adversity as the emotions of their parents can be biochemically transmitted through the germ cells altering the genetic expression from a stressful environment occurring in utero. Bruce Lipton, a cellular biologist puts it this way: "When stress hormones cross the human placenta...they cause fetal blood vessels to constrict in the viscera, sending more blood to the periphery preparing the fetus for fight or flight behavioral response."[45] The mother's emotions, thoughts, and perceptions can cross the placenta in the form of hormones, reprograming and preparing how the child will adapt to his or her environment.[46] This cutting-edge research has momentous implications for our work as educators, as it lays out a framework for understanding students who bring the genetics of family trauma and adversity into our classrooms.

In the following chapter, we will delve into tangible brain-aligned strategies that address attachment and relationships. These strategies provide students of all ages an opportunity to practice emotional regulation, an executive function that develops over time in the frontal brain regions, and can be grossly underdeveloped in students who carry with them adverse childhood experiences. A few regulation strategies are shared below. Our brains are created and wired to bend and not to break. Healthy connections and attachments can buffer those early childhood adversities. The Harvard Graduate School of Education has written a two-part report that recommends the following:

- Use scientific knowledge to help identify children with significant adversities and support children whose needs are not being addressed adequately by existing services.
- Enhance "serve and return" interactions between babies and children, who live in disadvantaged environments, and adult caregivers. This can strengthen the building blocks of resilience.

• Target the development of specific skills needed for adaptive coping, sound decision-making, and effective self-regulation in children and adults. Use scientific knowledge to help identify and support children whose needs are not being addressed adequately by existing services.[47]

How to Help Regulate Students

Put simply, we meet the child or adolescent where they are in brain development. Just as homes are built from the foundation up, so are our brains. We must begin with the foundation.

This foundation can only be built with the help of adults. All student regulation begins with adult regulation. However, it must be noted that all the students have private realities that become their operating belief systems. These systems can be both positive and negative depending on not just the experiences themselves, but how those experiences have been interpreted by the individual student. Some students, for example, may believe that teachers and other adults can provide support when they have a problem. Our most difficult and troubled young people, however, often have very different belief systems that are filtered through their own experiences that can diverge from what is considered "normal."

Children who have grown up in a chaotic environment with unpredictable adult support, for instance, may view adults as anything but helpful. They may believe that adults cannot be trusted or relied upon for help. Often this is perceived as a "lack of respect" from the child towards the adult. However, we need to see these belief systems that troubled children and youth bring into our schools as protective responses, not hostile challenges. These young people, because of their real life experiences are relationships, are reluctant and resistant. We must first create a different reality about adults for these young people. We must be quicker to listen and slower to speak. Calming the lower brain and draining high levels of emotion are the first steps in the process of changing these young people's belief systems and private realities, demonstrating for them that adults can be of help and can be trusted when they have difficulties. If we fail this first critical step, and respond with hostility and anger, we will actually reinforce and confirm the troubled students' belief systems, solidifying their personal realities that all adults are hostile and cannot be relied upon. Educators must mindfully change this dynamic.

While all this is helpful to understand theoretically, in reality, it is often difficult for teachers to take this understanding approach. What can we do when a student comes into our classroom "rough and ready" for the fight? Some strategies are below:

1. Be proactive. Schools know their students who walk in "rough" and dysregulated much of the time. We can be proactive by meeting them as they enter school and checking in with them early. As we get to know our students, we can recognize subtle clues that can inform us when a young person enters school stressed. We can preemptively connect with them and provide that sense of safety and support, calming them prior to starting their day.

2. Provide a space for a few rocking chairs for students to slowly rock as they listen to sounds produced by a white noise machine or from an app on their phones. To regulate means to meet the student in the lower regions of the brain. This is part of a preventative system of discipline. Our students who have experienced adversity do not respond to or

need punishment, which often just escalates their behavior. They first require a chance to regulate, which means moving out of the fight or flight response and into the thinking part of the brain. We must regulate their stress response, or we will find ourselves trying to handle escalating hostile behaviors from a student who is reacting from the lower regions of his or her brain. Once the student is calm, we can then begin to communicate using words that do not point to blame but to understanding. Here are some examples:

"I am wondering what happened. Can you help me? "

"I am feeling very confused, today. How are you feeling?"

"Please help me to understand, as I feel we have talked about this before."

"I need to know what you need."

"How can I help?"

"What can we do to make this better?"

"Please let me know when we can make a plan."

"I will work hard to find ways to help myself not to feel so irritated or angry."

"I can do this better, too!"

3. Going to an amygdala reset area within the room can serve as the space for a stressed brain to begin to calm. Students can be taught how to use this space, and it can be part of the routines in the classroom. Once they are regulated, we can teach them how breathing can calm their stress response. Coloring books can also be provided to allow students to find ways to dampen down their activated stress response. The amygdala reset (or first aid station) could include an ice or heat pack that students can choose to put on the back of their necks, providing a comforting sensation and pressure to sooth elevated emotions. By doing this, we are actually modeling how to regulate emotions for students, a

skill that will serve all of them well in their future lives.

This, it must be said, is not a waste of instructional time. Stressed brains do not learn. Until the student is in a relaxed and calm brain state, no learning can occur, even if a great lesson is being taught. It is important to model the amygdala reset station in a positive and celebratory way, as these areas need to be perceived positively by the students. When the class has worked hard on an assignment and needs a break, for example, this section of the class could be used as an area of relaxation and renewal for the remainder of the morning or afternoon.

4. Remember, stress is stored in the body. Keeping a jar of menthol muscle cream in the amygdala reset area is a great idea, as it provides a wonderful sensation for bringing students back to the present moment. An exercise roller is an effective tool in helping a student feel pressure and sensation in the body, which helps him or her focus within the frontal lobe regions of the brain, creating a sensation of feeling the body in the "here and now."

5. Notice what is going on around you, and speak to what you are noticing. Noticing is a form of what Larry Brendtro calls "preemptive connecting." This should be unobtrusive so as not to create impressions of favoritism. Connecting does not require a major investment of time. Bonds can be built in natural moment-by-moment interactions. Small doses of connecting behavior are most effective. Those with histories of negative encounters with adults are strongly influenced by small cues of respect, humor, and goodwill.[48] Notice a student's new shoes, a haircut, a smile, an emotion, or an action. These small observations go a long way and tell the student, "I am here, and I see you." Noticing provides psychological visibility for students. Noticing allows us to

reach out to our most difficult students who are often more familiar with negative interactions from the adults in their lives than positive ones.

6. Adversity leaves a child feeling powerless and without a voice. Validation, though, is powerful because it gives our students an opportunity to have a voice and be heard. Validation does not mean agreeing or approving. Validation is the recognition and acceptance of another person's thoughts, feelings, sensations, and behaviors as "understandable ways of being" and interacting with the world. Some examples of this type of validation are below:

"That must feel awful."

"I cannot imagine how frustrating this feels."

"This must feel scary."

"That must have made you feel_____."

"I hear you saying_____."

"Sounds like you are so angry."

7. Questions can create alertness and assist in locating patterns and contexts of behaviors. Below are examples of questions we have created that help us discover the primary needs of our most vulnerable students:

What else is going on here?

What does this child need?

What keeps me only looking at the behavior?

What is this behavior communicating right now?

What in the environment could be triggering this behavior?

Remember, relationships and regulation drive academic success and well-being!

CHAPTER FOUR

Trauma, Adversity, Toxic Stress, and School Discipline

It is easy to understand the outrage people feel when they hear the disturbing statistics about the state of children's lives in the United States. For most of us, our hearts ache when we hear the stories of mistreatment, harm, and neglect that many young people deal with on a daily basis. We watch the stories on the evening news, see stories on the internet, and read statistics that many people struggle to comprehend. To add to some of the dismal statistics mentioned earlier in our book and to reframe them in the context of school-level discipline practices, a quick review of the state of children in America can be found below.

- The United States has 14.7 million children living in poverty. That number exceeds the population of twelve of our states combined: Alaska, Hawaii, Maine, Montana, New Hampshire, North Dakota, Rhode Island, South Dakota, Vermont, West Virginia, and Wyoming.
- The country's poorest age group is its youngest children. The younger our children are, the poorer they are.
- Around three million children in the United States live in families trying to survive on two dollars a day for each family member. Our child poverty rate rivals some of the world's poorest countries.[49]

As more and more educators and community members learn about the Adverse Childhood Experiences (ACEs) studies, we are becoming more aware of how many of us faced adversity growing up as well as how many of our students carry with them the effects of growing up in environments that can change their neurobiology. To review, the adversities that the ACE studies examine are the following:

Abuse

- **Emotional abuse:** If a parent or other adult in your home ever swore at you, insulted you, or put you down.
- **Physical abuse:** If a parent or other adult in your home ever hit, beat, kicked or physically hurt you.
- **Sexual abuse:** If an adult or person at least five years older ever touched you in a sexual way, or tried to make you touch their body in a sexual way, or attempted to have sex with you.

Household Challenges

- **Intimate partner violence:** If parents or adults in home ever slapped, hit, kicked, punched or beat each other up.
- **Household substance abuse:** If a household member was a problem drinker or alcoholic or used street drugs or abused prescription medications.
- **Household mental illness:** If a household member was depressed or mentally ill or a household member attempted suicide.
- **Parental separation or divorce:** If parents were ever separated or divorced.
- **Incarcerated household member:** If a household member went to prison.[50]

The 2015 National Survey of Children Exposed to Violence indicates that nearly 60% of children have been exposed to trauma in the past year; more than one in ten children reported five or more exposures.[51] According to a survey on ACEs, conducted by the National Survey of Children's Health (NSCH), almost half of the nation's children have experienced at least one or more types of the serious childhood traumas listed above. According to the NSCH, this translates into an estimated 34,825,978 children nationwide. This report goes on to say that nearly a third of the youth ages twelve to seventeen in America have experienced two or more ACEs that are likely to affect their physical and mental health. Across the fifty states, the percentages ranged from a low of 23% in New Jersey to a high of 44.4% in Arizona. The survey results are not too surprising, in that they show that childhood ACEs increase as a child grows older and decrease as family income rises. Nevertheless, ACEs are still experienced by more than one in three children under the age of six. Even in higher income families, more than one in four children have ACEs.[52] ACEs, however, can also be found in community environments, which Wendy Ellis and Bill Dietz have described in their research (see Chapter 1 for more on this). Community violence, poverty, and unaffordable housing all play a vital role in the lives and behaviors of many of the young people we serve in our schools. Stressed brains, and brains in pain, cannot learn.

The increased awareness of this work has led the field and many school districts toward becoming "adversity and trauma informed." This is a positive and encouraging movement. After working with troubled and troubling children and youth for forty years, it is exciting to be a part of this movement. The students who carry high levels of adversity and toxic stress into our schools are our most challenging students. School systems, however, have historically not had much success with these young people. Our experience tells us that this shift will require school districts, and the adults within them, to change many long-held beliefs about how we handle, correct, and, yes, discipline children and youth in our schools and classrooms. To transform our current school practices, we must be able to see, feel, and think very differently about our most difficult young people.

Who Are These Kids? The Prevalence of Youth Trauma

Prior to reading this chapter, follow along with this exercise that we often ask teachers to complete. To begin, draw a response to intervention (RtI) triangle or Multi-System of Support (MTSS) triangle, and create your three tiers that are standard with both models. These tiers represent levels of emotional, regulatory, and connection support for our students. Read the following descriptions of each tier below. As we explore these tiers, we can begin to understand how achievement gaps may be aligned with adversity gaps.

• **Bottom Tier:** This tier represents the emotional and behavioral supports for all students. These children and adolescents who fall under this tier are students who come to you every day and rarely cause any behavioral difficulties. They meet their schoolwork responsibilities, pay attention, and try to cooperate with our classroom procedures. These are students who are easily redirected and rarely need any negative sanctions like detentions or suspensions. What percentage of your students meets this description?

• **Middle Tier:** These are students who are "off and on." We call these students "fence sitters," meaning they have moments of both meeting expectations and needing high levels of redirection and support. They often push limits, but sometimes respond to our structure and requests. What percentage of your students meets this description?

• **Top Tier**: These are your most difficult students and they are rarely, if ever, regulated. These students are well known in the school office and the faculty area. These students are difficult to engage constructively and can be oppositional and volatile. They are angry, often in conflict with teachers, adults, or their peers. They can also appear depressed and very hard to motivate, and often miss a lot of school. These are students who seem to always be receiving negative sanctions, including moving in and out of school suspensions and detentions. These negative sanctions, though, do not change their behavior. They do poorly in school and have sometimes been held back. By high school, they are often not on track to graduate and most likely have experienced failure since they first stepped into a school. What percentage of your students meets this description?

This exercise can be a great conversation starter with colleagues. Thinking about these tiers, specific students come to mind for each one. Those in the top tier tend to be a school's most difficult and troubled children and youth. We all know who they are in the classroom. But what do we know about their lives? Looking through the lens of the ACE surveys, how do their lives look? Is the anger we often see in students from these top tiers directed outwardly, inwardly, or is it more generalized and less focused?

Dr. Nicholas Long and Dr. Frank Fecser, both experts in working with troubled young people and founders of the Life Space Crisis Intervention Training Institute, categorize patterns of thinking, feeling, and behavior in children and youth who come to school with complex developmental trauma. Most troubled young people can be roughly broken down into three groups: those who externalize; those who internalize; and those who are in a persistent state of alarm (i.e., PSAs). Young people who become "externalizers" carry into schools self-serving thinking patterns and defense mechanisms and have a lack of empathy toward others. They can be narcissistic, impulsive, often rejecting any feedback from adults. According to Long and Fecser, "externalizers" see the world this way: "I do what I have to do, even if it hurts others. I have to take care of Number One. I have a reputation to maintain and I won't be disrespected. I have no need to change." These patterns, importantly, are not conscious in these young people. These children and adolescents are functioning from lower brain regions that chronically activate the fight/flight response. To change their surface behaviors will require interventions that work to change their unconscious patterns of thinking, feeling, and behavior. We need to provide patterned repetitive experiences that place an emphasis on emotional regulation strategies while building sustainable connections with these students through their conflicts.

"Internalizers," in Long's and Fescer's framework, have internalized their traumatic stress. These young people get angry in schools, but when they settle down, they tend to end up blaming themselves for something else that went wrong in their lives. They act out impulsively but feel bad afterward. These young people are at high risk of drug and alcohol use, and they can be students who harm themselves, are depressed, and are anxious. These young people, though, are also in pain. According to Long and Fecser, these students can be described as "Kids who internalize their anger tend to take responsibility for all that is wrong with life and learn to punish themselves at an early age....The students' self-perception can be described in this fashion: 'I'm a terrible person. I can never do anything right. I can't control myself so I need to be punished.'"[53]

"PSAs," the third group of our top tier students, often act similarly to students with attention deficit hyperactive disorder or ADHD. These young people have trouble organizing their belongings, materials, thoughts, and feelings. These young people usually come from disrupted environments, and have been living in chaotic situations that are often unpredictable. We can feel their stress and see it in their bodies, which are often unable to be still or calm. When a child is exposed to chronic levels of stress, their brain sensitizes pathways for the fear response and it becomes a reactive and almost automatic response. This brain state is called a hyper-arousal state and these young people are hyper-vigilant. Their brains are on high chronic alert, and any nonverbal cues may feel threatening. Often, these children and youth are medicated and labeled ADHD, yet underneath the diagnosis is their trauma and pain.[54]

These three broad groups of students are students who have experienced toxic levels of stress and adversity in their lives. These are children and youth with complex developmental trauma. They are all demonstrating pain-based behavior. As you read this chapter, these are the children and youth we would like you to keep in mind as we discuss the changes necessary to become a school that is truly trauma- and adversity-responsive and brain aligned within this new discipline paradigm.

In their 1994 book about adolescent suicide, *No One Saw My Pain*, Andrew Slaby and Lili Garfinkel describe the deep pain that many of the young people who walk into our classrooms daily are experiencing. Clearly, these authors understand the issues we face as we begin to examine how school discipline policies and practices interconnect with these young people in our schools. According to Slaby and Garfinkel:

> While our hearts go out to children who hurt, when their behavior troubles others, concern quickly turns to blame. We call these kids

disturbed, delinquent, disordered, and disruptive. Many seriously troubled kids are treated as damaged goods to discard. Their troubled behavior is a cry of pain, a call for help that often goes unheard.[55]

How do trauma, adversity, and toxic stress interconnect with school discipline? Just a short examination of school discipline tells the tale.

- In America, a public school student is suspended every two seconds.
- In America, a public school student is corporally punished every forty-three seconds.
- In America, a public school student drops out of school every nine seconds.[56]

In Indiana, the state where my co-author Lori lives and teaches, during the 2013-2014 school year, more than 75,000 students were suspended. That is about one out of every fourteen students.[57] Indiana, however, is not alone. During the 2015-2016 school year, Virginia schools, for example, issued over 131,500 out-of-school suspensions to over 70,000 individual students. Virginia schools continue to use exclusionary discipline with very young students at an astonishing rate, issuing over 17,300 short-term suspensions and at least 93 long-term suspensions to children in pre-Kindergarten (pre-K) through third grade alone.[58] Following this pattern, during the 2016-2017 school year, the country's two largest school districts—the New York City Department of Education (NYCDOE) and the Los Angeles Unified School District (LAUSD)—suspended or expelled students for a total of 47,558 days.[59]

Along with the large numbers of students who are suspended or expelled from public schools across America, however, also important to note is the the disproportionality of who is receiving this form of "discipline." In my state of New Jersey, for example, African Americans make up 15 percent of students enrolled in our public schools, but receive 40 percent of the out-of-school suspensions state-wide. Similarly, Latino students in New Jersey public schools make up 23 percent of the student population and receive 29 percent of our state's out-of-school suspensions. Adding to this, special education students in New Jersey make up 15 percent of the student population yet receive 29 percent of our out-of-school suspensions.

For the 2013-2014 school year, this disproportionality could be seen on a national basis. In this year:

- Students with disabilities were more than twice as likely to receive out-of-school suspensions as students without disabilities.
- African-American K-12 students were 3.8 times as likely to receive out-of-school suspensions as white students.
- African-American students were 2.2 times as likely to receive a referral to law enforcement or be subject to a school-related arrest as were white students.
- American Indian or Alaska Native, Latino, Native Hawaiian or other Pacific Islander, and multiracial boys were also disproportionately suspended from school, representing 15 percent of K-12 students but 19 percent of K-12 students receiving out-of-school suspensions.[60]

The suspension and expulsion problem starts early, in pre-school. On every school day in 2016, for instance, some 250 preschool children across the country were suspended or expelled for bad behavior, and black children were more than twice as likely to receive this type of discipline. In total, about 50,000 preschoolers—kids who are three and four years old—were suspended from both public and private preschools at least once in 2016, and an additional 17,000 are estimated to have been expelled, according to findings from the nonprofit Center for American Progress.

Black children were 2.2 times more likely to be suspended or expelled than other children, the analysis reported, and boys were given 82 percent of the suspensions and expulsions, even though they represent 51 percent of the population of preschool children.[61]

These young people are in a persistent state of alarm and are in pain. What schools have viewed as their most difficult discipline problems are children and youth demonstrating externalized or internalized pain-based behaviors. Pain-based behaviors look like disrespect, disengagement, disobedience, willfulness, moodiness, excessive anger, not being able to sit still, and a whole host of behaviors that are "punished" in our schools. The majority of our schools use the term "consequences" rather than "punishments," but in effect they are often one and the same. They are meant to cause some form of pain to teach a child a lesson. The vast majority of the time they are used over and over again with children and youth who have experienced trauma and neglect and are already in pain. We are unintentionally reactivating the stress response systems of these students and reigniting the trauma with our interventions in an attempt to teach a lesson. Simply put, it does not work!

James Anglin, from the University of Victoria in Canada, has studied at-risk youth extensively. He concludes that each of the young people in his research is experiencing deep and pervasive emotional pain. Anglin states that the central challenge in working with these young people is dealing with their primary pain, without adults inflicting secondary pain through our punitive or controlling reactions.[62] This, however, will require school systems to move beyond becoming only "trauma informed" toward becoming "trauma- and adversity-responsive" with brain-aligned strategies that build attachments and enhance the skills of emotional regulation. As we explore how significant adversity has affected the development of the brain and our stress response systems, we will all need to rethink many of the traditional ways we have handled children and adolescent behavior in school. It is time to move beyond the simplistic and traditional view of rewarding good behavior and punishing bad behavior.

Discipline is not something we do to children. It is something we help them to build from within.

Far too often school district discipline policies and procedures equate discipline with forms of punishment. For many schools, the code of conduct is made of long lists of possible behavioral infractions and the associated consequences (i.e., punishments). To properly engage with this debate, an overview of terminology is needed.

"Discipline," on the one hand, is prevention focused and looks forward. Discipline connects the relationship and enhances communication. Discipline helps a young person solve a problem. It enhances communication. It is done with a high degree of respect and dignity modeled for the young person. Discipline provides guidance and structure. It teaches fairness, responsibility, and life skills. Discipline focuses on solutions, not retribution. Discipline in the context of trauma responsiveness needs to be preventative and built into our procedures, routines, and classroom cultures. It occurs through bell work and community morning meetings, alongside moments of novelty and times set aside for regulation and awareness. This shift in how to discipline children who carrying with them toxic levels of adversity will require a change in perception, thinking, and behavior by us, the adults working with our children and youth. Discipline issues with children and youth need to be viewed as regulation issues. Dr. Daniel Siegal defines discipline in this manner: "Too often we forget that discipline really means to teach, not to punish. A disciple is a student, not a recipient of behavioral consequences."[63]

A child's greatest innate resource is their ability to emotionally regulate. This is a skill that needs to be learned. As many of us moved towards adulthood, we learned to regulate our emotions by being regulated by another person (mother/father/or other caregiver) when we were dysregulated. It is through patterned repetitive experiences that the brain begins to change structurally and functionally from fighting and fleeing to a relaxed alertness where learning and academics are possible. The children and adolescents who have developmental trauma did not receive these critical and healthy brain-developing experiences.

"Punishment," on the other hand, looks backwards and is a negative consequence that a more powerful person inflicts onto a less powerful one. It is designed to cause pain and discomfort in order to change the person's behavior. Punishment attempts to force compliance and obedience. Punishment disconnects relationships. It is usually done in anger and leads to resentment. It predictably leads toward passive aggressive behaviors or outright rebellion. The emphasis of punishment is retribution. Punishment comes from the Latin word *poena*, or pain. By design, punishment leads to physical, emotional, or social pain. As Larry Brendtro and Scott Larson have written, punishment is using pain to try and change the behavior of young people who are already acting out their pain.[64]

Creating Trauma and Adversity-Responsive
School Discipline Systems

All the strategies in the next chapters, as well as the resources in the back of this book, are brain-aligned preventative discipline strategies that change the emphasis from retribution/punishment toward regulation and our ability to calm a stressed brain. Prior to working out solutions to any difficulty, both the student and the adult must be in a regulated state. As Dr. Bruce Perry reminds us, we must first REGULATE then RELATE and then REASON.[65]

In thinking about how schools are moving towards responsive perceptions, we can begin to rethink and reconceptualize discipline. The seven-step process outlined in the work of the ECHO parenting organization is a helpful guide in moving toward a trauma- and adversity-responsive school or classroom. The seven steps include: (1) Creating safety; (2) Regulating the nervous system; (3) Building a connected relationship; (4) Supporting the development of a coherent narrative: (5) Practicing "power-with" strategies; (6) Building social emotional and resiliency skills; and (7) Fostering post-traumatic growth.[66]

1. Creating safety

The bedrock experience of any child or adolescent that has experienced complex developmental trauma is that of feeling unsafe. These young people carry into schools and classrooms their mistrust of adults. If they have already been in school, their experiences have usually not been ones of feeling safe and accepted. Over time and with good reason they have become relationship resistant.[67] Often, schools believe they are safe places. In the context of working with at-risk and traumatized children, however, youth safety is a much deeper and pervasive need then many may at first understand. Safety within the context of not just the children and youth we are focusing on, but all kids in a school, is about a "felt" sense of safety.

Felt safety is determined by each individual child and includes emotional, physical, and relational security. Felt safety goes well beyond the surface behaviors and protection from abuse and neglect, teasing or bullying, arguing and fighting, and includes protection from subtle threats to a person's self-worth and self-esteem. Historically our school cultures and climates have themselves been traumatic for many of these young people. Dr. Venus Evans-Winters, a professor at Illinois State University and a clinical social worker, argues schooling is a traumatizing place for many young people. When you examine some of the data earlier in this chapter, you can begin to get a sense of the pain schools can cause children and youth who carrying with them pain-based behaviors from their traumatic backgrounds. Evans-Winters states:

> Traumatizing schooling looks like teachers and administrators who unintentionally verbally or emotionally abuse students; labeling students as mentally impaired, learning disabled, or emotionally and behaviorally disturbed; and schools that look and feel more like prisons or mental health wards than learning communities. Traumatizing schools are school environments where students are routinely punished and sent home from school for minor infractions like "insubordination" (read: talking back) or "being out of uniform" (e.g. no belt or sleeveless tops).
>
> To adult school personnel these may be minor infractions with consequences, but for many students such punishments are actually acts of humiliation and intimidation.[68]

Human beings who have been devalued experience deep pain. To be devalued is to be disrespected at your core. Young people who have experienced the effects of prolonged devaluation have unconsciously become hyper-focused on the need to feel and be "respected." These young people can become so focused on the need to be respected that they can easily misinterpret benign messages that feel disrespectful. They can also accurately perceive subtle disrespectful messages delivered by adults through gestures, facial expressions, postures, eye contact, and tones of voice inflections, or even in their choice of words.

Underneath the surface concern of being "respected," however, is the felt sense of being devalued. In schools, these young people often demonstrate disrespectful behaviors to their teachers and other adults attempting to work with them. The paradox is that young people who have been the most disrespected often become the most disrespecting young people that enter our schools. From this perspective, respect must be earned in any way possible. Kenneth V. Hardy and Tracey A. Laszloffy put it this way:

> Neither the adolescent nor many of the adults working with them are consciously aware that their behavior is so heavily driven by the connection between devaluation and the desire for respect. The adolescents are too often distracted by their "the end justifies the means" philosophy, while most adults get trapped into focusing on the bad, or antisocial, behavior. In both cases, devaluation and the all-consuming concern with respect are overlooked.[69]

To begin, we suggest that schools truly interested and invested in becoming trauma responsive ask their students how they feel at their school. Climate and culture surveys that focus on collecting perceptual data from all the school's community (students, parents, guardians, teachers, staff, and community members) will provide an excellent starting point for this work.

2. Regulating the nervous system

One of the hallmarks of students who carry with them toxic levels of stress and trauma is that they remain in a persistent state of alarm. This is what causes these young people to be either a combination of hyper-aroused, anxious, angry, irritable, and explosive, or of hypo-aroused, withdrawn, exhausted, and depressed. We can learn and implement brain-aligned strategies that will calm the nervous system. All these strategies and interventions are discussed and shared in the next two chapters and are preventative and placed in the school procedures, routines, and structures that create a sense of felt safety. Recall that the brain learns best in a state of relaxed alertness and these strategies can be universally used with *all* students. The dosing can be changed as we move up our tiered system of emotional supports.

Human beings learn to regulate their nervous system as they interact with caregivers. Babies do not have the ability to regulate their emotional responses and need a calm regulated brain and a soothing presence to help them manage fear, frustrations, and anger. Babies calm down by experiencing a caregiver's calmness. Put another way, it takes a calm brain to calm another brain. Caregivers provide a sense of nurturing with their voice, touch, pressure, and actions like rocking back and forth with a baby, creating gentle rhythms as the infant's primary needs are met when they are wet, tired, hungry, cold, or experiencing discomfort. These sensory stimulations and co-regulation interventions are ways we help children develop the ability to regulate themselves. Dr. Bessel van der Kolk maintains that a primary function of parents and guardians is to help their child learn to manage their own arousal.[70] Over time, according to author and psychologist Dr. Louis Cozolino, with repeated cycles of emotional upset, followed by a relaxed state that comes after a caregiver provides a calming intervention, a sense of safety and trust develops and the child slowly learns to calm themselves and self-sooth.[71]

Children learn self-regulation through their attachment to caregivers, in effect borrowing their caregiver's regulated brain. Many of the children and youth in our schools who are our most difficult to engage and manage have not had these experiences of co-regulation, and therefore do not have the ability or brain architecture to regulate on their own. Without co-regulating with another human regulated brain in early development, these children and adolescents are experiencing and living in a chronic dysregulated state of arousal.

It is important to reflect upon the fact that the need for co-regulation never goes away in any of our lives. Think about the last time you had a crisis in your life and were helped by another calmer human brain that provided you with a soothing presence and felt sense of safety because of your relationship with this person. The practice of co-regulating with children and youth begins when adults change their focus from the surface behaviors they see in class to the emotions and sensations driving that behavior. As Dr. Erik Laursen, an internationally recognized developer of innovative programs for high-risk youth states: "At the core of healing presence is the ability to respond rather than react to the emotions of others."[72] As educators working with students who carry with them toxic levels of stress, we need to lend our "calm" to our unregulated kids. Co-regulation in schools can take many different shapes, but at its core involves an adult who has a connection with that child and who is able to assist in draining off the child's intense emotions in as private an area as possible and communicating through a soothing tone of voice that affirms and acknowledges the student's distress. Supportive silence and a calm presence, alongside the ability to absorb a child's hostility and frustration, enable us to provide a sense of "felt safety" as the child or adolescent learns to self-regulate. Breathing work and movement exercises are ways we can begin to teach children and youth to calm themselves when they feel triggered. Many of the activities and resources in the next chapter can also be implemented as we co-regulate and calm a dysregulated student.

There is a gap in many school programs, however, as they move to become trauma- and adversity-responsive. A teacher cannot teach a class filled with other children and co-regulate a dysregulated child at the same time. Schools will need to develop processes and predictable patterns of interventions that allow for adults who are available, and have relationships with the children or adolescents they serve, to be able to quickly come to a student's aid with the proper training and the skills to co-regulate a dysregulated student. Students do not become dysregulated by appointment. They will need to be regulated safely and then reintegrated back into their classrooms. This will require some training and coordination by the school leadership and the entire school staff as everyone in the school community will need to make the shift toward a culture that prioritizes connection and regulation at the core of its trauma- and-adversity discipline system.

3. Build a connected relationship

The number one way to regulate the nervous system of a dysregulated child or adolescent is to have a positive and ongoing connected relationship with them. These young people have been hurt in relationship and will only be healed within a relationship that is connected, positive, and sustained. Research on resiliency has drawn the same conclusion, namely, that caring relationships between a child and a teacher, mentor, coach, or other adult who is in a caregiving role is the critical element to supporting these young people.[73]

Relationships provide the critical supports needed for positive change. Being in a relationship with another is not the same as having a relationship. Everyone has relationships with other people. Connecting and being in relationship is different. Being in relationship with another person means you recognize the sacredness of the connection, and it means engaging in a deep manner which impacts both the young person you are serving and you. Thom Garfat describes this kind of relational care as the co-created space between us. To form connected relationships with these young people, we must constantly be attending to the co-created space between us and the children and youth we serve and are working beside. This will require us to be mindful of this co-created space, and ask ourselves reflective questions concerning this space. Some of these questions include:

Is this space calm and safe? Is this space accepting of who this young person is today?

Is this space developmentally appropriate for this student? Is this space a learning space for this child or adolescent?

Is the child able to relax in this space?

Each of these spaces enveloping us and our students will be unique and different. The focus of our reflections are not simply on the surface relationship, but rather on the connections made in the co-created space that is generated between us and every student we serve and work beside.[74] The co-created spaces we can intentionally build can create a space that will allow healing to occur. Relationships and connections are the critical intervention with students who have toxic levels of stress and pain. We can build such kinds of deep connections by meeting our students where they are in their current brain development, accepting them for who they are at their current stage as we interact with them. We can also build rituals of encounter, where we give conscious and intentional thought to the manner in which we engage our students. This will certainly be a new experience for them. We can use the daily experiences that we will encounter in their daily life space to facilitate change. The day-to-day unpredictable moments that bubble up throughout the school day can be used as opportunities to problem solve together, while also moving toward change.

Every child needs to be loved, and these children and youth need this experience, too. Dr. Bruce Perry puts it this way: "Troubled children are in some kind of pain, and pain makes people irritable, anxious and aggressive. Only patient, loving, consistent care works; there are not short-term miracle cures. This is as true for a child of three or four as it is for a teenager."[75]

4. Support the development of a coherent narrative

When a young child or adolescent lives in chronic stress, their environment is largely unpredictable. These young people carry in their bodies toxic levels of stress and are in a state of alarm. They need predictability in their lives: that is, they need adults who are predictable and present. They need adults, in other words, who they can rely and count on. They need and begin to thrive in predictable structure and routines that allow them to know what is coming next. Provide them with a daily visible schedule, and use it as your class approaches transitions. They need adults who can co-regulate them when they are too stressed and dysregulated. Build into your class schedule frequent movement and rhythm breaks, as well as many of the ideas mentioned in Chapter Five.

5. Practice "power-with" strategies

Trauma and significant adversity are about a felt lack of control. At its core, complex developmental trauma occurs when a child experiences multiple, chronic, and prolonged traumatic events, often of an interpersonal nature. These children have a sense of helplessness and a felt sense of being unsafe at their very core. They have lived the experience of little to no control over the events in their lives. It is critical to provide these young people with a sense of control. To help them with this, structure the choices we provide for them within the structure of our day.

Choices build a cooperative environment. They emphasize positive consequences—desirable outcomes available with cooperation. Choices create less stress and fewer power struggles than rules and demands, which are typically "win-lose situations" and often focus on punishments or other negative outcomes for non-compliance. Choices build mutual consideration and respect. Treating these children, regardless of their behaviors, with dignity and respect is critical if we are to build their inner resiliency. Examples of how to frame your choices could include:

- "You are welcome to __ or ___."
- "Feel free to __ or ___."
- "What would be best for you, __ or ___?"

If you are using incentive systems, they need to be set up in a "win-win" manner and should be implemented to provide young people a sense of accomplishment, meaning they should not wielded as a control mechanism that is so often seen in programs for our most traumatized children and youth. Students need to begin self-assessing their behaviors and efforts, followed up with a safe and actionable discussion when both the teacher and the student are communicating from their prefrontal cortex, where words are heard, experiences shared, and solutions are viable.

6. Formally build social, emotional, and resiliency skills

We can formally teach social and emotional literacy skills to all students. Lori has created a program, "Brain-Aligned Social Emotional Learning Competencies," that is foundational to the more common and highly cognitive social skills of self-awareness, self-management, relationship skills, social awareness skills, and responsible decision-making skills. These competencies can be found in our resource section. The developmental framework created by the Search Institute is an excellent resource for the creation of environments that can help build resiliency in our young people. It includes five elements that adults can focus on with the children and youth they support:

1. Expressing care: Show me that I matter to you.
2. Challenge growth: Push me to keep getting better.
3. Provide support: Help me to complete tasks and achieve my goals.
4. Share power: Treat me with respect and give me a say.
5. Expand possibilities: Connect me with people and places to broaden my world.[76]

7. Foster post-traumatic growth: Changing our view of discipline in school

Here, we want to reemphasize the perception of brain-aligned prevention. When a student is working from a brain that is chronically in the stress response system, he or she does not attend to what is right or wrong about his or her behavior. When a child or adolescent feels an impulse or desire in the moment, he or she will make it happen in the moment no matter the consequences. Consequences *do not* register in lower brain regions where our fight, flight, and freeze responses live. Our issues with these students are not behavioral, they are regulatory. In this brain-aligned model of discipline, we must begin to teach the behaviors that we want to see laying the ground work for prevention systems and strategies. Here are some preventive brain-aligned strategies:

1. Students are taught about their neuro-anatomy understanding and what happens in their brains when they become stressed, angry, fearful, or anxious. This is where we shift our behavioral lens to a science lens. When we understand what happens in our brains, we feel relieved and empowered, knowing that "I am not a bad kid, or that something is wrong with me." In morning meetings or whole class time, discuss the prefrontal cortex, amygdala, and neuroplasticity with all our students when they are calm and settled.

2. Use morning meetings and bell work time to identify and make lists of emotional triggers and coping strategies. Highlight and share these as a class or individually, continually learning new coping strategies as everyone explores and learns the science of behaviors and feelings.

3. Teach students to use their breath and movement to calm their stress response systems, implementing these individually or during whole class time when needed. Focused Attention Practices and Brain Intervals are critical for high engagement, all of which is part of preventative discipline.

4. Notice your own triggers and nonverbal communication with students. Is your facial expression, tone of voice, and posture inviting or provoking? Use questions that invite problem-solving skills, such as:

- What do you need right now? What can we do to make this better?
- I'm wondering what just happened? Help me to understand.
- I am feeling unclear about what led up to this. Let me try and see if I am understanding correctly.

5. Are you providing choices and creating incentives for this student to be successful and feel "felt?" For example: Would you like to work on these three math problems and take a break for a minute or would you rather finish the page and have your time on the IPAD?

6. Is there an adult in the school who connects with this student and has a space where he or she can go if they need to regroup and calm their nervous system? Are you teaching these procedures ahead of time when a student needs to regulate away from the class? Could our schools create an "amygdala reset area" for both teachers and students to go to when we need to reset our emotional state? This area could be filled with paper, markers, crayons, water, soft music and lighting, a jump rope, stationary bike, hand lotion, lavender scented cotton balls, a jar of affirmations, rocking chair, a worry jar, books on the brain, or a computer to show one- to two-minute videos that are uplifting. We will discuss more of these preventive options in Chapter Five.

We can create school level "Adversity Teams" that are made up of adults in our schools who are on call when a student is unable to regulate in our classroom. These teams of educators could be teachers, administrators, counselors, security personnel, paraprofessionals, office staff, or other individuals in our schools who are prepared to calm a child first through regulating the nervous system. These teams are trained and prepared in understanding how adversity and trauma intimately affect behaviors and deeply understand that discipline must occur when there is a regulated and safe adult co-regulating the nervous system of the student. Words, plans of actions, consequences, and a reframing of a negative experience all fall upon deaf ears when a student is reacting from a fight, flight, or freeze brain state. The adversity teams should meet regularly to discuss, explore, and plan preventative measures for our students who come to school rough and dysregulated. The purpose of these teams is to provide an adult who models the behaviors we want to eventually see from the student. When we time-out, or seclude a child or adolescent, we often are reactivating their stress response systems, and unintentionally producing no sustainable behavioral change. Often times, our traditional discipline systems become caught up in a consequences and rewards mentality. We have found that the most organic brain-aligned consequences of a child or adolescent's impulsive and inappropriate choices can begin to replace old behaviors with new shifts that are sustainable and purposeful. Below are some examples of brain-aligned organic consequences.

- **Name calling:** Create a book of positive affirmations for the class or assign this student the role of kindness keeper for a week. This student could create a list of "kind words" and teach these words to a younger class.

- **Low-level physical aggression (e.g., pushing, kicking, hitting):** All behavior is communication, so what is this behavior saying to me? What does this student need? New learning space in the room? Teaching strategies to use his or her words? Maybe we begin to model an act of kindness or service for the person we hurt?

- **Inappropriate school language:** This calls for a discussion when both student and teacher are in a calm brain state. Sometimes the words that are inappropriate at school are used at home, so we need to understand the cultural context and have a discussion with the student.

- **Incomplete assignments:** A one-on-one discussion of what this behavior is communicating. Do you see patterns? Has something changed at home or school? Is there a lack of understanding? Organization? After discussion, a plan needs to be made with the student and possibly a parent for making up the work that has been missed; or creating a mentor or an incentive plan that shortens assignments and creates shorter periods of time for students to complete an assignment, tapping into the student's interests, passions, and expertise.

- **Disruptive behavior:** Provide opportunities to be a classroom leader in positive capacities.

- **Disrespectful:** Connect. We need to be intentional about building connection when students feel disrespected.

- **Late/Tardy:** What do you need? How can I help? Warning bells, more time, early release pass, restroom break at the beginning of class to eliminate stopping during passing, storing materials in classroom for use. What patterns do we see and notice with this student?

- **Out of seat:** Allow students opportunities to move and regulate without punishment. Thank students for taking care of themselves. Provide areas to stand during instruction.

- **Destruction of property:** Time to provide service to property owner. Create videos, posters, or announcements about the importance of caring for property.

- **Walking out of room:** Breaks, passes for walks, and brain intervals throughout instruction. Ask students what they need during class and the three activities/ routines that would assist them in staying focused and engaged for an agreed-upon amount of time. Start with small successful periods of time so children and adolescents can meet with success immediately.

- **Impulse control:** Regulation activities throughout the learning block or class period that are taught ahead of time and are a part of the student's routine and procedures. Some of these strategies can be found in Chapter Five.

We have created a road map within this chapter for all of us to reconsider how traditional discipline is done in our schools. Our traditional discipline/punishment techniques work best for our students who need them the least and are completely ineffective with the students we think need them the most. These traditional techniques unintentionally escalate and elevate the neurobiology of children and adolescence that carry with them significant adversity and trauma. Rather than solving problems, our traditional techniques make things worse. This is the road map to the creation of schools that can work with and support students who come to us struggling to make sense of their lives, and desperate for connection and purpose.

To close this chapter, we included an essay by Sarah Dorsey, Lori's daughter. In this essay, Sarah, a brand new teacher, describes her first year teaching young children in pain.

A First Year Teacher's Journey:
Working with Children in Pain
Written by Sarah Dorsey, Lori's daughter

The bell rang and a slow rumble of voices and shuffling sneakers grew louder as the students in my Title One, F-Rated elementary school entered the building on a hot August morning. Four years of undergrad, followed by a brief phone interview at the end of July, and there I was on my first day of teaching.

It didn't happen as I thought it would, my first teaching job. That phrase—it didn't happen as I thought it would—could be applied to everything I experienced my first few months teaching. To begin, I didn't know if I was even going to teach immediately after finishing college. Having a fiancé in the Air Force doesn't make planning easy, and we were relocated at the last minute, arriving at the base after most elementary schools had already started their semesters. I contacted a few schools for possible subbing opportunities, but was blown away by their immediate responses and full-time job offers. I soon took one of these, and I found myself in the classroom only four weeks later.

I'm sure most teachers have the same feelings I had on my first day. I was optimistic, ambitious, and had my nicely written lesson plans ready to go. I had mental images of the personalities and capabilities of my students. Of course, I was nervous, too, wondering if I would be able to live up to the educational philosophies I had learned during my undergraduate years.

Although I had been given a bit of information about the school's limited resources, (I knew I had been hired quickly and that there was a major teacher shortage), I didn't understand how dire the situation really was. I didn't know how teachers—if they stayed for more than a year—struggled with such strong behaviors from their students. I didn't understand the amount of traumatic experiences (ACEs) most of my students had when they walked through my door. Put simply, I just wasn't prepared for what I would see, hear, experience, and be expected to do. What I saw, however well intentioned, seemed counterproductive—nothing we did took the brain state of our students into account.

When my mom, Dr. Lori Desautels and Michael McKnight offered me the opportunity to contribute to their book, I jumped at the chance, knowing I wanted to offer a glimpse of a first year teacher's classroom to a wider audience. There seems to be broad agreement that our nation's schools are in a state of crisis: whether its violence, dropping test scores, teacher shortages, or a whole host of other issues. But the crisis I saw in my first year—a lack of emotional regulation for both students and teachers alike—affects all these. Feelings and emotions were not being validated and worked through; spaces were not being created for reflection and regulation. Most disciplinary solutions emphasized intimidation or scare tactics, rather than truly trying to change student behavior.

In short, I saw a lot of short-term solutions to difficult, complex issues.

After my second day of teaching, I called my mom in tears. Already, I felt defeated, emotionally drained, and inadequate. Seven boys, and one sweet girl, were in my classroom, and I had never imagined the extent of poverty, gun and gang violence, physical, emotional, and sexual abuse, broken homes, and frequent moves my students would be coming from. Many were hungry; most were exhausted. One had a TBI, two were labeled ED, and the majority was classified as Developmentally Delayed—but all had undergone some significant trauma and adversity. They were a hodgepodge of different grade and ability levels, ages, labels, and backgrounds. Most were outright scared, which showed itself through rage and violence in the classroom, sometimes directed at me, sometimes at each other, and sometimes at themselves. The seven boys had been in the same self-contained classroom since kindergarten. I had never seen such a level of hostility before, and had no idea of where to start. I immediately recognized that although I had four incredible years at a university studying education, none of it prepared me for this class.

I talked with my mom for a couple of hours that afternoon. I looked at each desk and envisioned my new students in each one. I knew in that moment that I would have to forego some of my lesson plans (located in my trendy teacher lesson planner) and just listen to my students. I had to gain their trust and hear them, and, more importantly, I had to allow them to get to know me. I knew the only way to start was to create a safe space full of routine and loving boundaries.

I spent the next several weeks sitting beside my students doing little else. They exploded, I removed them, and we walked the halls. We would walk and sometimes stop for water and sometimes run our hands against the yellow lockers. Then, once their breathing and emotions relaxed, I gently asked for their account of what happened. I listened to my students, and then I listened some more. I nodded, made eye contact, and said, "Wow that must have really felt awful to you" or "I bet that was so frustrating" or "I can see that you are scared/hurt/upset."

This, I quickly noticed, surprised my students. I recognized that no one had taken the time to hear them when they'd knocked down a bookshelf or started a fight. No one had ever asked them why they did it; they had just been given a punishment of some type. Sometimes, I even chose to explain to them how their actions made me feel, telling them that I loved them, but not the choice they had just made. I told them I knew their actions came from a place of frustration and hurt, but also explained to them that I knew they could make a different choice next time around. As needed, we decided on a natural consequence (e.g., apologizing to the hurt student, putting the upside down bookshelf back together, taking some additional time out of our day to reflect), and we went back to try again.

You can't reason before regulating, so I never began a reflective conversation with a student prior to getting them to move in some way. For some of them, this meant taking a short walk; for others, it was sitting in a chair and rocking it back and forth. For one, in particular, it was putting on my Garmin watch and taking deep breaths to try to make the heart rate number decrease. Knowing they had never been taught these exercises, I had to help teach them these strategies. To be sure, oftentimes, after these exercises were over, the same episode would repeat itself, and we would begin again—much like a bad version of Groundhog Day. Admittedly, it was exhausting work. But consistency and routine is key for some students, so I kept at it. Gradually, over the course of the year, the outbursts slowed and the self-regulating became more innate. The outbursts never ceased, but the intensity diminished and the duration became shorter. There was a genuine, whole class transformation that I attribute to consistency, emotional regulation, and above all, listening to my students and validating them as humans.

Along these lines, I established a regular morning meeting. It went about as well as you imagine it would at first—screaming and punching, running away and refusing to sit down on our small square carpet—so we started for just a few minutes at a time. We practiced how to sit and how to make eye contact. Little by little, the consistency of this routine, coupled with small, positive interactions, established a sense of community and safety in our classroom. We even played games that helped students regulate. These were helped with breathing activities and rhythmic motor activity.

The first game we played we called, "The Shadow Game." In it, one student would lead us all in a series of large motor movements, and the rest of us would have to silently follow. The leading student had the choice of picking three to five big or small movements before passing on the leadership role to the next student in the circle. Another game was something we called, "Chief," during which one student would be deemed the "guesser" and would go to a corner of the classroom and close his or her eyes. The teacher would then pick the "Chief" who would start a body percussion pattern (e.g., clapping hands, patting legs, snapping fingers, etc.), constantly switching up the pattern/rhythm. The guesser would be invited back into the circle to try and guess who the Chief was. My students loved the secrecy and anticipation of this game, and I loved how it helped to regulate their stress response system.

Although these games helped, the biggest challenge I had with my students was that of hostility. Our morning routine certainly helped improve this, but I wanted to provide as many opportunities as possible for my students to show kindness to each other. I didn't just want them to show it, though; I wanted them *to want to show it.* To help, I bought a large thermometer, placed it on the wall, and labeled it "Kindness Points." The "Kindness Keeper," a role we created as a class, was tasked with charting acts of kindness throughout the day on this thermometer. When we reached ten points, the whole class received a "kindness mystery prize." Like everything else, the class seemed initially motivated by the prizes they won for their acts of kindness. Little by little, though, I noticed more and more small acts of kindness occur—a compliment here, a sharing of the toy there—and the students seemed to really develop a rapport with each other.

These strategies helped me during my first year in a tremendous way. Although there were growing pains for everyone involved—my students and me—my first year will have a lasting impact on the type of educator I will be in the future. Some of these pains were natural for any first-year teacher, but others were aggravated due to a lack of emotional, mental, and moral support. I wasn't taking adequate care of my brain state, and neither was my school or district. To be sure, this wasn't intentional; it simply wasn't seen as a necessity. I met wonderful people doing extraordinary things on a daily basis, but the district was facing crisis after crisis, and providing adequate teacher support tended to be put on the back burner.

Of course, individual staff members provided help at certain points in the year (and for that, I am extremely thankful). But professional development, especially in special education, was almost nonexistent.

During the year, I felt isolated and overwhelmed by both the daily workload and the emotional baggage students brought with them into my class. The lack of community and support in the school, and in the district as a whole, made the whole process more difficult than it needed to be. Admittedly, the administration—like most in our country—was under serious pressure from the state government regarding letter grades and test scores, the "visible" aspects of learning. But the school was lacking fundamentals and good support structures to help teachers grow into the best versions of themselves. Only in this way can we take care of our students.

My first year, in the end, was raw. It was extremely difficult and an enormous reality check. It broke me down, but at the same time instilled hope and inspiration. I don't have all the answers to how to handle the types of behaviors I saw in my class or those that you will see in yours. But I can share my experiences, reflect on them, and hope they can help you. Through this process, we can all grow together. I hope, moreover, that some of these experiences are relatable and demonstrate how brain-aligned strategies can help you work with your students and fellow co-workers.

CHAPTER FIVE

Brain-Aligned Preventative Strategies:
Addressing Regulation from the Brain Stem Up

"Remember, everyone in the classroom has a story that leads to misbehavior or defiance. Nine times out of ten, the story behind the misbehavior won't make you angry. It will break your heart."

— ANNETTE BREAUX

As we shared in Chapter Four, discipline is not something we do to children, but something we develop within them. At the heart of discipline with pain-based behaviors is co-regulation. These children and youth need the means and assistance of a regulated nervous system before they can learn new coping strategies and understand the consequences of their choices and decisions. As Dr. Bruce Perry, director of the Child Trauma Academy, points out, the brain develops from somatosensory, rhythmic, patterned, and repetitive activities.[77] This chapter offers an overview of several preventative brain-aligned strategies that we have implemented over the last few years. These preventative discipline measures, moreover, not only address regulation and attachment in our students, but also their engagement. At the end of this chapter, there is a separate section addressing early childhood regulation, and regulation strategies for children with significant adversities.

"Buffet Table" Strategies to Regulate the Brain

In our classrooms, we have a sensory diet buffet table

with choices of items students can use to get ready for the day. This buffet table of regulation is a part of our procedures and routines. Below are some of the items and their purposes. These are taught and modeled much like our traditional classroom roles, procedures, and responsibilities, such as sharpening pencils, passing out paper, or any other traditional classroom job. These suggestions can be modified for all grade levels.

(1) **Worry jar**. Students can choose to write down or draw a worry or concern on a post-it note, color-coding it red, yellow, or green. Red indicates this worry should be thrown away. Yellow implies the student is not sure what to do, and he or she may decide at the end of class what to do about it. Green suggests that at a convenient time, they would like to share their concerns with a teacher or another adult in the building. This strategy, in line with what Dan Seigel argues, helps the student express his or her concern, angst, and negative emotion. Remember, what we can name, we can tame, and what is sharable, is bearable.

(2) **Hand lotion**. This is available for students to use. Pass the lotion around during the morning meeting, allowing students to begin the day with a thirty-second hand massage. The students should be instructed to feel their palms, fingers, and joints, noticing every sensation they feel in their hands. This hand massage brings attention back to the present moment, away from the bus, hallway, lockers, or home. It creates a pressured touch that can calm or dampen the stress response systems.

(3) **Water and food**. This is critical not only for survival, but can also greatly affect how our students learn and behave. Simply put, water plays a big role in our students' days. Dehydration can lead to higher levels of glutamate, one of our body's excitatory neurotransmitters. Elevated levels of this neurotransmitter can produce increased levels of violent

and aggressive behaviors.[78] Children and youth who carry with them adversity may also have lower levels of serotonin, an inhibitory neurotransmitter referred to by Dr. Purvis as our "master regulator." Low serotonin levels can also produce chronic feelings of hunger. A snack and some water can greatly affect brain chemistry, especially with children and adolescents who have highly sensitized stress-response systems. Brain chemistry can predict mental health or mental illness and water and food contribute to these brain states.[79]

(4) **Sensation word wall**. When students walk into the classroom, they may choose a sensation from the list that aligns with how they feel. Sensation is the language of the brain stem, as our sensory and motor systems develop in this lower region. Therapist and author Dr. Peter Levine describes sensations as the sense of the physiological happenings inside us.[80] When we name how we are experiencing this physicalized emotion, it frees up the body from a static state of immobility and alerts us to the present moment.[81] In our classrooms, we model our own sensations by choosing a "sensation word" from the word wall and sharing how it feels and what it looks like. We use drawings, colors, and any other medium that can assist students in creating the sensation that mirrors what they carried into the classroom that morning or afternoon. Here are some examples:

- Cold, warm, hot, sweaty, twitchy, butterflies, stuck, soft, sharp, dull, itchy, shaky, trembly, tingly, jittery, weak, empty, full, relaxed, calm, peaceful, flowing, spreading, strong, tight, tense, dizzy, fuzzy, blurry, numb, prickly, jumpy, tearful, goose-bumpy, racing, and tired.

(5) **Clothespin drop**. As students enter class, they clip a small note to a clothespin and drop it into either a "celebration" or "challenge" bucket. Much like the worry jar, the clothespin drop can provide an opportunity for students to

share pent up feelings and thoughts through the symbolic ritual of releasing them.

(7) **Weighted vest**. Allow students to wear a weighted vest during class. Weighted pressure, as research has shown, can help regulate the nervous system of children and adolescents who are hyposensitive or hypersensitive to pressure and tactile stimulation.[82] Dampening the stress response systems for children and adolescents who carry an over-activated stress response primes the frontal lobes for stronger connections, allowing cognition to occur.

(8) **Feeling textures**. On the sensory buffet table, we have bowls filled with marbles and others with lentil beans. The textures from these items feel pleasurable and calming, and students can run their hands through both of them.

(9) **Chewing**. According to Dr. Karyn Purvis, eating a healthy snack or chewing a piece of gum regulates the lower brain regions. The crunching and chewing motions provide muscular input and help regulate the nervous system.[83]

(10) **Temperature changes**. Just as we injure our bodies when we are hurt, we can also explain to younger students that they feel anxious or angry because a part of their brain is injured, so an ice pack, frozen apple juice, or frozen grapes (really, anything frozen) can be offered to a student if he or she needs a few minutes in the morning to sit with these cooler sensations. A jar of the menthol rub can also be used for students who feel tense, stiff, or painful.

Attachment and Regulation

Young people have the innate capacity to bounce back from adversity. You can create an environment that feels safe and connected by helping students understand how negative emotions hijack our learning. To facilitate a predictable and consistent environment, create class guidelines, procedures, and engagement systems so each student knows the class expectations and routines. Here are some strategies to help with this:

(1) **Brain-aligned centers in the classroom**. Students can go to an area in the classroom to recharge and calm down from negative emotion. This corner is called the "amygdala first-aid center," as the amygdala is the fight/flight/freeze center in the brain. Students needing a quiet area with tables to study or to complete work can go to the "hippocampus area," named after the part of the brain that memorizes and connects new information to what we already know. Finally, the "prefrontal cortex area"—named after the problem-solving center of the brain—includes tables and collaborative spaces for students who are ready to discuss projects or ideas, watch documentaries, and collaborate. When we teach students about their brain anatomy and its functions, connecting them to specific activities, they become more self-aware and fluent in their cognitive processes.

(2) **Locked journal**. When we write down our thoughts and feelings, we clear space in the frontal lobes for positive emotion and higher cognitive processes. A locked journal can give students a safe place to release anxiety while maintaining control over their own privacy. If a student chooses to write or draw their feelings and thoughts in this format, we discuss how this journal can become a trusted friend, and how they might be able to use it to prototype creative forms of expression to be shared under the appropriate circumstances.

(3) **Focused-attention practices**. Research continually points to the statistically significant changes in calming our stress response systems through breathing and

movement. Brain scans of individuals who encountered adversity in childhood often show a loss of connectivity between the lower and higher brain regions that are foundational in creating relationships and downshifting an inflammatory response. When these connections are sparse or underdeveloped, we have less self-awareness in how we feel or experience the sensations in our environments.[84] Dr. Ryan Herringa, assistant professor of child and adolescent psychiatry at the University of Wisconsin states, "When children practice mindfulness, they may strengthen the same circuits of the brain weakened by early adversity and childhood trauma, including the frontal lobe and hippocampus."[85] When we breathe deeply and bring oxygen into our lungs, we begin to strengthen the underactive parasympathetic nervous system, thereby lowering respiration, heart rate, and blood pressure.

Five years ago, we began developing these "mindful practices" in our schools, referring to them as "focused-attention practices." As educators, we do not need a program for implementing these focused-attention practices. We can model them and lead these exercises at the beginning and end of the day or when difficult transitions have occurred. A focused-attention practice is a brain exercise for quieting the thousands of thoughts that distract and frustrate us each day. When the mind is quiet and focused, students can be present with a specific sound, breath, sight, or taste. Quieting our minds ignites our parasympathetic nervous system, reducing heart rate and blood pressure while enhancing our coping strategies to effectively handle the day-to-day challenges that keep coming. In other words, our ability to think improves while our emotions begin to regulate so that we can approach an experience with variable options. These are procedures and are built into our daily routines. Below is a list of several of these focused-attention practices. With each of them, the goal is to start small and build them up as the school year progresses.

(1) **Breathing.** Use the breath as a focus point. Have students place one hand close to their nose (not touching) and one hand on their belly. As they breathe in, have them feel their bellies expand. As they exhale, they can feel the warm air hit their hand. Students will focus on this breath for only one minute. Let them know that it is okay when thoughts sometimes come into the mind uninvited. Tell them to exhale that thought away.

(2) **Colors.** Visualize colors while focusing on the breath. Inhale a deep green, and exhale a smoky gray. Have the students imagine the colors as swirling and alive with each inhale. If a student is de-escalating from an angry moment, the color red is a great color to exhale.

(3) **Movement**. For younger children, direct students to stand and, as they inhale, lift an arm or leg and wiggle it, exhaling it back to its original position. For younger grades beginning these focused-attention practices, it's good to include an inhale and exhale with any type of movement.

(4) **The deep-dive breath**. Inhale for four counts, hold for four counts, and exhale slowly for four counts. You can increase the holding of breath by a few seconds once the students find the rhythm of the exercise.

(5) **Energized breathing**. We pant like a dog with our mouths open and our tongues out for thirty seconds, continuing for another thirty seconds with our mouths closed as we take short belly breaths with one hand on the belly. We typically take three energizing panting breaths per second.

After a full minute, the students return to four regular deep inhales and exhales.

(6) **Sound**. The use of sound is very powerful for engaging a calm response. You can use rain sticks, bells, chimes, and music.

(7) **Rise and fall**. As students breathe in and out through their noses, have them lie on the floor and place an object on their stomachs, enhancing their focus by watching the rising and falling of their bellies. When we are focused and paying attention to our thoughts, feelings, and choices, we have a much greater opportunity to change those thoughts and feelings that are not serving us well in life and in school. When we grasp this awareness, we see and feel the difference.[86]

(8) **Ice cubes**. Give each student an ice cube and a paper towel. As they hold the ice cube, ask them to focus on what it feels like in their hands and what the sensation reminds them of.

(9) **Deep breathing**. Have students scrunch their toes and cross their legs at the ankles. Then they should cross the left arm over the right arm, clasp their hands together, and—keeping their hands clasped—bring them toward their chest. Have them hold that pose for thirty seconds as they take five deep breaths, and then have them take another thirty seconds to uncurl their toes, uncross their legs, extend and unclasp their hands, and uncross their arms while taking another five deep breaths.

(10) **So what?** As students close their eyes and sit up nice and tall in their chairs, they should visualize a golden thread

that connects their hearts to their stomachs. As they breathe in, have them picture a pulse in the thread moving from their stomachs to their hearts; with each exhale, the pulse travels from the heart back down to the stomach. As the students breathe, have them say, "So what?" to themselves if a negative thought occurs.[87]

(11) **Cross and uncross.** For thirty seconds, have the students cross and hold their toes, ankles legs, wrists, and arms tightly while they take five deep breaths. Have them slowly begin to uncross each part, one at a time, as they continue to breathe deeply.

Brain Intervals

A brain interval is a short period of time when we change the dull routine of incoming information arriving via predictable, tedious, well-worn pathways in the brain. When we take a brain interval, it refreshes our thinking and helps us discover another solution to a problem or see a situation through a different lens. During these few minutes, the brain moves away from learning, memorizing, and problem solving, and towards processing new information. Brain intervals, moreover, provide movement for the body. Research has shown correlations between activity and cognitive improvements following this activity, along with an increased ability of our organs to carry oxygen to various brain regions. As a result, generalized brain effects, such as an increase of synapses, increasing brain volume, and decreasing age-related brain atrophy, have all been reported. Movement also can regulate our stress-response systems, which is critical to learning and well-being.[88]

Focused-attention practices and brain intervals can also be a part of your routines and procedures in the classroom.

Following are some examples:

Examples of Brain Intervals

(1) **The junk bag**. Have a bag of household objects containing markers, scrap paper, and anything that one would find in a junk drawer—for example, a can opener or a pair of shoelaces. Pick any object out of the junk bag and ask students to come up with two ways this object could be reinvented for other uses. They can write or draw their responses. Once students have drawn or written about an invention, they can walk the room for one minute sharing and comparing.

(2) **Squiggle story**. On a blank sheet of paper, a whiteboard, or a Promethean Board, draw one squiggly line. Give students one minute to stand and draw with their opposite hand, turning the line into a picture or design of their choice.

(3) **Opposite sides**. Movement is critical to learning. Have students stand and wink with the right eye while snapping the fingers of their left hand. Repeat this with the left eye and right hand. Students could also face one another and tap the right foot once, left foot twice, and right foot three times, building speed as they alternate toe tapping with their partner.

(4) **Symbolic alphabet**. Sing the alphabet with names of objects rather than the letters.

(5) **Other languages**. Teach sign language or make up a spoken language. In pairs, students take turns speaking or interpreting this new language for thirty seconds each.

(6) **Mental math**. Give a set of three instructions, counting the sequence to a partner for thirty seconds. Example:

Count by twos until twenty, then count by threes until fifty, finishing with sevens until eighty. Switch and give the other partner another set of numbers to count.

(7) **Invisible pictures**. Have a student draw a picture in the air while their partner guesses what it is. You could give them categories such as foods, places, or other ways to narrow the guessing.

(8) **Story starters**. A student or teacher begins a story for one minute, either individually or with a partner. The students continue it or complete it with a silly ending.

(9) **Funny talk.** Have students loosely touch the roof of their mouth with their tongue and begin to speak.

(10) **Class chants**. Create a class chant to all say together, or the teacher can address the class, modeling what he or she would like students to say.

(11) **Tongue stretch.** Have students use clean hands or a Kleenex to stretch their tongue as far as it can go. This relaxes the throat, palate, upper neck, and brain stem.[89]

(12) **Hum**. There are many ways you can incorporate humming as a break or to begin class. Lead students in "Simon Says" or "Name That Tune," or have students move their arms and legs to someone's humming. This activity releases stress and blockages in the brain stem.

(13) **Horse lips**. Loosen your lips and blow... allow the air to wriggle your lips and do these with a large inhale and even bigger exhale. We can laugh, too, as we calm the brain stem areas where the stress response begins.[90]

Rhythm: Strategies to Increase Movement

Rhythms are a part of our neurobiology. As Dr. Bruce Perry reports, "If our bodies cannot keep the most fundamental rhythm of life, our heartbeat, we cannot survive."[91] The brain works in many rhythms. If these rhythms are disrupted early in life, we often see depression and other disorders follow. Before birth, a baby's heartbeat aligns with the mother;s providing a patterned, repetitive cadence that is critical for the organization of these lower brain regions and our neurotransmitter systems.[92] When a baby cries, a caregiver co-regulates and thus the pattern of a healthy "serve and return" rhythm is established. When this rhythm is missing, educators can create opportunities in the classroom for rhythmic repetitive patterns that assist in rebuilding and organizing the lower brain regions. Following are four activities that can be incorporated into morning meetings or at the close of the day to build the capacity for rhythm movement and understanding.

(1) **Routine**. Providing routines and procedures is predictable and rhythmic. Students will begin to anticipate what is next and how to prepare with these boundaries and structures in place. Many of our children and adolescents walk into our classrooms with no sense of predictability and routine. Chaos feels comfortable for them, but having routines can help.

(2) **Rhythm circles**. Take just a few minutes as the class mimics the leader in claps, snaps, stomps, or drumstick patterns. Use music, sounds, or other students to follow the lead of the designated drummer or rhythm maker.

(3) **Rocking**. Place rocking chairs, a stationary bike, or

an elliptical machine in the "amygdala first-aid station" in the classroom so students can choose to move and rock, deescalating the dysregulated brain state.

(4) **Resting heart rate**. Keep pulse oximeters in the classroom so students can locate a resting heart rate, and then they can note and track the changes in their heart rates during the day. Then, they should name the sensations and feelings they are experiencing in their bodies as their pulse rate rises and falls.

Tapping: An Emotional Freedom Technique

Anxiety disrupts our ability to focus and concentrate, can create dysregulation of our stress-response systems, and also interferes with our perception, compromising optimal brain and body functions of students.[93] As already mentioned, the amygdale in the limbic region of the brain is the emotional smoke detector, sending messages to various parts of the brain and body readying our fight, flight, or freeze responses. Recent research reports that stimulation to specific meridian endpoints can decrease survival brain activity in this limbic region.[94] This past year, Amy Gaiser, professor at Purdue University, trained all the educators at Indianapolis Public School 60 in Emotional Freedom Techniques (EFT; also known as "tapping"). In this school, tapping is being modeled through whole classes, small groups, and also individually. Students are encouraged to tap independently whenever they feel the sensation of anxiety or negativity. Tapping is a skillset that children and youth can take with them throughout the day, incorporating movements and breathing exercises that dampen the stress-response systems while also lowering elevated levels of one of our stress hormones, cortisol.[95]

Tapping can be done during morning meetings with students. The sequence can be initiated by tapping on "end-points," or the areas on the skin's surface that contain nerve endings correlated with pathways to the limbic regions of the brain. This can begin to dampen the stress response system.[96] Then, students can take turns leading the exercises individually or with a partner.

Brain-Aligned Bell Work: Strategies to Calm the Brain and Get It Ready for Learning

(1) **Bilateral scribbling.** With a large sheet of paper and two markers—one in each hand—students will follow your directives. Have them make random marks vertically and then horizontally. Next, have them make large arcs across the page, followed by large circles, first fast and then slowly. Finally, have them make dots all over the page. As they look at their drawings, ask them the following questions:
- Is there anything about this scribbling that resembles you or any part of you?
- Is there anything about this scribbling that is nothing like you?
- Are there any pictures or designs you see in this scribbling?
- What word comes to mind as you look at your scribbling?
- Would that word describe something about you or someone you know?

Then, give students a chance to share their artwork with a classmate. Sharing is always a choice and discussions may alternate between groups of students and the entire class. This bilateral scribbling exercise also provides the educator with perceptual data. Students will sometimes project their sense of self into their artwork.[97]

(2) **Animal symbols**. Have students view pictures of animals and then choose an animal that they are most connected to, either positively or negatively. After they choose, ask the following questions and have students write out, draw, or verbally share their responses:

- What is it about this animal that you like or dislike?
- How is this animal like you in any way? How is this animal nothing like you?
- What are the two best qualities about this animal? What are the two worst qualities?
- What would the home of this animal look like?
- Who is in this animal's family, and do they get along with one another?
- If you could give this animal magic power, what would it be?

This exercise promotes connection and emotional regulation in a safe environment. Most children and adolescents can identify with an animal and it feels safe to talk about an animal's home, characteristics, and behaviors. Through this strategy, we may be able to gather some strong perceptual data about how our students feel, think, and process their worlds and relationships.[98]

(3) **Fill your paper with color**. After students fill their paper with color, ask them these questions:

- Which color is the biggest?
- If it had a voice, what would it say? Which color is in charge? Which color would like to be in charge?
- Which color likes to hide? Why? What color is the happiest? Why?
- What color is the saddest or angriest?

When we can use color, shapes, and art to express the emotional self, there is increased organization in the lower regions of the brain.[99]

(4) **Draw your initials**. Have students draw their initials.
- Which letter is most developed? Which letter is least developed?
- Which letter do you like best? Which letter is most powerful?
- Which letter is most vulnerable or gets picked on?
- What message do you receive from your initials?

(5) **Bucket inventory**. Take a bucket inventory. Explain to your students that we each carry two internal buckets with us each day. One is a stress bucket, which sometimes is so full it just takes a drop or two for it to overflow. The other is a bucket of good feelings that needs to be filled by those around us and ourselves.
- Which bucket is full? Which feels empty?
- How can we help fill or empty each bucket?[100]

(6) **Create trigger lists.** Older youths (those in grades five to twelve) who have experienced trauma sometimes know their "triggers"—those sounds, sights, and experiences that spark negative emotions. A few times each week, check in with all students and have them create a list of triggers that can block learning and relationships, while also listing those experiences, people, or celebrations that enhance positive emotions.[101]

(7) **Fantasy interview**. When students enter the class, they choose a half sheet of colored paper with a set of instructions displayed on the smart board. An empty chair and

a few props to create a comfortable setting stand in the front of the class. Begin with a question: "If you could spend fifteen minutes with any person in the whole world discussing, questioning, and sharing, who would this be and why did you choose him or her?" The students can write or draw their responses and, if they choose, share them following the exercise.

(8) **The things I carry**. At the front of the room is a backpack containing five items, pictures, or words that I identify with or hold close to my mind and heart. As I model for my students the contents of my own backpack, I begin sharing who I am as a person. This is a powerful way of not only getting to know your students, but also tying in the backpack's contents with a class novel, science experiment, or any standard that you are teaching. Students can also guess what items might be in the backpack before you reveal them.

(9) **Ten-word story**. Write or draw a ten-word story on a specific topic that you are teaching, or have students write a ten-word story describing their strengths and expertise. Another option for those who do not want to write is to create an infographic.

(10) **Belief infomercial**. Using images, words, colors, or technology, have students design an infomercial about a strong belief that they hold.

(11) **Reinvent gum**. Place a stick of gum on every desk as students walk in. On five notecards, have them design five new inventions for chewing gum. Students can share and compare at the end of the bell work.

(12) **Meeting of the minds**. Students select characters

from a book, historical figures, or any author, inventor, scientist, or individual whom they have been studying. Given a twenty-first-century challenge, how would these individuals solve it? What would their discussion look like, and how would they relate to one another?

(13) **The traveling pants**. Place an old pair of trousers or blue jeans on a table in the front of the room. Present a variety of questions and activities about these pants, such as:
- Where have they been? Where would you travel?
- Describe three places you would travel to or goals you would accomplish while wearing these pants.
- What will it take for you to get there?
- How can you begin creating these destinations or goals today?

(14) **Invent a new language**. Either individually or with a partner, have students create a new language that we need today. It could be a language of feelings, kindness, service, or just a silly variation by adding or deleting words, parts of words, vowels, or consonants.

(15) **Legibility test.** With their opposite hand or blindfolded, students write a short review paragraph about a topic on the upcoming test or something that needs to be remembered. Then they trade papers with a classmate to see if they can read and understand what was written.

Trauma and Tension Releasing Exercises (TRE)

TRE are exercises intended to release pent up stress and anxiety in the body. These exercises stimulate the body's innate tremor mechanism and target the psoas muscles, which are our fight or flight muscles in the pelvic region. Structurally, your psoas muscles are the deepest core muscles and these are the only muscles connecting your spine to your legs. Below are some simple exercises that promote a healthy contraction and release of muscle groups where stress and anxiety are held in a child's developing nervous system.

(1) Spread your feet slightly wider apart than your shoulders and point them straight forward. Roll onto the sides of your feet rolling them in the same direction. You should be on the outside of one foot and on the inside of the other foot. Hold this position for a few seconds then sway the body in the opposite direction and invert your feet. Continue swaying back and forth like this very slowly five to eight times in each direction. To end the exercise, shake out your feet.[102]

(2) Place one foot in front of you and put all your weight onto the front leg. The back leg is on the floor just for balance. With the front standing foot—come up and down onto your toes, raising your heal as high as possible then lower your foot to the floor. Repeat coming up onto your toes and back down five to eight times, depending on the strength and flexibility of your legs. If it becomes painful or begins to produce a burning sensation, stop the exercise.

(3) Come to a standing position on both legs and vigorously shake the leg you just exercised to eliminate any pain, burning, or discomfort. Repeat this same exercise with the other foot. When finished, vigorously shake the leg to relax the muscles.[103]

(4) Keep your feet in the same position as the previous exercise. Place your hands partly on the lower back and the buttocks to support the lower back. Gently push your pelvis slightly forward so that there is a gentle bow in your lower back. You should feel a stretch at the front of your thigh. This exercise is not about arching the back but about pushing the pelvis forward so that the back naturally arches. This should be a gentle stretch according to your body's ability. Gently twist at the hips (keeping the bowed position) looking behind you in one direction. Take three deep breaths. Turn again from the hips in the opposite direction looking behind you (keeping the bowed position). Take three deep breaths. Return to the forward position (keeping the bowed position) and take three more deep breaths. To finish, release the bow and come to a normal standing position.[104]

Early Childhood Regulation Strategies

Prenatal infants, newborns, and young children are the most at risk to chronic toxic levels of stress and traumatic events. This is because a child's nervous, motor, and perceptual systems are vulnerable while development occurs in these beginning years.[105] When chronic unpredictable stress surrounds the mother, and traumatic events take place while the child is in utero and through the first few years of life, these physiological systems remain underdeveloped. Trauma, in other words, compromises development. Children and infants who experience high levels of toxic stress will often move to the frozen stress response because they cannot physically flee or fight the experiences that are happening to them. According to Dr. Peter Levine, author and trauma specialist in biomedical physics and psychology, "the emotion of fear has a very specific neural circuit etched in the brain corresponding to specific physiological sensations held in the body."[106]

Although the memory of a tragic or traumatic experience may not be conscious, the body remembers, and when the stress response is unceasingly activated, the brain can be reprogrammed in such a way that feelings of terror and helplessness become a new level of normal under ordinary circumstances.[107] Our bodies are designed to always return to a normal rhythm following adversity and trauma, but this homeostatic balance can become impaired and elevated when the adversity is chronic or perceived to feel unsafe or threatening, and there is not a caregiver to buffer and attune to the pain and despair following these toxic experiences. Young children will often show duress through distorted sleep patterns, play, exaggerated emotional responses, and altered activity levels as words in the form of narratives and explanations are not developmentally present during these times.

When early developmental stages have been compromised and the child needs an adult caregiver to co-regulate these bodily sensations, early childhood education provides a place, and a time for children to repair and heal through the loving relationship and co-regulation of another adult. When we address the sensory and motor systems through pressure, rhythms, movement, breathing, and art, these strategies and activities can calm the nervous system and help to organize the wide world of stimuli that enter into our brains each moment of the day. Several brain-aligned co-regulation strategies follow.

(1) **Create rhythm.** Using drumsticks, children mimic a rhythm from the leader in the circle. Vary this drumming from soft to loud, slow to fast, and the children can even move their bodies as everyone drums together. Children can also listen to the beat of a piece of music and taking crayons, they can draw how they visualize and imagine the beat with colors, shapes, and different sizes.

(2). **Take a sensory bath**. Gather a group of three or four children into an area in the room with a large beach towel, a bath time luffa, and a tube of lotion. Students could choose to take their own luffa and press on their arms and legs pretending to scrub and clean, or they could choose an adult to give them the sensory bath. Model this activity by pretending to step into a warm sudsy tub. Sit down and sing, "We're taking a brain bath, a brain bath, a brain bath, we're taking a brain bath to help us feel_____." Once we had patted the luffa up and down our arms and legs and on top of our heads, we pretended to carefully step out of the tub. We wrapped up each child tightly in the oversized beach towel, one at a time, while swaying and rocking back and forth continuing to rock and sing. This time we sang about drying off and feeling ready for the day. Students could then select a drop of hand lotion to massage onto their hands, leaving the area with three deep breaths as they entered into their day of learning. Addressing the sensory and motor systems of these young children through this exercise helped to regulate their nervous system so that learning could occur.

(3) **Wake up the singing bowl**. Patterned repetitive activity that works with our body's rhythms and senses is calming to a child's nervous system. The singing bowl can be a part of your morning circle time, as students listen to the sound that the bowl creates while placing their fingers on their vocal chords, trying to match the sound of the singing bowl's tone. Follow this with three deep breaths and then take turns "waking up" the bowl, matching the sound, increasing breaths to five or six long inhales and exhales. Some children may be sensitive to these sounds, so we paid close attention to each child's response and adjusted this activity as needed.

(4) **Walk the lines**. Movement and breathing calms the nervous system. Create a labyrinth of colorful lines and

shapes with various types of foot work and animal walks that the children can follow as they walk, hop, crawl, and skip along the lines and shapes. Model the crab walk along the purple line, and then the students can follow. This regulation strategy gave us a deep look into student balance, along with their gross and fine motor skills.

(5) **Squishy pillow sandwich**. This method requires two large pillows. Laying one pillow on the floor, the child lies across the pillow on his tummy. Then ask the child, "What would you like on your squishy sandwich?" and when they respond, use your hands and spread or sprinkle the next few ingredients using generalized touch and pressure along their backs. Then take the second pillow and lay it on the child's back, pressing into the sandwich with pressure to create the most delicious mushy sandwich.

(6) **Toothpaste squeeze**. The child lies on his or her stomach and, with a large exercise ball, you roll, roll the ball, starting at the child's feet all the way up to his or her head, up the child's back. As we roll the ball along the backside of the child, we narrate that we are squeezing the toothpaste out of the tube very slowly.

(7) **Vacuum cleaner**. Children lie on their backs with their arms behind their heads. Gently grab their ankles, swaying them back and forth to warm up the vacuum cleaner. Then the adult begins to slowly scoot the child back and forth just as a vacuum moves along the carpet. This is a powerful sensory practice for calming the nervous system.

We hope that these regulation brain-aligned strategies can become a daily part of your routines and procedures, providing the students with opportunities to calm down and attune their nervous systems so that emotional, physical, and cognitive well-being can become grounded in self-awareness and an understanding of how regulation affects all areas of our lives.

CHAPTER SIX

Touch Points Matter

"If a child is to keep alive his inborn sense of wonder, he needs the companionship of at least one adult who can share it, rediscovering with him the joy, excitement, and mystery of the world we live in."

—RACHEL CARSON

As author, psychiatrist, and neuroscientist Dr. Bruce Perry has shared, relationships are the carrier and foundation of brain development. Numerous studies share how relationships are the oxygen to healthy emotional, social, and cognitive development.[108] When youth have experienced chronic adversity, they often have not experienced the quantity and quality of relationships, where trust, predictability, and safety are a part of their worlds. The human brain needs to feel felt, seen, and heard. Trauma specialist Dr. Bessel van der Kolk states that our attachment bonds are our greatest protection against threats.[109] Traumatized human beings recover in the context of supportive relationships, and the role of these relationships is to provide a sense of emotional and physical safety. Chronic levels of stress and adversity damage the young child's developing neurobiology.

Millions of children in our country are victims of, or witnesses to, violence in their own homes.[110] Although it is estimated that less than 5 percent of domestic violence is actually reported, research reports that the home is the most violent place in our country for children.[111] Poverty of relationships, a form of neglect, is a significant adversity in our children's lives because neglect occurs when the brain does not receive the instructions or directions it requires to grow and flourish.[112] Early childhood trauma is characterized by environments of traumatic, stress, and exposure to maltreatment and neglect. The impact of long-term neglect is a major problem in America.[113]

Adverse childhood experiences (ACEs) deeply affect brain development and behavior, along with the emotional, mental, and physiological health outcomes of our students. Childhood adversity impacts the brain's ability to self-regulate, form healthy relationships, and also impairs learning. Currently, we are learning how chronic unpredictable stress causes the brain and the body to marinate in toxic inflammatory chemicals. Dr. Bruce Perry repeatedly argues that when adversities are met with relational care, the brain and body can repair and heal, lessening the dose-dependent relationship of negative and adverse emotional, mental, and physiological health outcomes.[114] Developmental trauma occurs in children and adolescents when chronic events and experiences do not meet the emotional and physical needs of the developing brain and body.

Schools can be a setting that produces positive attachments and relationships for our most troubled children and adolescents. Within this environment, we, as educators, need to create new patterns and associations of relational permanence that can begin to trump the adversity that has left the child or adolescent without healthy (and repetitive) social interactions. This can help our students begin to emotionally regulate on their own. One of the ways to do this is through "touch points."

Touch points are the deep connections we have with other people who provide a consistent base for us. Our touch points can be individuals we trust and interact with on a daily basis. These people see and notice our strengths, interests, passions, and the challenges facing us. They provide us psychological air and a place that we know we can be ourselves and be accepted for who we are. Many of our most difficult and troubling students, though, do not have people to provide these touch points for them in their lives.

By creating "resiliency touch points encounters," however, schools can help their most disconnected and discouraged young people. These encounters are brief connections throughout the school day created by school personnel who have been made aware and informed about this student's experiences. These encounters must not be long; their purpose is to create a dyadic exchange between adult and child. The goal is to see underneath the young person's surface behaviors and all their various defense mechanisms and to let them know that we see them. For older students, this might be a verbal exchange with validation, listening to learn, asking a question, or noticing a smile. In younger children, these touch points might include play, a hug, sensory or art activity, and rhythm and movement strategies that help to calm the nervous system while sharing connection with another.

How should all this work in praxis? These "resiliency touch points" are targeted and intentional. In a school, we can quite easily identify our top "tier three" students who enter school with chronic elevated and activated stress response systems. These are our students who may be chronically shut down and disengaged. These might be our students who continually test the boundaries of the adults who are trying to connect with them. Following are some guideposts for implementing this approach in our schools:

(1) **Provide information**. Our schools must be adversity/trauma informed before they become responsive. Our staff and educators need to understand what happens to the neurobiology of these students because of significant adversity. Schools must begin to embrace the fact that all negative behaviors arise from a stress-response brain state, and that

the behavioral issues we are seeing are intimately correlated to attachment and regulation challenges inside the brains and bodies of these students.

(2) **Start small**. Students need predictable and safe environments, along with ongoing support where a team of educators check in frequently and consistently with identified top tier students. Grade level meetings and professional development can be used to teach everyone in the school community about what adversity does to the young people we serve and what that looks like in the behaviors they see every day. We need a fundamental shift in our thinking from "What is wrong with these children?" to "What happened to these children?"

(3) **Assess**. Assess these touch points with office referrals, absences, truancies, as well as in-school and out-of-school suspensions. We can also collect perceptual data from our students, parents, community members, and staff to examine our school climate and culture.

We now know enough about the intersection of neuroscience, psychology, child development, and pedagogy to change the dynamics in our classrooms. It will benefit all our students, not just the young people who carry with them toxic levels of stress from the adversity in their lives. Following are attachment and connection strategies that can be implemented throughout the school day.

(1) **Validation.** Before our children and adolescents have reached the point of no return in their behavior, we can use the brain-aligned strategies of validation and questions. Validation, so powerful when used correctly, allows the child to feel felt and heard. When we validate, we do not praise or

ask questions, we simply listen to learn. We try and step inside our students' minds and hearts, experiencing the frustration, pain, and perceived anxiety they feel in the moment.

(2) **Structured emotional support.** The "2x10 Strategy," developed by psychologist Raymond Wlodkowski, is a powerful brain-aligned strategy to implement with our most challenging students. For two minutes, ten days in a row, teachers engage in a personal conversation with a student about anything the student is interested in, as long as the conversation is "G-rated."[115]

(3) **Take your order.** To connect with and create consistency for a diverse array of students with different needs, implement "waiter checks" as a way of personalizing communication throughout the day. Select two or three students a day, and ask them, "What do you need from me today? I would love to take your order. I may not be able to provide everything you want, but I will work hard to ensure one or two items." Once the task, item, or goal has been ordered and received, you can create fun ways to make a payment.

(4) **Noticing.** Noticing is much different from praising. When a child or adolescent feels noticed, they interpret this relational strategy as being heard and seen. Create a "noticing sheet" in your classroom for all ages. Every hour, to let the student know that you noticed, write down a note about what the student!

(5) **Dual brain sheets**. Many schools and classrooms require students to fill out thought sheets after a conflict or altercation and, oftentimes, students will resist filling these sheets out because of a sense of unfairness coupled with a brain that is still functioning from a reactive response. We

are learning that as educators, we could always do it better! Even if we feel the student made a poor choice, and they need to write up a plan of action for the next emotional classroom challenge, we still want to model for our students what a clear and thought-out plan of action could be, showing them how we are willing to work for them and change up a bit of our reactions and responses. Following is an example of what this could look like; for younger students, the words could be replaced with images in a simpler form.

• What is our challenge?
• What led up to this challenge?
• How did we handle this together and/or apart?
• Could we have prevented this challenge?
• What are two adjustments we will make the next time?

(6) **Adversity and the new story**. Reframing a negative experience with a child can provide new sensory associations for the child. This could take place in the midst of the adversity or following and reflecting with a student who has already experienced this difficult situation. Children and adolescents that have chronically walked through adversity and trauma carry the sensations of those events through pieces of visual imagery, and visceral sensory fragments from these challenges felt in the body and the brain. These sensations from negative memories can be buffered and reappraised with a trusting and safe adult who guides and helps them create a new narrative, reframing the positive aspects by exploring new sounds, smells, sights, tastes, and perceptions for the adversity experienced. The following is an example.

Jon sauntered into his fourth-grade classroom, head down, dark circles under his eyes, no book bag in sight, and angry! He explained that he was not taking the "fucking test" and his homework was gone! His teacher was beginning to see patterns similar to this during the school week. Mr. A, his teacher, took a few deep breaths, and turned towards Jon with a warm gentle greeting. "Let's not worry about the test right now or the homework. What do you need from me that would help you to feel better?" Jon looked at him with biting anger and said nothing. He flung himself into his chair, covered his head with the hood of his sweatshirt and slumped over in his chair. Mr. A gave him some time and space as he continued to check in with other students. After a few minutes, he walked over to Jon, and laid a handwritten note on the corner of his desk that read, "You don't need any more anger or sadness today and I have some ideas!" An hour later, Jon and Mr. A. sat in the back of the room and together began to rework and reappraise this negative situation. Shuffling through his notes and papers, Mr.A leaned back in his chair with his hands folded in his lap. "Jon, I want you to know that what happens at home or away from this classroom is none of my business, but when you are with me, I work for you, just like you work for me. You and I can devise a plan to finish this homework, just small chunks at a time and when you are ready this afternoon or tomorrow afternoon, we can review for the test. I know how creative and innovative you are, so I trust that you can help me create a new plan of action for how we can use our time together in here. Actually, I am grateful we have this time together so I can see you in action! I rarely get to see how you conquer an assignment or solve problems that I know are within your reach." Jon took a deep breath and a slight look of relief crossed over his face. Mr. A. continued, "I brought some extra water bottles and a bag of goldfish crackers for anyone who needs a little pick me up. Help yourself and then we will get to work!"

(7) Emotional and academic designer. These techniques are implemented for students in a frozen stress response state, which often takes the form of a student looking like he or she just does not care. This seemingly uncaring surface attitude, though, often masks a sense of hopelessness and despair in young people coming from adverse places. This strategy is process oriented and builds over a one- to six-week time period. In a neutral time, suggest a variety of ways to complete small chunks of assignments. These suggestions could range from drawing, painting, sketching, voice recording, video creation, or a medium of the child or adolescent's choice. "Chunking" refers to shortening assignments so that completion feels possible and doable. Occasionally, act as the "scribe" who takes the thoughts and notes as the student speaks. Begin with short, bite-sized assignments that students may feel more comfortable in attempting. Ask for their input, questions, direction, and thoughts, agreeing to check in with one another during this process. The check-in is not implemented for an evaluation or assessment but for mutual feedback and dialogue. These are young people who have really given up, not just in school, but with themselves. We need to recognize them and work to slowly restart them.

(8) Active constructive responding. Shelly Gable, professor of psychology at the University of California at Santa Barbara, has shown that how you actively share, celebrate, or respond to an event or experience with another individual is critical for the development of a connection with that person.[116]This process means stepping into the experiences with another and responding with questions, details, and interest. It is a form of questioning that asks and focuses on details when another individual shares something about an experience, event, idea, or relationship. Here are some examples of questions that may be used to build this skill:

Where were you when you saw this or heard this? Who was with you? What were you doing right before this happened? What were you doing when this happened? How did this feel? Now, how will this change things for you?

(9) **Life space crisis intervention.**[117] Create a timeline with a student in stress in order to bring order back into a student's crisis situation, and to problem solve to correct the difficulty. The timeline is a way to listen, to make decisions, to sort out thoughts, and to bring order to chaos. The objective of the timeline is to gather enough information about the student's perspective that you can put yourself in his or her psychological world. Timeline skills have to do with getting the story from the student's point of view, while reading between the lines and decoding the meaning behind the behavior. Students under stress do not recall or relate events in sequence. They offer a feeling, a behavior, a thought, and it can be difficult for an adult to follow. During the creation of the timeline, structure the interview by focusing on the student's experience of the event, his thoughts at the time, his feelings, how those feelings were expressed (behavior), and the consequences. As we build the student's recollection of the events, we create a climate of cooperation. We are on the same side, and we use abundant affirming to keep the interchange moving along. Kids want to tell their story to a trusting adult, but they do not want to be ridiculed, humili-

ated, or punished. When we respond, we affirm and we validate, and we also check for understanding by rephrasing what the student says to us. As you do this, you bring order to chaos. You create a clearer sequence of events. The Life Space Crisis Institute offers training in this advanced strategy if desired (for this, visit their website: https://www.lsci.org/).

(9) Building relationships with parents. At the beginning of a school year, semester, or grading period, write letters to parents, sharing what you have noticed about their children, especially their strengths. Sharing our interest in this way builds bridges. We often celebrate students of the week or month, but we can also celebrate parents of the week or month. Even if we have to dig deep for an affirmation, such celebrations could propel parents to collaborate with us.[118] We know that positive calls home can be effective, but we can also bring the home into our classes by having a family section in our class newsletters or website where families share celebrations, such as new babies or siblings, new homes, new pets, or "shout outs" for specific academic skills students have mastered. A family shout out could be something like: "Thank you for bringing David in early this week, as we really got a chance to work on his math skills." Try having a special recognition highlighting an entire family once a week to celebrate the cultures and composition of each unique family. These relationships can also be built during parent-teacher conferences. At the initial conference, ask some of these questions to forge stronger relationships:

- How I can work with you this year to help make this year a positive and exciting experience for your child?
- Please share your favorite memories of your child. What makes him or her smile and laugh? What do you need from me that would be helpful for everyone?

- What are two changes you would like to see in our classroom or school? Are there any changes at home that would be helpful for me to know?
- Is there anything you would like to teach or share with our class this year?

As argued throughout this book, our most challenging students carry into our classrooms and schools toxic levels of stress and adversity. On the surface, we see poor behavior. Adversity shows up in students who are chronically angry, upset, have difficulty regulating their emotions and are easily triggered by adults. These are the young people who are constantly at the center of problems, do not get along with their peers, and do not respond to any of the negative sanctions schools typically use for "misbehavior." They can be disrespectful and most are relationship resistant. This is what childhood mistreatment and trauma looks like. We must recognize it as behaviors of children who have been mistreated and hurt, and we must intentionally work to change this dynamic.

Dr. Bruce Perry, neuroscientist, author, and leading expert on trauma and brain development, shares, "These powerful regulating effects of healthy relational interactions on the individual—mediated by various key neural networks in the brain—are at the core of relationally-based protective mechanisms that help us survive and thrive following trauma and loss. Individuals who have few positive relational interactions—a child without a healthy family/clan—during or after trauma have a much more difficult time decreasing the trauma-induced activation of the stress response systems."[119]

The brain acts like a muscle, but is an organ that is use-dependent and changes in response to patterned, repetitive activity. Thus the more any neural network of the brain is stimulated, the greater chance of that region changing. This patterned repetitive activity in various brain regions is the foundation for creating memory, learning, and development.[120] This is such good news for educators because we have the opportunity to develop those missed attachment opportunities within the social milieu of the classroom and school.

All of strategies that are covered in our work will create the opportunity to connect and build touch points in the lives of these children. All children need these critical connections with supportive adults in their lives in order to begin to grow beyond the adversities they encounter. Children have been hurt in relationship and they will only heal while in relationship. Near the end of this book, we have added a resource section of the working standards and competencies for Indiana's new Social and Emotional Initiative for our state educators. This is a work in progress, but we are excited that these competencies address the child and adolescent's brain development through a triune brain model. We have also created an Applied Educational Neuroscience Toolkit that will support these competencies with activities, strategies, topics, and resources that align with each grade-level section.

Epilogue

We are so very grateful for the educators, students, parents, and communities who have informed this book with much research and shared interventions and practices over the past couple of years. It is through experiences that our brains continually grow, evolve, and create. Our nation and world have never experienced a time when there has been such a great need to embrace the mental and emotional health of each and every child and adolescent who enter into our schools, districts, and communities. We are living in a state of crisis with the adversities and trauma intimately affecting the mental, emotional, and cognitive health of our youth. We are also experiencing greater awareness and opportunities within this crisis leading to the resiliency of the human brain and spirit.

We also deeply see and understand the levels of toxic stress our educators are feeling and experiencing with the task and responsibility of meeting our students' emotional, mental, social, and cognitive needs. We now are learning that adversity and achievement gaps are intimately connected and when we meet students in brain development, we are addressing the regions of the brain that must be activated and integrated for academic growth to occur. Since we wrote *Unwritten, The Story of a Living System*, we have delved through higher education into the world of adverse childhood experiences as it relates to early childhood education. We have had the honor to see how adversity affects the developing brain within all age groups and within a variety of schools, districts, and communities across the country. We have also seen the effects through our own adversities and emotional challenges within our families and circles of friends; we have grown professionally and more important, personally, during these past few years. We want to thank each and every one of you for exploring and implementing this discipline and framework of Applied Educational Neuroscience /Adversity and the Brain into your homes, classrooms, schools, and all the environments where you sit beside our nation's youth. We will continue to research, write, and work beside each of you in the upcoming years, as the resiliency and the plasticity of the human brain is far greater than we could ever have imagined. May we meet each adult and child in our lives with gentle touch points knowing that their stories, pain, and adversities form the landscapes of their experiences and perceptual maps. We will continue to ask, "What happened to this child or adolescent," not "What is wrong with this child or adolescent?" In the resource section of this book, you will find many strategies, interventions, social and emotional competencies, and an educational neuroscience toolkit that will guide your educational practices for all ages of students. The online resource section for this book and more can be found at www.revelationsineducation.com. We will continue to add and share research, brain-aligned strategies, and instruction for creating social and emotional well-being for all our students, educators, families, and communities.

Dr. Lori Desautels

Assistant Professor, Butler University's College of Education

IN GRATITUDE
From Lori

First things first: I could not have written this book without Michael McKnight! Our work has created so much learning for me over the past few years. Our discussions, presentations, professional developments, and interfacing with educators from around the country have been blessings that are indescribable.

This book has been a collaborative effort and I want to acknowledge so many brilliant educators who have contributed to *Eyes Are Never Quiet*. Thank you to Austin, Indiana educator Ms. Kelly Stagnolia for her clear and transparent narrative of not only sitting beside students with significant adversity, but one that engaged with her own adversities with awareness. She demonstrated an openness to model healing and repair for her students. I want to thank my beautiful loving daughter, Ms. Sarah Desautels Dorsey, for her openness in sharing her life as a first-year teacher working with a group of severely traumatized young students in a self-contained classroom with children classified as "emotionally disturbed." Thank you to Mr. Chad Brown, certified trainer in TRE, who has worked so hard to create a series of tension and trauma-releasing exercises for students in our classrooms. Thank you to Dr. Shelia Dennis who spent the past two years creating case studies and research that support the framework of Applied Educational Neuroscience/Adversity and Trauma. The research, interventions, and resources were so lovingly and generously created and formatted by my colleagues and graduate students, including Deanna Nibarger, Sara Midura, Mary Kate Daniels, Dr. Shelia Dennis, Becky Pokrandt, and Courtney Boyle. You will be able to discover their powerful resources and contributions in the resources section of this book and online at:
www.revelationsineducation.com.

I want to thank Dr. Cathy Pratt for a beautifully written Preface. Cathy has been so supportive of this work and is my shoulder to lean on when frustrated, anxious, and a little down! Dr. Ena Shelly, Dean of Education at Butler University, has been the wind beneath my wings during these past two years, always exploring and creating ways for this discipline and framework to grow and develop within the university and in the community. Thank you, Ena, for writing the heartfelt foreword for this book. Dr. Deb Lecklider, Associate Dean of Education at Butler University, has been the quiet, gentle giant of a presence in my life, someone who believes in me when I begin to doubt myself! Thank you, Deb, for the lovely forward to this book. I want to also thank my friend and colleague, Christy Gauss, an advocate like no other for attending to the emotional and social health of all children and adolescents in every corner of Indiana and beyond! Thank you to the Butler University College of Education faculty who always sit by my side and share in the wonders of childhood and adolescence.

To the students, educators, parents, and communities all over this country and world, I want to thank you from the bottom of my heart for bringing this story to life! I want to thank you for your courageous service as you wake up each morning and walk into your classrooms, schools, and districts with so many emotions and life experiences that have brought each of you to this moment on your path of discovery! A heartfelt thank you to our editor, Douglas McKnight who has provided endless hours, energy, and a talent that has breathed life into this book and story. Michael and I could not do this without our publisher, Nancy Cleary at Wyatt-MacKenzie. Truly, Nancy, you bring joy to this challenging process and Michael and I are so grateful.

My heartfelt gratitude to my forever partner in this life, Michael Desautels, and to our three children: Andrew, Sarah, and Regan. My children have taught me about "eyes that are never quiet" and the unique spirit and love that is within every human being. These acknowledgments would be incomplete if I did not share the love, strength, and loyalty of our sweet rescue dog, Nellie, who grew up with so many traumas. Luckily, she is now beginning to settle into a more peace-filled existence. Finally, I want to dedicate this story to "T.," a young boy who has stolen my heart. He has experienced more trauma and adversity in his nine years than we can even imagine. "Nothing changes if nothing changes."

IN GRATITUDE
From Michael

"Chance encounters play a prominent role in shaping the course of human lives."

– ALBERT BANDURA

There is absolutely no way I would have written two books without meeting Lori Desautels back in 2012. Our chance encounter occurred when we met online. I was instantly drawn to the title of her first book, *How May I Serve You? Revelations in Education,* and the photograph on its cover, a picture of an adolescent young woman. What really captured my attention, looking back on it though, was that woman's eyes!

I would have never imagined that five years later, we would be writing our second book together and titling it, *Eyes Are Never Quiet!* Lori and I have become very good friends over these last five years. Our collaborations as co-authors and as co-staff developers have not only been extremely growth producing, but they have also been tremendous amounts of fun! She has deepened my understanding of what is underneath the surface behaviors of at-risk youth and the underpinnings of neuroscience. She is a passionate learner, a supporter of kids and the adults who work to support them. Her passion is contagious.

As a young teacher working with what our system still calls "emotionally disturbed students," I had another chance encounter with Fritz Redl and David Wineman's book, *Children Who Hate* (1951). Redl and Wineman both taught at Wayne State University (Detroit), and, although I have never met either of them, I am extremely grateful for their work. Reading that book allowed me to find Dr. Nicholas Long who, along with Frank Fecser, was just starting the Life Space Crisis Intervention Institute (LSCI). Both of them allowed me to become a senior trainer in some of the best training programs I have had the opportunity of working with in my almost forty-year career.

At my first training with Dr. Long, I heard about a group of people doing great work with at-risk kids in South Dakota, and I went to learn from the founders of Reclaiming Youth International (Dr. Martin Brokenleg, Dr. Steve Van Bockern, and Dr. Larry Brendtro). The 1990 book, *Reclaiming Youth at Risk*, along with the Long and Fecser's work at LSCI put me firmly on a new path of learning that continues to this day. I have enjoyed reading Dr. Brendtro's work (he is the author or co-author of over 200 articles and 15 books) on strength-based interventions with challenging youth. Dr. Long and Dr. Brendtro, former students of Fritz Redl, have carried his work forward for a new generation of strength-based professionals who support some of our most traumatized young people.

One of my goals in co-writing these books was to share the strength-based work of these pioneers. In a field that is often looking for the next "best thing," their work has withstood the test of time. Programs do not change people, people change people. Keep in mind that chance encounters can happen in all kinds of ways, even within the pages of a book!

Chance encounters come in many forms. I was privileged to have the opportunity to work with Pat Dannenberg for over a decade as we led a school for troubled children and youth between the ages of five and twenty-one. That was a critical decade that drove my learning, and it allowed us to put into practice many of the things we were learning as we worked to create a reclaiming environment for the students we served, as well as all the professionals who supported them with great care.

Another chance encounter that changed my life was when I met my future wife, Joan. That chance encounter, now over four decades in the past, has led to a great love, partnership, and journey. She has continued to support my passion for this work. The journey we have taken together over these years has truly been the best part of my life. This chance encounter has also produced our two children, Maya and Nate, who have continued to teach me about how deeply humans can love. Watching them unfold over the years has been an amazing experience that continues. These chance encounters could have easily been missed. As the pace of our lives continues to speed up, and we continue to be bombarded with information from all directions, we must learn to pause and reflect, to be on the lookout for these special encounters that come into our lives.

The students and the staff you are working with are also affected by the chance encounters with others they come into contact with. As a teacher, every year new students encounter you. It is a huge privilege and opportunity to influence the direction of their lives. This is not just a one-way interaction, though. You, hopefully, can be influenced by the lives of the young people you serve as well.

I want to thank our editor Douglas McKnight, my twin brother's middle son, for providing support during our writing process. You helped this book come to life. Doug, you did a wonderful job. Lori and I will always be grateful.

Lastly, I want to thank you, the reader, for having a chance encounter with our book. We are hopeful that this encounter will allow you to continue working—in whatever capacity—with children and youth who are waiting for a "turnaround adult" to appear in their lives. Remember, each encounter you have with a student is an opportunity to influence their lives and for you to be influenced by theirs!

ENDNOTES

[1] Larry Tobin, *What Do You do With a Child Like This?* Whole Person Associates, West Michigan Duluth MN, 1991, page 204.

[2] Nelson Mandela, "A Fabric of Care," in *Nelson Mandela. From Freedom to the Future: Tributes and Speeches*, ed. Kader Asman, David Chidester, and Wilmot Godfrey James (Johannesburg, South Africa: Jonathan Ball Publisher, 2003), page 418.

[3] Larry Tobin, *What Do You Do With a Child Like This? Inside the Lives of Troubled Children* (Duluth, MN: Whole Person Associates, 1991), page 10.

[4] James P. Anglin, "Pain Based Behavior with Children and Youth in Conflict," *Reclaiming Children and Youth* 22, no. 4 (2014): 53-55.

[5] James P. Anglin, *Pain, Normality, and the Struggle for Congruence: Reinterpreting, Residential Care for Children and Youth* (New York, NY: Howarth, 2002).

[6] Larry Brendtro, Martin Brokenleg, and Steve van Bockern, *Reclaiming Youth at Risk: Our Hope for the Future* (Bloomington, IN: Solution Tree, 2002).

[7] Children's Defense Fund, *The State of America's Children 2017* (Washington, D.C.: The Children's Defense Fund, 2017), 1-79. Available at: http://www.childrensdefense.org/library/state-of-americas-children/2017-soac.pdf.

[8] CNN, "Opioid Crisis Fast Facts," *CNN*, June 6, 2018, https://www.cnn.com/2017/09/18/health/opioid-crisis-fast-facts/index.html.

[9] Bruce Perry and Maia Szalavitz, *The Boy Who Was Raised As a Dog: What Traumatized Children Can Teach Us about Loss, Love and Healing* (New York: Basic Books, 2006), 51.

[10] *Based on 180 school days a year. For more, see Children's Defense Fund, *The State of America's Children 2017*, 10.

[11] "Philadelphia Urban ACE Study," Public Health Management Corporation, last accessed July 30, 2018, http://www.instituteforsafefamilies.org/philadelphia-urban-ace-study.

[12] Wendy Ellis and Bill Dietz, "A New Framework for Addressing Adverse Childhood and Community Experiences: The Building Community Resilience (BCR) Model," *Academic Pediatrics* 17, no. 7 (2017): 586-593.

[13] "Child Abuse and Neglect Prevention," Centers for Disease Control and Prevention, last modified April 10, 2018, https://www.cdc.gov/violenceprevention/childmaltreatment/index.html.

[14] Kristin Turney and Christopher Wildeman, "Mental and Physical Health of Children in Foster Care," *Pediatrics* 138, no. 5 (2016): e20161118.

[15] Michael Baglivio et al., "The Prevalence of Adverse Childhood Experience (ACE) in the Lives of Juvenile Offenders," *Journal of Juvenile Justice* 3, no. 2 (2014): 1-23.

[16] Kenneth V. Hardy, "Healing the Hidden Wounds of Racial Trauma," *Reclaiming Children and Youth* 22, no.1 (2013): 25-28.

[17] "Toxic Stress," Center for the Developing Child, Harvard University, last accessed August 1, 2018, https://developingchild.harvard.edu/science/key-concepts/toxic-stress/.

[18] Bessel van der Kolk, "Developmental Trauma Disorder: Towards a Rational Diagnosis for Children with Complex Trauma Histories," *Psychiatric Annals* 33, no. 5 (2005): 402.

[19] Bessel A. van der Kolk and Rita Fisler, "Dissociation and the Fragmentary Nature of Traumatic Memories: Overview and Exploratory Study," *Journal of Traumatic Stress* 8, no. 4 (1995): 505-525.

[20] Nicholas Long and Frank Fesser, *Life Space Crisis Intervention: Managing Troubled and Troubling Students in Crisis* (Hagerstown, MA: Life Space Crisis Institute, 2000), 34-35.

[21] Nicholas Long, "Why Adults Strike Back: Learned Behavior or Genetic Code?" *Reclaiming Children and Youth* 4, no. 1(1995): 15.

[22] Bessel van der Kolk, *The Body Keeps the Score: Brain, Mind, and Body in the Healing of Trauma* (London, Penguin Books, 2015), 122, quoted in Michael McKnight, "Teaching Adult Wary Children and Youth," *ACES Connection,* November 1, 2016, https://www.acesconnection.com/blog/teaching-adult-wary-children-and-youth.

[23] This section was previously written as part of an essay for *Edutopia*. See Lori Desautels, "Teachers, Students, and the Hero's Journey," *Edutopia*, August 4, 2016, https://www.edutopia.org/blog/teachers-students-and-heros-journey.

[24] Katherine T. Volk et al., *What about You? A Workbook for those Who Work with Others* (Newton Centre, MA: The National Center on Family Homelessness, 2008), 17. Available at: http://508.center4si.com/SelfCareforCareGivers.pdf.

[25] Jason Moser and Andy Henlon, "Talking to Yourself in the Third Person Can Help You Control Stressful Emotions," *MSU Today*, July 26, 2017, https://msutoday.msu.edu/news/2017/talking-to-yourself-in-the-third-person-can-help-you-control-stressful-emotions/.

[26] Lori Desautels and Michael McKnight, *Unwritten The Story of a Living System* (Oregon: Wyatt-MacKenzie Publishing, 2016), 38-39.

[27] Ken Robinson, *Out of Our Minds* (Oxford, UK: Capstone Publishing, 2011), 141-142.

[28] Linda Chapman, *Neurobiologically Informed Trauma Therapy with Children and Adolescents* (New York: W.W. Norton and Company, 2014), 21.

[29] Bruce Perry and Maia Szalavitz, *The Boy Who Was Raised as a Dog* (New York: Basic Books, 2006), 83.

[30] Peter Levine and Maggie Kline, *Trauma through a Child's Eyes* (California: North Atlantic Books, 2007), 34.

[31] Ibid., 6.

[32] Ibid.

[33] Ibid., 16.

[34] Ibid., 14.

[35] Ibid., 80.

[36] "Any Anxiety Disorder," National Institute of Mental Health, last modified November, 2017, https://www.nimh.nih.gov/health/statistics/any-anxiety-disorder.shtml.

[37] Donna Jackson Nakazawa, *Childhood Disrupted* (New York: Atria Books, 2015), 52.

[38] "Include: Supporting Young Carers and Their Families," The Children's Society, available from: http://www.youngcarer.com/sites/default/files/childrens_services_booklet_2011_3rd.pdf.

[39] Nadine Burke Harris, *The Deepest Well* (New York: Houghton Mifflin Press, 2018), 48.

[40] Ibid., 49.

[41] Bessel van der Kolk, *The Body Keeps the Score: Brain, Mind, and Body in the Healing of Trauma* (London, Penguin Books, 2015), 154.

[42] Mark Wolynn, *It Didn't Start with You* (New York: Viking Press, 2016), 29.

[43] Ibid., 16.

[44] Wolynn, *It Didn't Start with You*. 33.

[45] Ibid., 27.

[46] Ibid., 27.

[47] Bari Walsh, "Public Policy and Resilience: How We Can Change our Policies to Help Disadvantaged Kids Cope and Thrive," *Useable Research, Harvard Graduate School of Education*, March 23, 2015, https://www.gse.harvard.edu/news/uk/15/03/public-policy-and-resilience.

[48] Larry Brendtro and James E. Longhurst, "The Resilient Brain," *Reclaiming Children and Youth* 14, no. 1 (Spring 2005): 52-60.

[49] Children's Defense Fund, *The State of America's Children 2017* (Washington, D.C.: The Children's Defense Fund, 2017). Available at: http://www.childrensdefense.org/library/state-of-americas-children/2017-soac.pdf.

[50] David Finkelhor et al., "Children's Exposure to Violence, Crime, and Abuse: An Update,"*Juvenile Justice Bulletin* (September, 20015), 5.

[51] Ibid.

[52] Jane Ellen Stevens, "Nearly 35 Million U.S. Children Have Experienced One or More Types of Childhood Trauma," *Aces Too High News,* May 13, 2013, https://acestoohigh.com/2013/05/13/nearly-35-million-u-s-children-have-experienced-one-or-more-types-of-childhood-trauma/.

[53] This quote originates from the LSCI training that is available on their web site. For more, see https://www.lsci.org/.

[54] Bruce Perry, "Neurodevelopmental Adaptations to Violence: How Children Survive the Intragenerational Vortex of Violence," *The ChildTrauma Academy*, last accessed August 26, 2018, http://www.childtrauma.org/CTAMATERIALS/vortex_interd.asp.

[55] Andrew Slaby and Lili Garfinkel, *No One Saw My Pain* (New York: W.W. Norton 1994), 22.

[56] Stats based on 180 school days per year. Children's Defense Fund, 10.

[57] Peter Balonon-Rosen, "7 Things To Know About School Discipline And Civil Rights In Indiana," *Indiana Public Media*, June 10, 2016, https://indianapublicmedia.org/stateimpact/2016/06/10/indiana-suspensions-expulsions-corporal-punishment-numbers/.

[58] file:///C:/Users/mmcknigh.CURRICULUM/Downloads/Suspended-Progress-2017.pdf.

[59] Laura Jimenez, "Public Schools Must Address Disparities in Discipline Rates," *Center for American Progress*, January 17, 2018, https://www.americanprogress.org/issues/education-k-12/news/2018/01/17/444972/public-schools-must-address-disparities-discipline-rates/.

[60] Education Law Center, "School Discipline in New Jersey: A Toolkit for Students, Families, and Advocates," last accessed August 26, 2018, http://www.edlawcenter.org/assets/files/pdfs/publications/Student_discipline_manual.pdf.

[61] Varlie Strauss, "250 Preschoolers Suspended or Expelled Every School Day, According to New Analysis," *The Washington Post*, January 7, 2017, https://www.washingtonpost.com/news/answer-sheet/wp/2017/11/07/250-preschoolers-suspended-or-expelled-every-school-day-new-analysis/?noredirect=on&utm_term=.0f39d59f1ba5.

[62] James P. Aglin, *Pain, Normality, and the Struggle for Congruence: Reinterpreting Residential Care for Children and Youth* (New York, NY: Howarth, 2002), 55.

[63] Daniel Siegal, *The Whole Brain Child* (New York, NY: Random House, 2011) 14.

[64] Larry Brendtro and Scott Larson, *The Resilience Revolution* (Bloomington, IN: National Education Services, 2005).

[65] ECHO, "Trauma-Informed Schools," last accessed August 26, 2018, https://www.echotraining.org/trauma-informed-schools/.

[66] ECHO, "Trauma-Informed Schools," last accessed August 26, 2018, https://www.echotraining.org/trauma-informed-schools/.

[67] John Seita and Larry Brendtro, *Kids Who Outwit Adults* (Bloomington, IN: Solution Tree, 2005).

[68] Venus Evans-Winters, "Racial Trauma and Schooling: The Silence Dialogue," *Dr. Venus Evans-Williams Blog*, April 25, 2018, https://www.venusevanswinters.com/blog.

[69] Kenneth V. Hardy and Tracey A. Laszloffy, *Teens Who Hurt: Clinical Interventions to Break the Cycle of Violence* (New York, NY: The Guilford Press, 2005) 45- 46.

[70] Bessel van der Kolk, "Developmental Trauma Disorder: Towards a Rational Diagnosis for Children with Complex Trauma Histories," *Psychiatric Annuals* 33, no. 5 (2005): 401-408.

[71] Louis Cozolino, *The Neuroscience of Human Relationships: Attachment and the Developing Brain* (New York, NY: W. W. Norton & Co, 2006).

[72] Erik K. Laursen, "Healing Presence: Being with Kids in Pain," *CFLearning* 2, no. 6: 2. Available at: http://growingedgetraining.com/wp-content/uploads/2017/10/Healing-Presence_Thriving_vol_2-6.pdf.

[73] Bonnie Bernard, *Resiliency: What We Have Learned?* (San Francisco, CA: West Ed, 2004).

[74] Thom Garfat, "The Inter-personal In-between: An Exploration of Relational Child and Youth Care Practice," in *Standing on the Precipice: Inquiry into the Creative Potential of Child and Youth Care Practice*, eds. G. Bellefeuille and F. Ricks (Alberta, Canada: MacEwan, 2008), 7-34.

[75] Bruce Perry and Maria Szalavitz, *The Boy Who Was Raised As A Dog: What Traumatized Children Can Teach Us about Loss, Love, and Healing* (New York: Basic Books, 2006), 244.

[76] The Search Institute, "The Developmental Relationships Framework," available at https://www.search-institute.org/wp-content/uploads/2017/11/DevRel_Framework-1-Pager-04-26-2017.pdf.

[77] Bruce Perry and Maia Szalavitz, *The Boy Who Was Raised as a Dog* (New York: Basic Books, 2006), 40, 95.

[78] Karyn B. Purvis et al., "Trust-based Relational Intervention (TBRI): A Systemic Approach to Complex Developmental Trauma," *Child & Youth Services* 34, no. 4 (October 2013): 360-386.

[79] Peter Levine and Maggie Kline, *Trauma through a Child's Eyes* (California: North Atlantic Books, 2007), 112.

[80] Levine and Kline, *Trauma*, 112.

[81] Purvis et al., "Trust-based Relational Intervention."

[82] Nancy L. VandenBerg, "The Use of a Weighted Vest to Increase On-Task Behavior in Children With Attention Difficulties," *The American Journal of Occupational Therapy* 55, no. 6 (2001): 621-628.

[83] Purvis et al., "Trust-based Relational Intervention."

[84] Donna Jackson Nakazawa, *Childhood Disrupted* (New York: Atria Books, 2015), 161.

[85] Nakazawa, *Childhood*, 161.

[86] Lori Desautels, "Energy and Calm: Brain Breaks and Focused-Attention Practices," *Edutopia*, January 14, 2015, https://www.edutopia.org/blog/brain-breaks-focused-attention-practices-lori-desautels.

[87] Lori Desautels, "Quick Classroom Exercises to Combat Stress. These Brain Breaks and Focused-attention Practices Can Help Students Cope with Stress and Trauma and Focus on Their Learning, *Edutopia*, October 23, 2017, https://www.edutopia.org/article/quick-classroom-exercises-combat-stress.

[88] Joyce Gomes-Osman, "What Kinds of Exercise are Good for Brain Health?" *Harvard Health Blog*, May 2, 2018, https://www.health.harvard.edu/blog/what-kinds-of-exercise-are-good-for-brain-health-2018050213762?utm_content=buffer0a91a&utm_medium=social&utm_source=twitter&utm_campaign=buffer.

[89] Levine and Kline, *Trauma*, 387.

[90] Levine and Kline, *Trauma*, 388.

[91] Perry and Szalavitz, *The Boy*, 142.

[92] Perry and Szalavitz, *The Boy*, 143.

[93] Perry and Szalavitz, *The Boy*, 143.

[94] Mike Shook, "Working with Anxiety in School-Aged Youth - Neuroplasticity, Optimizing Stress, and Emotional Freedom Techniques with Amy Gaesser," *The Thoughtful Counselor*, 2017, podcast, https://player.fm/series/the-thoughtful-counselor/working-with-anxiety-in-school-aged-youth-neuroplasticity-optimizing-stress-and-emotional-freedom-techniques-with-amy-gaesser.

[95] Ortner, *The Tapping Solution*, 9.

[96] Shook, "Working with Anxiety."

[97] Linda Chapman, *Neurobiologically Informed Trauma Therapy with Children and Adolescents* (New York: W.W. Norton and Company, 2014), 89.

[98] Chapman, *Neurobiologically Informed Trauma Therapy*, 115-116.

[99] Chapman, *Neurobiologically Informed Trauma Therapy*, 117.

[100] Lori Desautels, "5 Ways to Help Students in Trauma. Teachers Can Create a Calm Classroom Atmosphere That Helps Troubled Students Be More Receptive to Learning," *Edutopia*, November 14, 2016, https://www.edutopia.org/article/5-ways-help-students-trauma-lori-desautels.

[101] Desautels, "5 Ways to Help Students in Trauma."

[102] David Berceli. *Shake It Off Naturally: Reduce Stress, Anxiety, and Tension with [TRE]* 298.

[103] Berceli, *Shake It Off Naturally*, 298.

[104] Berceli, *Shake It Off Naturally*, 298.

[105] Levine and Kline, *Trauma*, 10.

[106] Levine and Kline, *Trauma*, 34.

[107] Levine and Kline, *Trauma*, 43.

[108] Bruce Perry and Maia Szalavitz, *The Boy Who Was Raised As a Dog* (New York: Basic Books, 2006), 92.

[109] Bessel van der Kolk, *The Body Keeps the Score* (New York: Penguin Books, 2014), 81.

[110] Peter Levine and Maggie Kline, *Trauma Through a Child's Eyes* (California: North Atlantic Books, 2007), 27.

[111] Ibid., 28.

[112] Center on the Developing Child, Harvard University, "InBrief: The Impact of Early Adversity on Children's Development," last accessed August 26, 2018, https://developingchild.harvard.edu /resources/inbrief-the-impact-of-early-adversity-on-childrens-development/.

[113] Center on the Developing Child, Harvard University, "InBrief."

[114] Perry and Szalavitz, *The Boy*, 232-233.

[115] Raymond Wlodkowski, *Motivational Opportunities for Successful Teaching [Leader's Guide]*, (Phoenix, AZ: Universal Dimensions, 1983).

[116] Shelly Gable, et al., "What Do You Do When Things Go Right? The Intrapersonal and Interpersonal Benefits of Sharing Positive Events," *Journal of Personality and Social Psychology, 87* (2004): 228-245.

[117] Nicholas J. Long, Frank A. Fecser, and Mary M. Wood, *Life Space Crisis Intervention, Talking with Students in Conflict,* (Austin: PRO-ED, Inc., 2001), 87-94.

[118] Lori Desautels, "Navigating Confrontations with Parents," *Edutopia*, May 21, 2018, https://www.edutopia.org/article/navigating-confrontations-parents.

[119] Perry and Szalavitz, *The Boy*, 80.

[120] Christine R. Ludy-Dobson and Bruce D. Perry, "The Role of Healthy Relational Interactions in Buffering the Impact of Childhood Trauma," *Working with Children to Heal Interpersonal Trauma: The Power of Play*, ed. Eliana Gil (New York, NY: The Guilford Press, 2010), 26-43.

RESOURCE SECTION TO FOLLOW

There are many links contained within the resources, therefore we've made this a *Kindle Matchbook* — if you purchase the print edition at Amazon, you can download the Kindle edition for free and the links will be clickable.

Brain Intervals and Focused Attention Practices

Why Do Brain Intervals and Focused Attention Practices Work on a Scientific Level?

Research shows that the brain develops from the bottom up (van der Kolk, 2014, pp. 55-64). When we are born, our brain stem is the only fully developed part of our brain. This is the primitive region of our brain that controls our breathing, our heart rate, our pulse, our temperature, and our balance. Our limbic brain or midbrain is the next to develop, which is the feeling, emotional part of our brain. Our limbic brain activates our fight or flight response when we register a threat, and it thrives on relationships, feeling safe, and positive emotions. The cortex is the third region of our brain, and it is the last to develop. The cortex's focus is on reasoning, learning, analyzing, planning, and imagining, all things that are really important to students being successful in schools!

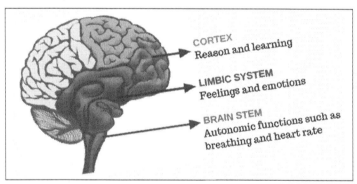

Most schools are good at taking care of students' limbic brain and cortex through having strong relationships with students as well as encouraging learning and inquiry; however, most schools miss activating and caring for the lowest part of students' brains—the brain stem. Caring for our students' lower brain region is especially important because many students who have experienced adverse childhood experiences have damage to their brains in the parts that were developing the most at the time the trauma happened—the brain stem and the limbic brain. We want to find more ways to reach our students at the lowest levels of their brains, and focused attention practices and brain intervals can help do just that. These practices speak the language of our lower brain regions, and they work to calm our students' from the bottom of the brain up. Just like you wouldn't build a house starting on the second floor, we need to tap into the bottom of our students' brains first.

"Bottom-up regulation involves recalibrating the autonomic nervous system, (which originates in the brain stem). We can access the ANS through breath, movement, or touch. Breathing is one of the few body functions under conscious and autonomic control."
— BESSEL VAN DER KOLK

BRAIN INTERVALS

"Parents and teachers can learn to use regulating interventions to help get their students and children back to a state where they can both learn and reason. In fact, unless we do regulate ourselves and then help regulate our children, no learning or reasoning is even possible. The lower regions of the brain need attention first."
—DR. BRUCE PERRY

Have you ever been driving for a long stretch of time, and then you realize that fifteen minutes have passed, and you don't remember thinking about driving because you were in such a relaxed state of alertness? That's not how we want our students to feel at school!

We want to keep our students' brains ENGAGED so their best learning can occur. We want to bring novelty, curiosity, and sometimes even a brief state of confusion into the classroom because the human brain pays close attention to these types of experiences, thanks to our RETICULAR ACTIVATING SYSTEN (RAS) in our brain stem.

Think of your RAS as the gatekeeper to your conscious mind. Your RAS filters and prioritizes sensory information to allow your mind to stay focused and alert. It decides what is important and what can be safely ignored.

You can use BRAIN INTERVALS to stimulate the reticular activating system in the brain stem and bring focus and alertness back to the conscious mind. Brain intervals can be used as a way to engage and alert students' brains, PRIMING them to be able to soak in new information. Additionally, brain intervals can be used after a period of intense learning to give the brain an interval of time to absorb the learning.

BRAIN INTERVAL IDEAS

Match My Tune
Have a student hum a pitch. Have other students match the pitch they're making while feeling the vibrations on their vocal chords.

Name That Sensation

Project a list of sensations onto the board such as warm, hot, sweaty, twitchy, soft, butterfly feeling, goosebump-y, tired, prickly, jittery, weak, empty, calm, etc. Have students identify where they feel that sensation in their body. The could think in their head, discuss with a partner, or draw a stick person and label where they feel the sensation.

Popsicle

Have students tighten all of their muscles as hard as they can. Then, have students "melt" each part of their body slowly, starting by softening their feet, then their shins, etc. Challenge them to see how slow they can "melt."

Brain Intervals for Peaceful Engagement:

Singing Bowl

Have students close their eyes, and make a singing bowl sing. Have them raise their hand when they can no longer hear the sounds. If you do not have a singing bowl, you could do this with a chime.

Tracing

Have your students continually trace their hand on a piece of paper while they take deep breaths.

Warm water

Have students run their hands under warm water, and then have them touch their face.

Invisible Ink

Have students partner up. Have one partner spell ONE word in the air that relates to what they just learned. Have the other partner guess the word. The drawer has to share why they picked that word. Switch and repeat!

Junk Bag

Grab an object from a designated "junk bag." Come with a new purpose for that object.

Music Scribble

Play a song and have students scribble what they envision they song to look like. When finished, students can share if their scribbles look like anything and give their art a name.

Brain intervals to Bring Laughter and Joy into Classroom:

Ice Cubes
Have students hold an ice cube in their hands and see how fast they can melt it. Then, have them touch their cheeks with their cold hands.

Check the Beat
Have students use pencils to create a beat as a class, or have one student create a beat and have others mimic the beat.

Trumpet Breathing
Have students fill their cheeks with air and blow out the air repeatedly.

Guess that Sound
On YouTube, look up the video "Guess the sound game" and play the video for students. It plays a sound, and students have to guess where the sound is coming from.

Brain Intervals to use simultaneously while having students talk to a partner about what they just learned:

Follow the Line
Create a line on the floor with tape about 10 feet long, or use an existing straight line in the hallway. Have students sit on the line and balance an object on their head (stuffed animal, eraser, etc.). Students have to scoot from one side of the line to the other while balancing the object on their head.

Bubble Wrap
Have students pop bubbles!

Pinky/L Swap
Have students hold up their pinky finger on one hand and create an "L" with their index finger and thumb on the other. Have them continue to switch simultaneously!

Wall Push-ups
While standing, have students create a push-up on the wall.

Tongue Talk
Have students tell their neighbor what they just learned while keeping their tongue on the roof of their mouth.

Wink and Snap
Have students wink with one eye and snap their fingers on the opposite hand. Switch!

Ear Grab
Have students grab their left ear with their right hand, and grab their nose with your left hand. Switch!

Arm Pulse
Have students put their arms straight out from their sides into a "T" shape. Have students close their eyes and pulse arms for 90 seconds.

"Lower areas are improved by good diet, steady doses of exercise, regular sleep habits, many positive relational interactions, and a steady dosing of patterned, repetitive, rhythmic movements that serve to bring calm and order to a clattering brain."
— DR. BRUCE PERRY

FOCUSED ATTENTION PRACTICES

Focused attention practices calm and soothe our limbic brain activity and sympathetic nervous system (responsible for the "fight or flight response"), and then they allow access to the parasympathetic nervous system (which relaxes the body and helps us return to homeostasis) through deep breathing and movement. Deep breathing is crucial to supporting people in accessing their parasympathetic nervous system because "there is no medication that can help to boost your parasympathetic nervous system.

"YOUR BREATH IS THE BEST CALMING TREATMENT KNOWN"

—NAKAZAWA

Focused attention practices also activate executive functions in the prefrontal cortex such as sustained attention and emotional regulation, which helps us to create a pause and bit of reflection. Focused attention practices are critical when priming the brain for cognition!

Focused Attention Practice Ideas:

Belly Breathing
Have student lie down on their back or sit straight up with hands on their belly. As they take deep breaths in through the nose and out through the mouth, they will feel their belly rise and fall.

Box Breathing
Breath in through the nose for 4 seconds, hold for 4 seconds, breathe out for 4 seconds, and then hold for 4 seconds. Repeat while tracing a box in the air for each breath as shown below.

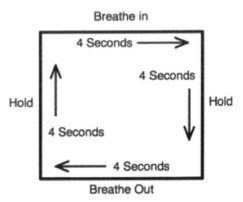

"There are scientifically supported and relatively simple steps that you can take to re-boot the brain, create new pathways that promote healing, and come back to who it is you were meant to be."
– DONNA JACKSON NAKAZAWA

Hoberman Sphere Breathing
Have student expand the Hoberman Sphere simultaneously as they inhale deeply. Close the sphere as they exhale slowly.

Hang Ten Breathing
Students make a Hang Ten sign with one hand. Cover left nostril with pinky finger and breathe in. Then switch and cover right nostril with thumb and breathe out. Repeat starting with inhale through left nostril.

Six Second Breathing
Have students take a deep, six-second inhale while reaching arms overhead. Exhale while counting backwards from six and slowly bring arms back down.

Object Breathing
Have students place a light object such as a cotton ball on their desk or in the palm of their hand. Have them inhale through their nose and exhale through their mouth. As they breathe out, they need to control their breath enough to move the object. You can make this more challenging by creating a path in which they need to move the object on or creating a finish line that the need to move the object to.

Paper Football Breathing
Have student make a paper football. Have students use their breath to move the football down the field. You can have students play against each other or alone at their desk., adding up their touchdowns.

Color breathing
Have students think of a favorite color and breathe in, then breathe out a worry.

Bubble Blowing
Have students pay close attention to breathing while blowing bubbles. Students could also pop bubbles while taking deep breaths.

Infinity
Have students hold their thumb about 10 inches from their face and create an infinity sign in the air, slowly with their thumb. Have them follow their thumb with their eyes while taking deep breaths.

Doodling
Allow students time to doodle. If you want to connect it to academics, give them the chance to doodle what they just learned.

Capture a Sound
Have students sit comfortably. Breathe in and out through the nose. If they hear a sound, have them "capture" it and put the noises into a "jar" in their head and continue breathing.

"When you control breathing, the vagus nerve links to everything else!
You have sensors in your lungs that when you slow your breathing, it slows your heart!
When you speed your breathing, it speeds your heart.
All of these organs are connected!"
– SETH PORGES

EMOTIONAL FREEDOM TECHNIQUES

Calming the lower region of the brain through tapping

Emotional Freedom Techniques, also known as EFT or Tapping, are evidenced-based strategies that promote stress relief and resiliency through activating a mind-body connection. "The basic Tapping technique requires you to focus on the negative emotion at hand—a fear, a worry, a bad memory, an unresolved problem, or anything that's bothering you. While maintaining your mental focus on this issue, you use your fingertips to tap 5-7 times on each of the 9 specific meridian points of the body. Tapping on these meridian points in sequence while concentrating on the negative emotions engages both the brain's limbic system and the body's energy system, encouraging a sense of safety and resolution" (The Tapping Solution, 2018). Thus, this is a bottom-up regulation strategy! By pairing Tapping with strength-based cognitive reframing, the brainstem is activated through the "language" of sensations.

1. Identify the stressor and any accompanying feelings, physical sensations, or challenging thoughts.

2. Determine the title and reminder phrase for your stressor.
Example of a title: "Feeling sick to my stomach when I have to get on the school bus." Reminder phrase: "Sick feeling in stomach."

3. Rate your stress level
Identity stress from a 0 (no stress) to a 10 (the most stress ever).

4. The set-up phrase and karate chop point
The set-up phrase is formed by inserting your title as follows: "Even thought I felt his [insert title here], I [insert positive affirmation here]." Tap on the karate chop point (shown here) while saying the set-up phrase. Repeat the sequence 3 times while repeating the set-up phrase.

5. The EFT Tapping Sequence
Following the Tapping Sequence in order, tap about 7 times on each spot using the balls of the fingertips of index and middle fingers on each specified acupoints in the diagram while repeating reminder phrase.

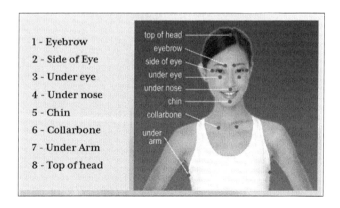

1 - Eyebrow
2 - Side of Eye
3 - Under eye
4 - Under nose
5 - Chin
6 - Collarbone
7 - Under Arm
8 - Top of head

6. Assess Progress

Rate stress from 0 to 10 again. If stress is the same or higher, repeat steps 4 and 5 up to five times. If it is still not helping, try thinking about a different stress. If stress is lower, repeat step 4, but change the set-up phrase to "even though I still have some of this [title], I [insert positive affirmation here]." At step 5, change the reminder phrase to "Remaining [title] at each tapping point. If stress is zero, it is not necessary to repeat tapping protocal.

Information from: Association for Comprehensive Energy Psychology. The ACEP Recommended EFT Research Protocol. Retrieved from http://energypsych.org/displaycommon.cfm?an=1&subarticlenbr=132

Bath, H. (2008). The three pillars of trauma-informed care. Reclaiming Children and Youth, 17, 17-21.

Lieberman, M., Eisenberger, N., Crockett, M., Tom, S., Pfeifer, J., & Way, B. (2007). Putting feelings into words: Affect labeling disrupts amygdala activity in response to affective stimuli. Psychological Sciences, 18(5), 421-428.

The Tapping Solution. (2018). What is Tapping and How Can I Start Using It? Retrieved from The Tapping Solution: https://www.thetappingsolution.com/tapping-101/

"Bringing to mind an emotional trigger, problematic scene, or unresolved traumatic memory activates the amygdala, arousing a threat response. Stimulating selected acupoints, according to the Harvard studies simultaneously sends deactivating signals to the amygdala. Repetition of the physical intervention resolves these opposing signals by reducing the arousal while the trigger is still mentally active. The hippocampus records that the memory or trigger is being safely engaged without a stress response, and the neural pathways that initiate the associated stress response are permanently altered. Being able to encounter the memory or trigger without limbic arousal becomes the new normal."
— DAVID FEINSTEIN, PH.D.

HOW TO USE EFT IN SCHOOLS:

- Tap together as a class with a shared worry such as an upcoming test
- One-on-one tapping in which the teacher taps with a student in need
- The teacher taps him/herself while vocalizing the stressor of the child
- A student or small groups taps about a stressor

STARTING YOUR DAY A BRAIN-ALIGNED WAY

Let's compare a zero-tolerance education system with a restorative practices-based, BRAIN-ALIGNED education system...

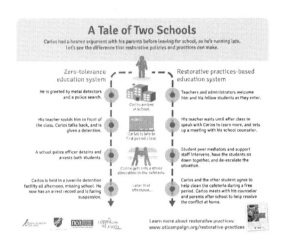

*Note: this is a thumbnail for reference only, download here: http://schottfoundation.org/sites/default/files/rp-carlos.jpg

Have you heard of the "school-to-prison pipeline?" When we implement these zerotolerance policies, research shows that "nearly six in ten public school students studied were suspended or expelled at least once between their seventh and twelfth grade school years" (Fabelo, et al., 2011, p. ix). That is a LOT of kids being suspended and/or expelled. Additionally, this is a racial equity issue because there are "disproportionately high suspension/expulsion rates for students of color: Black students are suspended and expelled at a rate three times greater than white students" (U.S. Department of Education Office for Civil Rights, 2014). Additionally, we know that once a student has been expelled or suspended that their likelihood of being involved in the juvenile justice system increases significantly in the following years (Fabelo, et al., 2011, p. xii). Is this racially biased, zero-tolerance system what we want for our children? I say no. That is why I urge you to make your first interaction with your students each morning count. Instead of making your first interaction with a student one that escalates them, perhaps you could give them a hug and ask them how they are before any needed redirections. We need our students to know from the moment they walk in the door to our classrooms and schools that they are known and loved—that we see them for who they are and not for their behavior.

I challenge you to shift the paradigm of behavior management from one of consequences and punishment to one of regulation, restoration, and teaching into the correct behavior. I urge you to shift your thinking from, "What is wrong with this kid," to "What happened to this kid," because many of our students are walking in with a lot of pain and trauma. Instead of always just punishing the negative behavior, we need to help them first regulate their brains and bodies, connect with them to show them we will stick with them through the conflict, and then help them find a way to repair any harm that they may have caused.

One way we as educators can begin to help our students regulate from the moment they walk in is through your classroom environment, brain-aligned bell work, and a morning meeting fueled with love and positive relationship building. In terms of environment, I like to start the day with lavender diffusing throughout the classroom, soft lighting, and the sounds and sights of the ocean by projecting a video of crashing waves on the screen in my room. When each student comes in, I greet them at the door with a good morning, and a hug or high-five. For students who need some extra help regulating in the morning, I sit with them as they do their morning work, talk to them about how they're doing, and even let them hold our classroom lizard to help them start off their day on a positive note. More ideas for brain-aligned bell work and morning meeting ideas to follow.

Take the time to know. Make your first interaction each morning count.
Let our children know that they are known and loved.

Written By: Becky Pokrandt, Indianapolis Public Schools Teacher

Fabelo, T., Thompson, M. D., Plotkin, M., Carmichael, D., Marchbanks III, M. P., & Booth, E. A. (2011, July). Justice Center. Retrieved from Breaking schools' rules: a statewide study of how school discipline relates to students' success and juvenile justice involvement: https://csgjusticecenter.org/wpcontent/ uploads/2012/08/Breaking_Schools_Rules_Report_Final.pdf

U.S. Department of Education Office for Civil Rights. (2014, March 21). Data snapshot: school discipline. Civil rights data collection. Washington D.C.

Brain-aligned
Bell Work Activities

1. **FANTASY INTERVIEW**
When students enter the class, they choose a half sheet of colored paper with a set of instructions displayed on the smart board. In the front of class is an empty chair and a few props to create a comfortable setting. I begin with a question: "If you could spend 15 minutes with any person in the whole world discussing, questioning, and sharing, who would this be and why did you choose him or her?" The students can write or draw their responses and, if they choose, share them following the exercise. When I implemented this experience with middle school and undergraduate students, the sharing and empathy in the room was palpable, and I learned so much about the emotional and social profiles of these students!

2. **THE THINGS I CARRY**
At the front of the room is a backpack containing five or six items, pictures, or words that I identify with or hold close to my mind and heart. As I model for my students the contents of my own backpack, I begin sharing who I am as a person. This is a powerful way of not only getting to know your students, but also tying in the backpack's contents with a class novel, science experiment, or any standard that you're teaching — simply by aligning items in the bag with what students need to know. Students can guess what items might be in the backpack before you reveal them. Prediction is an effective brain state which increases the brain's dopamine levels that are responsible for pleasure- and goal-seeking behaviors.

3. **JUST TEN WORDS**
Write or draw a ten-word story on a specific topic that you're teaching, or have students write a ten-word story describing their strengths and expertise. Another option for those who don't want to write is creating an infographic.

4. **PREDICT AN OUTCOME**
Choose a short TED Talk or documentary and watch the first minute. Following this one-minute presentation, students will predict two or three outcomes as to how this presentation will end. This can be related to subject matter that you're teaching, or it could be a motivational video addressing social and emotional skillsets.

5. **BELIEFS OUTCOME**
Using images, words, colors, or technology, have students design an infomercial about a strong belief that they hold. It could be a longtime personal belief, one that they've developed through recent experiences, or one that they're beginning to question.

6. REINVENTING GUM

Place a stick of gum on every desk as students walk in. On five notecards, have them design five new inventions for chewing gum. Students can share and compare at the end of the bell work.

7. MEETING OF THE MINDS

Students will select characters from a book, historical figures, or any author, inventor, scientist, or individual whom they've been studying. Given a 21st-century challenge, how would these individuals solve it? What would their discussion look like, and how would they relate to one another?

8. THE TRAVELING PANTS

Place an old pair of trousers or blue jeans on a table in the front of the room. Present a variety of questions and activities about these pants, such as: Where have they been? Where would you travel? Describe three places you'd travel or goals you'd accomplish while wearing these pants. What will it take for you to get there? How can you begin creating these destinations or goals today?

MORNING MEETING ACTIVITIES:

THE EMOJI SHARE

Project the "How are you Feeling Today?" poster on the projector. Have students share what emoji(s) they are feeling today and why.

PITS & PEAKS

Students can share a "pit" and a "peak" about their day, week, etc. A "pit" is something not great happening in their life, and a "peak" is something great happening. You can also call this "highs" and "lows" if you prefer.

*"We tend to view **misbehavior as resistance** because we understand where we want children to go. Children view **misbehavior as protection** because they know where they've been."*

- L. TOBIN

Trauma Releasing Exercises (TRE)

The "Fight or Flight" Response

Imagine a caveman. When a caveman encountered a threat such as a lion, the caveman could either fight the lion or flee from the attack. When this happened, the caveman's heart would beat faster, his blood pressure would rise, and his cortisol and adrenaline levels would rise. He would then fight or flee, and his stress hormones would be discharged, and his body would go back to homeostasis.

The "Freeze" Response

When fighting or fleeing isn't an option, animals can also go into what is called the "freeze" mode to try and stay safe. Since the animal did not engage in the fight or flight response, the chemicals released during the stress response are still in their body. After the predator leaves and the animal is now safe, their body starts trembling and shaking to release all of the chemicals and muscle tension built up from the stress response.

What "Fight, Flight, or Freeze" looks like today, and how TRE can help!

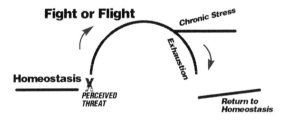

The problem is that today when humans encounter stressors, our bodies still react as if there was a physical threat to our lives such as a lion, although the stressors often come from unmanageable deadlines, relationships, violence, etc. Our bodies can also go into the "freeze" response; however, it has become socially unacceptable to allow our bodies to shake after the stressor has passed, so we do not release the built up chemicals and tension from the stress response. This leads to muscle pains, headaches, and psychological symptoms such as anxiety, depression, poor concentration, and more. TRE "exercises safely activate a natural reflex mechanism of shaking that releases muscular tension, calming down the nervous system. When this muscular shaking/vibrating mechanism is activated in a safe and controlled environment, the body is encouraged to return back to a state of balance. Tension & Trauma Releasing Exercises (or TRE®) is based on the fundamental idea, backed by research, that stress, tension and trauma is both psychological and physical" (TRE, 2018).

TRE-inspired exercises to use with your students:

Grounding Exercise
Bend your knees slightly, and rock to one end of your feet. Take a couple nice full breaths. Switch to the other edge of your feet and take a nice deep breath again with a sigh. Repeat one more time on each side.

Wall Sits
Engage in a wall sit until your legs start to shake. If it becomes slightly painful, move up the wall about two more inches. The quivering may get a little stronger and the pain should subside. Find a position in which your legs are quivering but there is no pain. After five minutes, come out of the wall sit and hang forward.

Prayer Push
Place your hands in prayer pose (palms together and elbows out). Push your palms together as hard as you can. Hold the pose while your arms shake. Release after a minute or two.

RESOURCES:

TRE. (2018). Trauma Prevention. Retrieved from Tension & Trauma Releasing Exercises:

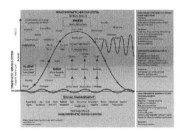

*Note: this is a thumbnail for reference only, download here:
https://traumaprevention.com/

NOTES:

100 DAYS
of Educational Neuroscience
TOOLKIT
Scope and Sequence

Teachers can use the 100 days of educational neuroscience to strategically implement lessons in the classroom. Use 2-3 lessons a week to discuss and reflect with students for five to ten minutes. The lessons are laid out in a manner that builds on previous understanding and knowledge. The guiding questions, strategies, and resources are intended to be a guide. The hope is that each teacher will bring a personal touch to each conversation, each year with uniquely different groups of students.

Teaching Brain Aligned Content for Engagement,
Relationship and Regulation

DAY 1
The Brain Neuroanatomy

Guiding Question: What is the brain like?

Strategies/Activity
Create brain storm lists in small groups so students can work together with guessing what the brain is like. After some guessing and wondering, provide them with a few objects like a three-pound weight, tofu, Jello, a jug of water and/or some type of fat. Discuss how the brain shares many of the characteristics from the objects.

To Do
Create "the brain is like" statements.
The brain is like...

Resources
https://www.coolkidfacts.com/facts-about-the-brain-for-kids/
http://www.sciencekids.co.nz/sciencefacts/humanbody/brain.html
https://www.healthline.com/health/fun-facts-about-the-brain

• • • • • • • • • • • •

DAY 2
The Brain Neuroanatomy

Guiding Question: What is the brain like?

Strategies/Activity
Watch and the discuss and reflect on video.

Resources
Elementary:
    https://www.youtube.com/watch?v=-nH4MRvO-10
Secondary:
    https://www.youtube.com/watch?v=XSzsI5aGcK4

• • • • • • • • • • • •

DAY 3
The Brain Neuroanatomy

Guiding Question: What is the brain like?

Strategies/Activity
Read Aloud and engage in discussion, questioning, wondering, all while adding new background understanding to learning.

To Do
Divide book into two day read aloud. Choose intentional stopping points for emphasis.

Resources
Elementary:
    Book: *The Fantastic Elastic Brain*, By: JoAnn Deak, Ph.D.
Secondary:
    Book: *The Brain* By: Seymour Simon

• • • • • • • • • • • •

DAY 4
The Brain Neuroanatomy

Guiding Question: What is the brain like?

Strategies/Activity
Read aloud and engage in discussion, questioning, wondering, all while adding new background understanding to learning.

To Do
Complete book in read aloud today.

Resources
Elementary:
>   Book: *The Fantastic Elastic Brain*, By: JoAnn Deak, Ph.D.
Secondary:
>   Book: *The Brain* By: Seymour Simon

• • • • • • • • • • • • • •
DAY 5
The Brain Neuroanatomy

Guiding Question: What is the brain like?

Strategies/Activity
Pass out brain shaped papers for exit slips as students write out or draw what they have done over the past 24 hours and what part of the brain did this occur or impact?

To Do
Post student responses to exit slip.

• • • • • • • • • • • • • •
DAY 6
The Brain Neuroanatomy

Guiding Question: What do you know about the brain?

Strategies/Activity
Pre-Assessment: Brain Jeopardy Online Activity
Complete the activity whole group and discuss as you work through the questions. At the end, note your score for later comparison to post assessment.

Resources
>   **Brain Jeopardy**
>   https://jeopardylabs.com/play/brain-aligned-teaching7

• • • • • • • • • • • • • •
DAY 7
The Brain Neuroanatomy

Guiding Question: What do you know about the brain?

Strategies/Activity
View Hand Model of the Brain video and discuss. Practice creating and iden-tifying parts of the brain with hand models. Remember to use partner's names at the beginning and end of the activity/share. How could using this

hand model be helpful to individuals, whole group, and in other environments.

To Do
Create an anchor chart identifying amygdala, prefrontal cortex, and hippocampus. Teachers and students can begin to create a Brain Area in the classroom where findings and questions are posted.

Resources
Hand Model of the Brain
https://www.youtube.com/watch?v=5CpRY9-MIHA

• • • • • • • • • • • • • • • •
DAY 8
The Brain Neuroanatomy

Guiding Question: What does the brain control?

Strategies/Activity
Watch and discuss areas of the brain from the Sentis video from resources. What new learning did we take away? What are the names of these parts of the brain?

To Do
Add new learning to anchor charts with labels, small sticky notes, and/or pictures.

Resources
Sentis Video: Areas of the Brain
https://www.youtube.com/watch?v=5_vT_mnKomY&index=2&list=PL

• • • • • • • • • • • • • • • •
DAY 9
The Brain Neuroanatomy

Guiding Question: What do you want to know about the brain?

Strategies/Activity
Spend time reviewing and looking over notes from the week and then create a KWL chart for future learning opportunities, relevancy, relationships, and engagement.

To Do
Display individual or group questions to return to in the near future. Use these guiding questions to support curriculum, morning meeting, advisory, discussion, and/or relationship connection.

Resources
https://www.youtube.com/watch?v=kMKc8nfPATI

DAY 10
The Brain Neuroanatomy

Guiding Question: What do you know about the brain?

Strategies/Activity
Post Assessment: Brain Jeopardy Online Activity

Resources
   Brain Jeopardy
   https://jeopardylabs.com/play/brain-aligned-teaching7

DAY 11
The Brain Neuroanatomy

Guiding Question: What three areas of the brain will we be focusing on when discussing and learning about educational neuroscience?

Strategies/Activity
We have spent time talking about what the brain is like and introducing the areas of the brain. This week we will look closely at the prefrontal cortex, hippocampus and amygdala. Today we are going to spend time reviewing, reflecting and connecting to what we will be learning throughout this week.

Resources
   What are the parts of the brain?
   https://www.youtube.com/watch?v=jdJ5eq6iNPA

DAY 12
The Brain Neuroanatomy

Guiding Question: What is the prefrontal cortex?

Strategies/Activity
Prefrontal Cortex
Where we do life (cognitive, emotional, behavioral functioning). The prefrontal cortex goes offline when faced with danger (fear or stress). The prefrontal cortex communicates through words, spoken language. Teach students that their prefrontal cortex is where decision making happens—we want to be in our prefrontal cortex at school! Teach students to put their hands over their forehead to find their prefrontal cortex. To Do: Create an anchor chart for executive functions and reflect throughout the day when we are using the prefrontal cortex.

Resources
> https://www.youtube.com/watch?v=tLKTJ8igZ9I
> https://www.youtube.com/watch?v=IfKLmqpjfWs
> https://www.youtube.com/watch?v=REo3fzja5xs

• • • • • • • • • • • • • •

DAY 13
The Brain Neuroanatomy

Guiding Question: What is the prefrontal cortex?

Strategies/Activity
Prefrontal Cortex
Where we do life (cognitive, emotional, behavioral functioning). The prefrontal cortex goes offline when faced with danger (fear or stress). The prefrontal cortex communicates through words, spoken language. Teach students that their prefrontal cortex is where decision making happens - we want to be in our prefrontal cortex at school! Teach students to put their hands over their forehead to find their prefrontal cortex. To Do: Review the anchor chart and add new learning from today's discussion.

Resources
> https://www.youtube.com/watch?v=FZLXggsK6oA

> https://www.understood.org/en/learning-attention-issues/child-learning-disabilities/executive-functioning-issues/3-areas-of-executive-function

• • • • • • • • • • • • • •

DAY 14
The Brain Neuroanatomy

Guiding Question: What is the hippocampus?

Strategies/Activity
Hippocampus
Formation of new memories and learning emotions. Chronic stress causes increased levels of cortisol and adrenaline that can damage and kill cells in the hippocampus. Why is memory important for learning at school?

To Do
Highlight the hippocampus on anchor chart and its function.

Resources
> https://www.youtube.com/watch?v=5EyaGR8GGhs

> https://www.youtube.com/watch?v=XvjrqOTNa8Y

• • • • • • • • • • • • • •
DAY 15
The Brain Neuroanatomy

Guiding Question: What is the hippocampus?

Strategies/Activity
Hippocampus
Formation of new memories and learning emotions. Chronic stress causes increased levels of cortisol and adrenaline that can damage and kill cells in the hippocampus. Why is memory important for learning at school?

To Do
Review the anchor chart and add new learning from today's discussion.

Resources
https://www.kidsdiscover.com/quick-reads/meet-hippocampus-memories-go-make-sense/

http://brainmadesimple.com/hippocampus.html

• • • • • • • • • • • • • •
DAY 16
The Brain Neuroanatomy

Guiding Question: What is the amygdala?

Strategies/Activity
The amygdala is the alarm center for the brain. It is the emotional station for our brain and it can make our prefrontal cortex go offline and disrupt our ability to think. The amygdala communicates through emotions. When the amygdala is firing we need to regulate/calm.

To Do
Label the amygdala on anchor chart and its function.

Resources
Bring in almonds or small rocks in the shape of the amygdala to support discussion of amygdala.

https://www.youtube.com/watch?v=d_5DU5opOFk&index=3&list=PLqlCitlObKYTqgMpmujruBllvXucAEwzD

• • • • • • • • • • • • •
DAY 17
The Brain Neuroanatomy

Guiding Question: What is the amygdala?

Strategies/Activity
The amygdala is the alarm center for the brain. It is the emotional station for our brain and it can make our prefrontal cortex go offline and disrupt our ability to think. The amygdala communicates through emotions. When the amygdala is firing we need to regulate/calm.

To Do
Review the anchor chart and add new learning from today's discussion.

Resources
http://brainmadesimple.com/amygdala.html

• • • • • • • • • • • • •
DAY 18
The Brain Neuroanatomy

Guiding Question: Where is the prefrontal cortex, amygdala, and hippocampus?

Strategies/Activity
Classroom community create Brain Hats from resources. Spend time wearing, discussing and reflecting on learning from the week.

To Do
Spend time creating brain hats to demonstrate knowledge of brain regions.

Resources
Brain Hat Activity
https://steameducation.wordpress.com/2012/03/21/brain-hat-activity/

Momentous Institute
http://momentousinstitute.org/video-library

• • • • • • • • • • • • •
DAY 19
Focused Attention Practices

Guiding Question: What is a focused attention practice?

Strategies/Activity
A focused attention practice is an exercise to quiet the body and focus the

mind. The practices calm and soothe the limbic brain and allow us to return to a calm baseline. Complete your first focused attention practice as a class. Discuss and reflect after focused attention practice. How do you feel? What do you notice about your body? Mind? Accept positive and negative feedback as this is creating a safe space to share.

To Do
Notice. Notice who is participating and providing feedback and connect with those students who need support.

Resources
Focused Attention Practice
Begin with tracing our fingers of each hand with an inhale and exhale! Start for only 30 seconds or less and build up time as a challenge for the class. Always make this a choice and reflect for a minute afterwards. (See Focused Attention Practice resource for a list of other practices.)

https://www.edutopia.org/blog/brain-breaks-focused-attention-practices-lori-desautels

DAY 20
Focused Attention Practices

Guiding Question: What is a focused attention practice?

Strategies/Activity
Review the purpose of a focused attention practice. Spend time completing the same focused attention practice from previous day, adding on a few seconds if students are ready. Discuss and reflect after focused attention practice. How do you feel? What do you notice about your body? Mind? Accept positive and negative feedback as this is creating a safe space to share. Anyone feel differently today than yesterday?

To Do
Create an anchor chart with essential agreements for focused attention practices in the classroom. Have students create definition and agree on essential agreements.

Quiet Body (hands, feet, mouth)

Choice to participate (respectful)

Resources
Videos to Support Buy-in

Kobe Bryant
https://www.youtube.com/watch?v=ucNODrsGdx0&list=PLmWktbOLl
ZuaHEVS4dhqz8DyOTQleYIWO&index=3

Celebrities that Meditate
    https://www.youtube.com/watch?v=XgtDPiZNefY

Teens
    https://www.youtube.com/watch?v=OKgWaBc6e38

Primary Elementary
    https://www.youtube.com/watch?v=9CdPQ7XlMzU

    http://www.mindfulschools.org/

    https://www.youtube.com/watch?v=7zpo04Xqzlw&list=PLmWktbOLl-ZuaHEVS4dhqz8DyOTQleYIWO&index=5

    https://www.youtube.com/watch?v=SCR7OfRuQd4&index=11&list=PLmWktbOLlZuaHEVS4dhqz8DyOTQleYIWO

    https://www.youtube.com/watch?v=_MqVd8XlShM&index=15&list=PLmWktbOLlZuaHEVS4dhqz8DyOTQleYIWO

    https://www.youtube.com/watch?v=GVWRvVH5gBQ

    https://www.youtube.com/watch?v=hKnRKy5Wu7c

• • • • • • • • • • • • • • •

DAY 21
Focused Attention Practices

Guiding Question: What are the benefits of focused attention practice?

Strategies/Activity
Focused Attention Practices have many benefits. First they calm the limbic brain activity and sympathetic nervous system inviting the parasympathetic nervous system in! They also activate executive functions in the prefrontal cortex in particular, sustained attention and emotional regulation helping us to create a pause and a bit of reflection. These two strategies are critical when priming the brain for cognition.

Resources
    Continuing sharing from video resources in Day 17. Take time each day at this stage to reflect on how the body and mind feels before, during and after focused attention practice.

DAY 22
Focused Attention Practices

Guiding Question: How is focused attention practice impacting me?

Strategies/Activity

To Do
Create an anchor chart displaying different focused attention practices as you try each one. Before introducing new practices, spend time mastering each focused attention before you move to another one. We want students to feel comfortable and confident with the practices before being introduced to more practices.

Resources
Continuing sharing from video resources in Day 17. Take time each day at this stage to reflect on how the body and mind feels before, during and after focused attention practice.

DAY 23
Focused Attention Practices

Guiding Question: How to breath during focused attention practice?

Strategies/Activity
Students should be feeling comfortable with the idea of focused attention practice, what it is, and the benefits of participating each day. Let's talk about how to breath during

Resources
https://www.youtube.com/watch?v=c3YyjUmDapc
https://www.youtube.com/watch?v=Jd78W66mA2U&t=124s
https://www.youtube.com/watch?v=WmLmu3PDyx0

DAY 24
Amygdala

Guiding Question: How do emotions impact our thinking and actions?

Strategies/Activity
Emotions are an important part of each day for all of us. What happens in the brain when we experience positive and negative emotions?
Connection: When we take time to engage in focused attention practices

each day, this helps create pause when we become overwhelmed with emotions in a difficult situation. Pausing allows us to respond to an incident rather than react to it.

Resources
Sentis: Emotions and the Brain
https://www.youtube.com/watch?v=xNY0AAUtH3g

Books About Emotions:
Today I Feel Silly and Other Moods That Make My Day Jamie Lee Curtis
The Feelings Book Todd Parr
The Way I Feel Janan Cain
What Do You Do with a Problem? Kobi Yamada
What Do You Do with an Idea? Kobi Yamada
What Do You Do with a Chance? Kobi Yamada

DAY 25
Emotions and The Brain

Guiding Question: How do emotions occur in the brain?

Strategies/Activity
Watch Inside Out clip and share that tomorrow the whole group will discuss the clip and how we are sharing our emotions. Watch what feelings you notice and how they change from the film Inside Out
Inside Out. When have you felt similar emotion?

Resources
"Inside Out" Clips
https://www.youtube.com/watch?v=8CnlpYnAZSE

DAY 26
Emotions and The Brain

Guiding Question: How are you sharing your emotions to support well-being?

Strategies/Activity
Let's talk about the Inside Out clip from yesterday and share the emotions we have most often each day and what is causing those in our brains. Here are some questions that will drive our learning over the next two days!

Resources
These questions were designed for promoting student discussion, self-reflection, and self-awareness. Dr. Dan Seigel's research reports that, **"What is sharable is bearable."** Sadness helped Joy in the film, and your

own sadness can help you.

How do you cope with Sadness?

    Can you use your Sadness to feel better? How?

    What would happen if we never felt Sadness?

    Is it sometimes good to keep Sadness inside a circle so that it does not spread and get out of control? Why?

    Fear and Anger can protect and motivate us.

    When was Fear needed in your life?

    How did Fear help you?

    What is the perfect amount of Fear?

    What happens to our thinking and problem solving when we carry too much Fear or Sadness?

    How does Anger show up in your brain?

    Has Anger ever helped you?

    How do you typically handle your Anger?

    Disgust keeps us from being poisoned physically and socially.

    How has the feeling of Disgust helped you?

    How has expressing Disgust hurt your relationships or experiences?

    Joy plays the leading role among the feelings in Riley's brain.

    Does Joy always play the leading role in our brains?

    What happened when Joy and Sadness left headquarters?

    How do we see Joy in your brain?

    What creates Joy to take over your brain?

    Imagine having no feelings at all.

    What would life be like if we didn't have feelings?

    Describe two positive changes in our life if we didn't have feelings.

    Describe two negative changes that could occur in a life with no feelings.

DAY 27
Emotional Contagion

Guiding Question: What is emotional contagion?

Strategies/Activity

Emotional contagion is the phenomenon of having one person's emotions and related behaviors directly trigger similar emotions and behaviors in other people. This happens because of mirror neurons. After watching the video spend quiet time reflecting on the question, "What are you sharing?"

Resources

Emotions and the Brian

https://www.youtube.com/watch?v=xNY0AAUtH3g&t=3s

Are Emotions Contagious?

https://www.youtube.com/watch?v=rNGeNzoTPq0

• • • • • • • • • • • • •
DAY 28
Emotional Contagion

Guiding Question: What is emotional contagion?

Strategies/Activity

It is important to be aware of our brain state and what we are sharing as we enter a space. Choose one of the videos from resources and discuss whole group. How does emotional contagion impact empathy in our classroom, school, state, country, and world?

Resources

Are Your Emotions Contagious?
https://www.youtube.com/watch?v=HTFdMwCXpMw

Empathy and Mirror Neurons
https://www.youtube.com/watch?v=XzMqPYfeA-s&list=RDQMDzvo_A7NaXY

• • • • • • • • • • • • •
DAY 29
Mirror Neurons

Guiding Question: What are mirror neurons?

Strategies/Activity

Mirror neurons allow us to communicate without talking. Mirroring is one brain reflecting and interpreting the actions, intentions, and emotions of another brain. Essentially, we are human magnets, picking up other's feelings, thoughts and actions subconsciously. Think of a time in your life when someone's actions or bad mood was felt by you even if you were not directly involved with that person. Share out.

Resources

Mirror Neurons Allow Us to Understand Each Other
https://www.livescience.com/11002-mirror-neurons-understand.html

• • • • • • • • • • • • •
DAY 30
Mirror Neurons

Guiding Question: How do mirror neurons work?

Strategies/Activity

Stand in front of the class with a big cold glass of ice water and drink it slowly. Take deliberate sips and watch students. Continue to talk to students about delicious this water tastes! Take time to process through whole group discussion.

How did this make you feel?

What did you experience as you watched this person slowly sipping and enjoying the ice cold water?

• • • • • • • • • • • •
DAY 31
Amygdala

Guiding Question: What role does the amygdala play in the brain?

Strategies/Activity
The amygdala is the alarm center for the brain and does not respond to words but emotions. When your amygdala is alerted, your prefrontal cortex goes offline. Your amygdala keeps you safe, helps you to process emotions, and decide between fight or flight.

Resources
Two Minute Neuroscience: Amygdala
https://www.youtube.com/watch?v=JVvMSwsOXPw

Quantum University–Amygdala
https://www.youtube.com/watch?v=xU5QmZp9Cmo

• • • • • • • • • • • •
DAY 32
Amygdala

Guiding Question: What is fight or flight?

Strategies/Activity
The bodies fight or flight reaction in the amygdala is common and biological way to prepare our body for action. It is important that we recognize and notice when our bodies are having these symptoms and that we respond in a way that is helpful and not hurtful.

Resources
https://science.howstuffworks.com/life/inside-the-mind/emotions/fear2.htm

https://www.youtube.com/watch?v=uxweRCXaLVA

https://www.youtube.com/watch?v=JtSP7gJuRFE

https://www.sfh-tr.nhs.uk/images/PIL3026_Fight_or_flight_and_relaxed_breathing.pdf

DAY 33
Amygdala

Guiding Question: What triggers your amygdala?

Strategies/Activity
It is important to know your triggers and be aware of others triggers. When we are aware of what alerts our amygdala we can anticipate, plan ahead, and have more success responding when triggered in our environment. Complete the trigger survey with students over the next two days with a class share at the end of the activity.

Resources
https://do2learn.com/activities/SocialSkills/Stress/IdentifyStressTriggers.pdf

DAY 34
Amygdala

Guiding Question: What triggers your amygdala?

Strategies/Activity
Continue completing the survey from Day 24. Once each person has identified their Top 5 spend class time sharing out, finding similarities and common triggers, and allowing students to explain their own triggers.

To Do
It can be helpful to post Top 5 lists in the classroom environment for accountability and reflection. Be sure to put these lists in a place for easy access during repair conversations.

Resources
https://do2learn.com/activities/SocialSkills/Stress/IdentifyStressTriggers.pdf

DAY 35
Triggers

Guiding Question: What causes my brain to go on alarm alert? (shift from prefrontal cortex to amygdala)

Strategies/Activity
Triggers, or hot buttons, are events or situations that cause irritation, irritability, anxiety, sadness, anger, etc. If we are aware of our triggers we can take action to avoid them in certain situations and/or anticipate when we

might be triggered. If we bring this to our conscious mind, we can prepare and better respond rather than react in the emotional moment.

To Do
Over the next several days, students and teacher will complete the Identifying Triggers at School Survey from resources. Chunk the survey into manageable pieces for appropriate age level. Younger students could complete independently as teacher reads questions aloud.

Resources
https://do2learn.com/activities/SocialSkills/Stress/IdentifyStressTriggers.pdf

DAY 36
Triggers

Guiding Question: What causes my brain to go on alarm alert? (shift from prefrontal cortex to amygdala)

Strategies/Activity
Review: Triggers, or hot buttons, are events or situations that cause irritation, irritability, anxiety, sadness, anger, ect. If we are aware of our triggers we can take action to avoid them in certain situations and/or anticipate when we might be triggered. If we bring this to our conscious mind, we can prepare and better respond rather than react in the emotional moment.

To Do
Over the next several days, students and teacher will complete the Identifying Triggers at School Survey from resources. Chunk the survey into manageable pieces for appropriate age level. Younger students could complete independently as teacher reads questions aloud.

Resources
https://do2learn.com/activities/SocialSkills/Stress/IdentifyStressTriggers.pdf

https://www.psychologytoday.com/us/blog/wander-woman/201507/5-steps-managing-your-emotional-triggers

DAY 37
Triggers

Guiding Question: What causes my brain to go on alarm alert? (shift from prefrontal cortex to amygdala)

Strategies/Activity
Review: Triggers, or hot buttons, are events or situations that cause irritation, irritability, anxiety, sadness, anger, ect. If we are aware of our triggers we can take action to avoid them in certain situations and/or anticipate when we might be triggered. If we bring this to our conscious mind, we can prepare and better respond rather than react in the emotional moment.

To Do
Over the next several days, students and teacher will complete the Identifying Triggers at School Survey from resources. Chunk the survey into manageable pieces for appropriate age level. Younger students could complete independently as teacher reads questions aloud.

Resources
> https://do2learn.com/activities/SocialSkills/Stress/IdentifyStressTriggers.pdf

DAY 38
Triggers

Guiding Question: What are my top 5 triggers that I need to share with my learning community?

Strategies/Activity
Share in partners, small groups, or whole group top 5 trigger list. Do you see common themes arise from class feedback? How could the class use this new learning to support essential agreements in the learning environment? To Do: Post and revisit top 5 lists as needed.

Resources
> https://do2learn.com/activities/SocialSkills/Stress/IdentifyStressTriggers.pdf
>
> https://tinybuddha.com/blog/how-to-identify-your-emotional-triggers-what-to-do-about-them/

DAY 39
Triggers

Guiding Question: How can we shift from reactive responses to proactive responses when it comes to our emotional triggers?

Strategies/Activity
On this day we will review and post our emotional triggers and the regulation strategies we have explored to support positive emotional regulation.

Resources
Sharing Triggers
    Classroom Jobs
    Assign new roles and responsibilities on your classroom that help everyone to regulate their emotions and take responsibility for one another.

Here are some choices.
    Kindness Keeper- notices and shares out kindness noticed

    Gratitude Keeper- notices and shares out gratitude noticed

    Inspirational Leader- finds and share inspiration

    Mystery Motivator- provides encouragement anonymously

    Resource Manager- looking up topics related to what we are studying and shares information

    Feeling Tracker- to recognize when a classmate or another student is beginning to feel negative emotion suggesting we might need a focused attention practice

    The Giver- what might this role be in your classroom?

DAY 40
The 90 Second Rule

Guiding Question: What is the 90 Second Rule?

Strategies/Activity
What do you think this is? Let's write down our answers or guesses!
ANSWER: Our brain can let go of negative emotion in 90 seconds. When a person has a reaction to something in their environment, there is a 90 second chemical process that happens in the body; after that, any remaining emotional response is just the person choosing to stay in that emotional loop.

To Do
Create an anchor chart for the 90 Second Rule.

Resources
    Complete a focused attention practice: Place one arm under your opposite armpit the other arm hugging your shoulder. Sitting tall in this position, breath for 90 seconds. Notice: How do you feel after letting go of emotions?

• • • • • • • • • • • • •

DAY 41
The 90 Second Rule

Guiding Question: How does the brain let go of negative emotion in 90 seconds?

Strategies/Activity
When you have a negative reaction to something in the environment, you release adrenaline and cortisol. Your brain does not know the different between you experiencing a negative event or you thinking the thought. The same release of chemicals takes place. Check out the first 3 minutes of Dr. Jill Bolte Taylor's Ted Talk.

Resources
Dr. Jill Bolte Taylor- The 90 Second Rule
https://www.youtube.com/watch?v=PzT_SBl31-s

• • • • • • • • • • • • • •

DAY 42
Negative Bias

Guiding Question: Why is the brain negatively biased?

Strategies/Activity
It is normal to feel negative emotion because our brains are wired to survive before we feel and think! And it is OK to go into survivor mode for short bits of time once in a while, but when our bodies are constantly going into that negative brain state, it becomes a hard wired habit!

To Do
Above or Below the Line! - Draw your own line and let's monitor our brain state changes all day to see where they fall and how they change!!

Resources
Negative Brain Bias
https://www.youtube.com/watch?v=fLqzYDZAqCI&list=
PLImZFIKE4ka8gRAVJUO-DzD0F9BXrzopz

• • • • • • • • • • • • • •

DAY 43
Senses and The Brain

Guiding Question: How does the brain take in senses?

Strategies/Activity
"We see the world not as it is, but as we are conditioned to see it." What are our senses and how do we use them each day?

To Do
In one minute, draw or write down everything in this classroom you are taking in through sight sound touch or smell! Share and compare your one-minute reflection. What are you conditioned to see?

Resources
Sentis: Limitations of the Brain
https://www.youtube.com/watch?v=9BdzhWdVaX0 &index=3&list=PL53nCCeNj-RQDhbjE9LjvnFad-wdB5bw7

How Do We See?
https://www.youtube.com/watch?v=Mbmt-6o-Bp0

DAY 44
Senses and The Brain

Guiding Question: What does the brain do with sensations?

Strategies/Activity
The brain stem takes in the sensations from the world around you. Perception of these sensations helps in regulating or dis-regulating our brain state. Humans are intended to connect with one another, but before we can connect in relationship the brain stem must be regulated.

Resources
The 3 Parts of the Brain
https://www.youtube.com/watch?v=yQetOVB_VZo

DAY 45
Senses and The Brain

Guiding Question: How do sensations impact our perception of the environment we are living?

Strategies/Activity
The brain can become overwhelmed by the amount of information there is to take in from the environment. Perception makes us aware of what is happening in our environment and attention helps focus in on what is important in the environment.

To Do
What is your strongest sense? What is your weakest sense? Can you recall an emotion from one of your senses being triggered? Get with a partner to share and provide feedback. Discuss whole group.

• • • • • • • • • • • • • • •
DAY 46
Senses and The Brain

Guiding Question: What is stress?

Strategies/Activity
Begin by discussing stress whole group. What is stress? Have students share their definition. How does your body feel when it is stressed? What sensations do you have? Explain to students that sometimes when we are feeling anxious, worried, angry, disgusted, or sad, we cannot always know exactly where we feel these emotions or even explain them! Sensations are physical feelings and these we can name! Naming the sensation allows us to acknowledge the stress we are feeling. Here are some examples: tired, tense, itchy, cold, icy, tingly, full, numb, frozen, flowing, goose-bumpy, butterflies, suffocating, closed, etc. What other sensations can you think of?

Resources
>   **What we can name, we can tame.**
>   **What is sharable is bearable!**

• • • • • • • • • • • • • • •
DAY 47
Senses and The Brain

Guiding Question: What is the stress response system?

Strategies/Activity
Our bodies have a stress response system that is supposed to take care of us under times of stress but sometimes it goes on overload and keeps pumping out stress hormones. The stress response system is the fundamental reorganization of how the brain manages perception. We have built in attachment programs that motivate us to seek out positive bonds with caring adults. A healthy stress response system supports cognitive flexibility, imagination, and empathy. Let's watch!

Resources
>   **How Stress Effects the Body**
>   https://www.youtube.com/watch?v=WuyPuH9ojCE
>
>   Breathing and Moving help us to relieve the stress and this is why we are learning about focused attention practices!

DAY 48
Senses and The Brain

Guiding Question: What is the stress response system?

Strategies/Activity

Our bodies have a stress response system that is supposed to take care of us under times of stress but sometimes it goes on overload and keeps pumping out stress hormones. The stress response system is the fundamental reorganization of how the brain manages perception. We have built in attachment programs that motivate us to seek out positive bonds with caring adults. A healthy stress response system supports cognitive flexibility, imagination, and empathy. Let's watch!

Resources
Managing Stress
https://www.youtube.com/watch?v=hnpQrMqDoqE

Breathing and Moving help us to relieve the stress and this is why we are learning about focused attention practices!

DAY 49
Senses and The Brain

Guiding Question: How can we support a healthy stress response system?

Strategies/Activity

Regulation occurs in the brain stem and it is not something we are born with. We learn to regulate through experiences with others. We model how to regulate and we support regulation through emotional contagion when we feel regulated (calm). Discuss and share whole group what regulates (calms) you. It can be helpful to identify a regulating activity when calm to help support emotional regulation when triggered.

Resources
Japanese Method of relieving stress/ thumb hold anxiety, first finger holds fear, middle finger holds anger, ring finger holds sadness, and pinky finger holds optimism and our self-esteem. As listen to soft instrumental music about 60 to 80 beats per minute holding each finger for 30 seconds to one minute we can dampen the stress response!

Music for relaxation, studying and dampening the stress response.
https://www.youtube.com/watch?v=pmoGdaOeUkQ&list=PL3K4bu5ml 6giU39ifLp_Z6Ope9dqVBqt_

• • • • • • • • • • • • • • •
DAY 50
Senses and The Brain

Guiding Question: What does it mean to regulate?

Strategies/Activity
It can be helpful to identify a regulating activity when calm to help support emotional regulation when triggered. The next couple of days, we will spend time in regulation stations discovering what feels good. We will spend time reflecting after each station; sharing how these activities make your body and mind feel.

Spend 3-4 minutes participating in the activity and then 1-2 minutes reflecting and sharing out noticings.

Other Regulation Station Ideas: word search, coloring, puzzle, stacking cups, take a walk, stationary bicycle, yoga, Legos, and more!

Resources
Regulation Stations
Taking deep breaths brings an oxygenated glucose blood flow to our frontal lobes. Taking just three deep inhales and exhales calms the emotional brain.

Movement is critical to learning, as it activates several areas of the brain at once while calming the brain. Clap out rhythms and have students repeat. The collective sound brings a sense of community to the classroom.

DAY 51
Senses and The Brain

Guiding Question: What does it mean to regulate?

Strategies/Activity
It can be helpful to identify a regulating activity when calm to help support emotional regulation when triggered. The next couple of days, we will spend time in regulation stations discovering what feels good. We will spend time reflecting after each station; sharing how these activities make your body and mind feel.

Spend 3-4 minutes participating in the activity and then 1-2 minutes reflecting and sharing out noticings.

Resources
Regulation Stations
Pass out a drop of lotion, and for 90 seconds students give their hands

and fingers a massage, noticing their palms, fingertips, and any sensations that feel uncomfortable or stiff.

Ask students to rock along their spine to help them feel present in their bodies. This provides a soothing rhythm that subtly grounds them with sensation and movement.

DAY 52
Senses and The Brain

Guiding Question: What does it mean to regulate?

Strategies/Activity
It can be helpful to identify a regulating activity when calm to help support emotional regulation when triggered. The next couple of days, we will spend time in regulation stations discovering what feels good. We will spend time reflecting after each station; sharing how these activities make your body and mind feel.

Spend 3-4 minutes participating in the activity and then 1-2 minutes reflecting and sharing out noticings.

Resources
Regulation Stations
Placing our fingers on our throats, we begin the day with a sound or class chant and feel the vibration of our vocal cords. This gives everyone a chance to participate and to see how we can mimic different animals, instruments, and random classroom sounds such as papers crinkling.

The students sit with their legs straight out and begin wiggling their toes and ankles, shaking knees and thighs, rotating shoulders, arms, and finally their heads, keeping all body parts moving at the same time. Then we reverse the process and stop our heads, arms, shoulders, and on down. This gives children a great body scan and a sequence for working memory.

DAY 53
Senses and The Brain

Guiding Question: What does it mean to regulate?

Strategies/Activity
It can be helpful to identify a regulating activity when calm to help support emotional regulation when triggered. The next couple of days, we will spend time in regulation stations discovering what feels good. We will spend time reflecting after each station; sharing how these activities make your body and mind feel.

Spend 3-4 minutes participating in the activity and then 1-2 minutes reflecting and sharing out noticings.

Resources
    Regulation Stations
    Sometimes I'll put on music and give the students old scarves, and we'll dance around the room waving the scarves and feeling the soft sensation as we dance and pass by one another. When the music stops, we freeze and notice our postures and movements. This strategy can be led by the teacher or a student to see if we can mimic a movement or create our own.

    Listen to calming music (60 beats per minute)

DAY 54
Brain Intervals

Guiding Question: What is a brain interval?

Strategies/Activity
The purpose of a brain interval is to stimulate the reticular activating stem located in the brain stem. When we begin to lose attention, no learning can occur. The brain intervals bring novelty and curiosity and a brief state of confusion which is healthy for activation while learning in robotic ways can lull the brain to sleep! Our brains need an interval of time, to soak in new information and this is also why brain intervals are so important to learning!!

Resources
    https://www.edutopia.org/blog/brain-breaks-focused-attention-practices-lori-desautels

    https://www.youtube.com/watch?v=QCnfAzAIhVw

    https://www.youtube.com/watch?v=T2zjlB4ctu4

DAY 55
Brain Intervals

Guiding Question: What is a brain interval?

Strategies/Activity
A brain interval is a quick opportunity to change up our predictable routines of receiving incoming information.

To Do
Notice. Notice who is participating and providing feedback and connect with those students who need support.

Resources
http://www.greatexpectations.org/brain-breaks

https://www.pinterest.com/parko/brain-break-activities/

http://minds-in-bloom.com/20-three-minute-brain-breaks/

• • • • • • • • • • • • • • •
DAY 56
Brain Intervals

Guiding Question: What are the benefits of brain intervals?

Strategies/Activity
Use brain intervals to stimulate the brain stem and bring focus and alertness back to the conscious mind. Brain intervals give students the chance to develop and apply social competence. A brain break allows students to rest and recharge, while simultaneously learning to cooperate, communicate, and compromise. **Frequent breaks boost attentiveness in class and maximize learning.**

Resources
http://fsnep.ucdavis.edu/trainings/town-halls/townhalls/copy2_of_14activitybreaks_000.pdf

http://www.squiglysplayhouse.com/BrainTeasers/

https://www.youtube.com/watch?v=FoypZyibQro&feature=youtu.be

• • • • • • • • • • • • • • •
DAY 57
Brain Intervals

Guiding Question: How are brain intervals impacting me?

Strategies/Activity
Create an anchor chart displaying different brain intervals as you try each one. Remember brain intervals should be a familiar activity, but not scheduled. Brain intervals should be used as needed and novel.

Resources
Take time each day at this stage to reflect on how the body and mind feels before, during and after brain intervals. Notice as students return to work focus, alertness and time on task.

• • • • • • • • • • • • • • •

DAY 58
Brain Intervals

Guiding Question: When is a good time to regulate and provide myself with independent brain intervals?

Strategies/Activity
Incorporate brain intervals into your daily schedule. Remember the rule:
Age + 2= Get Up & Move

Resources
> https://funandfunction.com/blog/wp-content/uploads/2014/10/Activity_Guide_web.pdf

> http://www.learningstationmusic.com/blog/2015/05/09/from-your-seat-brain-breaks/

> https://sharpbrains.com/resources/1-brain-fitnessfundamentals/brain-functions-perception-attention-memory-and-more/

• • • • • • • • • • • • • • •

DAY 59
Neuroplasticity

Guiding Question: What is neuroplasticity?

Strategies/Activity
Neuroplasticity is the brains ability to reorganize itself by forming new neural connections through experiences. Students spend an average of 1000 hours a year at school. As teachers, we know behaviors are hard-wired, but we also know that because of neuroplasticity and the important role school plays in young people's lives, we are able to share knowledge with students to change thinking.

Resources
> **Sentis: Neuroplasticity**
> https://www.youtube.com/watch?v=ELpfYCZa87g

• • • • • • • • • • • • • • •

DAY 60
Neuroplasticity

Guiding Question: What is neuroplasticity?

Strategies/Activity
Need an example of a brain rewired? Take a look at the Backwards Brain

Bicycle and then reflect and share as a whole group. What habits are helping and/or hurting you?

To Do
Choose a habit (personally or within school) you are going to try to rewire for a week. Track those new neural pathways.

Resources
>   **Backwards Brain Bicycle**
>   https://www.youtube.com/watch?v=MFzDaBzBlL0

DAY 61
Neuroplasticity

Guiding Question: What circuits are you firing and wiring?

Strategies/Activity
Watch video from resources and discuss circuits in your brain that are strong and connected. These strong circuits are your habits (neurons that are firing and wiring together)

To Do
Discuss with a partner something you do well? Discuss a challenge for you or something you would like to get better at!

Resources
>   **Stacking Cups with Austin**
>   https://www.youtube.com/watch?v=-nhRPVWM9A0

DAY 62
Neuroplasticity

Guiding Question: What is a neuron?

Strategies/Activity
A neuron is cell in the brain that receives information and passes it along. A single neuron is useless; as it requires millions of neurons to transmit information. When neurons receive and send messages they transmit electrical impulses across the synaptic gap. The human brain has 86 BILLION neurons.

Resources
>   **What is a neuron?**
>   https://www.youtube.com/watch?v=6qS83wD29PY
>
>   **Neuron Models**
>   http://faculty.washington.edu/chudler/chmodel.html

Secondary
https://www.youtube.com/watch?v=HZh0A-IWSmY

Elementary
Structure of a Neuron
https://www.youtube.com/watch?v=HZh0A-IWSmY

Neuron Song
https://www.youtube.com/watch?v=NzjMljo_8AU

Neurons for Everyone!
https://www.youtube.com/watch?v=HZh0A-IWSmY
https://www.youtube.com/watch?v=DLNlUsvmVvM

https://www.youtube.com/watch?v=UDpydfpEads

DAY 63
Neuroplasticity

Guiding Question: How do neurons work?

Strategies/Activity
We will play a game today and connect neurons to what we know about telephones.

Resources
   Game: Chain Reaction: What is the connection to neurons?
   https://originsonline.org/educator-help/chain-reaction

DAY 64
Neuroplasticity

Guiding Question: What is a neuron?

Strategies/Activity
One neuron by itself means nothing. It takes hundreds of thousands of neurons connecting just to remember your name! Open with this video and discuss after stopping and starting at different points or give students certain terms and definitions to listen to as they capture the answer as they listen!

To Do
Make candy models of neurons with licorice, M&M's, and different candies that resemble the cell body, dendrites and axons!

Resources
   https://www.youtube.com/watch?v=UDpydfpEads

DAY 65
Neuroplasticity

Guiding Question: What are synapses, dendrites and axons?

Strategies/Activity
A synapse is a chemical message sent between two neurons connecting them to one another (like when we send a Snap Chat). After watching the video, create a human synapses. Create a circuit as we link hands and arms mimicking an axon and dendrite. As we link arms and then hands, squeeze the person's hand next to you indicating a signal has passed.

Resources
Synapses

https://www.youtube.com/watch?v=LT3VKAr4roo

https://www.youtube.com/watch?v=g7FdMi03CzI

https://www.youtube.com/watch?v=WhowH0kb7n0

DAY 66
Neuroplasticity

Guiding Question: What am I choosing to rewire?

Strategies/Activity
Today is a day for neuroplasticity reflection. A week ago you chose a habit (personally or from within school) and tried to rewire for a week. How did you do? What did you notice? Was it difficult? Did it get easier? What are your plans moving forward? Can you think of other behaviors that could benefit from some rewiring?

DAY 67
Neuroplasticity

Guiding Question: What does neuroplasticity look like in the brain?

Strategies/Activity
Break the word neuro-plasticity apart. What does neuro mean? (brain) What does plastic mean? (malleable or able to change) What does neuro-plasticity mean?

This activity demonstrates that repetition and practice create a fast circuit of connection and the more we do anything the better we become!

Resources
Circuit Ball Toss
Activity: Circuit Ball Toss
Form a circle and choose a leader who will begin and end the ball toss. That leader, often the teacher, will time the circuit from start to finish. There is one rule! You must remember the person who you throw the ball to in the circuit. Before starting, all participants stick both hands straight out in front of the body (to show they have not received the ball). After you have received the ball and thrown it, you place your hands behind your back. The circuit is complete toss when it is tossed back to the leader who started the circuit. Round 1: What did you notice about our circuit? Was it efficient? Why or why not? Complete the circuit following the same circuit two more times noticing time changes and other aspects making the circuit more efficient. This activity demonstrates that repetition and practice create a fast circuit of connection and the more we do anything the better we become!

● ● ● ● ● ● ● ● ● ● ● ● ● ● ● ●
DAY 68
Adolescent Brain

Guiding Question: How is the adolescent brain unique?

Strategies/Activity
The greatest stage of brain development occurs in the last trimester throughout two years of age. Adolescence is an important time in brain development because it is the second greatest time of brain development. What is happening in the adolescent brain during this time?

- Natural pruning of neurons
- Increasing mastery skills
- Less serotonin and more testosterone
- Heightened dopamin
- Hyperrationality

Resources
Brain Development in Teenagers (4th- 12th)
https://www.youtube.com/watch?v=dISmdb5zfiQ

Teen Brain
https://www.youtube.com/watch?v=EGdlpaWi3rc

DAY 69
Adolescent Brain

Guiding Question: How is the adolescent brain unique?

Strategies/Activity
What wires together fires together.

Resources
> **The Teenage Brain Explained**
> https://www.youtube.com/watch?v=hiduiTqlei8
>
> **The Teenage Brain**
> https://www.youtube.com/watch?v=aIqVvyHeSiY
>
> **The Neuroanatomical Transformation of the Teenage Brain**
> https://www.youtube.com/results?search_query=
> 90+second+rule+jill+bolte+taylor

DAY 70
Adolescent Brain

Guiding Question: What is happening in the adolescent brain?

Strategies/Activity
Watch clip from *Inside Out* and take notes whole group or individually.
Use notes from viewing to support tomorrow's class discussion. Use the
Edutopia article from resources to support whole group discussion.

Resources
> **The Adolescent Brain: Leaving Childhood Behind**
> https://www.edutopia.org/blog/adolescent-brain-leaving-childhood-
> behind-lori-desautels
>
> **Video clips of Bing Bong and the Adolescent Brain**
> https://www.youtube.com/watch?v=tXj6lBXEy2M

DAY 71
Adolescent Brain

Guiding Question: What is happening in the adolescent brain?

Strategies/Activity

Yesterday we watched a clip from *Inside Out*. Today we are going to share our reflections and uncover the symbolism from this scene in the movie.

- What or who was your Bing Bong? Could it be an object (like a blanket or teddy bear) or something abstract?
- What does Bing Bong symbolize?
- Why is it important for Riley to let go of Bing Bong?
- Why did Bing Bong jump off the wagon?
- What makes it so *sad* for the audience (especially parents and adults) as we watch this part?
- Do we really ever lose Bing Bong? Explain.
- Do you have a core memory of an experience from your imagination? What is it like?

Resources
> **Video clips of Bing Bong and the Adolescent Brain**
> https://www.youtube.com/watch?v=tXj6lBXEy2M

DAY 72
Core Memories

Guiding Question: What is a core memory?

Strategies/Activity

What is the difference between a core memory and a regular memory? A core memory is a memory that holds significant emotion or meaning to the individual.

Memory Games
1. Bring out ten items on a tray and show students for 10 seconds. See what students remember?
2. Put a short sequence and then build a longer sequence of numbers and letters together!

What strengthens memory?

Resources
> **Your Memory Under Stress**
> https://www.youtube.com/watch?v=FKzUSfzqh5A

• • • • • • • • • • • • • •
DAY 73
Core Memories

Guiding Question: What is a core memory?

Strategies/Activity
A core memory is a memory that holds significant emotion or meaning to the individual. Share one of each and list the details of each memory! Which memory has more details? Can you write down the different details?

Resources
Hippocampus and Memory
https://www.youtube.com/watch?v=eu_zOYHeGrg

• • • • • • • • • • • • • •
DAY 74
Core Memories

Guiding Question: How does positivity impact the brain?

Strategies/Activity
Your brain state matters and when you believe you can, you are actually more likely to be successful. Go ahead spread positive vibes!

Resources
The Power of Positivity
https://www.youtube.com/watch?v=kO1kgl0p-Hw

• • • • • • • • • • • • • •
DAY 75
Core Memories

Guiding Question: Can happiness spread?

Strategies/Activity
Spreading gratitude will increase your happiness. Try it out.

Resources
The Science of Happiness
https://www.youtube.com/watch?v=oHv6vTKD6lg&t=17s
    Quiet from 5:15-5:30 for language edit.

• • • • • • • • • • • • • • •
DAY 76
Short Term Memory

Guiding Question: What is short term memory?

Strategies/Activity
Short term memory is the phase of memory responsible for temporary storage of information.

Resources
How Does Your Memory Work?
https://www.youtube.com/watch?v=TUoJc0NPajQ

• • • • • • • • • • • • • • •
DAY 77
Long Term Memory

Guiding Question: What is long term memory?

Strategies/Activity
Long term memory is the phase of memory responsible for the storage of information for an extended period of time.

Resources
How Does Your Memory Work?
https://www.youtube.com/watch?v=TUoJc0NPajQ

Short Term, Long Term, and Working Memory
https://www.youtube.com/watch?v=iPEog8Wd8po

• • • • • • • • • • • • • • •
DAY 78
Memory

Guiding Question: How are short term and long term memory different?

Strategies/Activity
Your brain is taking in millions of signals all day. It is not possible to remember everything. The brain must do something with a memory to store it in long term and make it easy to retrieve from memory.

Resources
Short Term vs. Long Term Memory
https://www.youtube.com/watch?v=b9aEeLGjR6M

DAY 79
Memory

Guiding Question: How does learning become memory? (encoding, consolidation, retrieval)

Strategies/Activity
Memory is learning that has persisted over time.

Resources
How We Make Memories
https://www.youtube.com/watch?v=bSycdIx-C48&t=510s

DAY 80
Memory

Guiding Question: How are you priming your brain for memory storage?

Strategies/Activity
What daily habits do you have that are helping you come to school ready to learn and socialize? (sleep, diet, exercise, mindfulness, planning ahead, schedule). Discuss whole group strategies for taking care of our body and brain to help support memory.

Resources
How We Make Memories
https://www.youtube.com/watch?v=bSycdIx-C48&t=510s

DAY 81
Gratitude

Guiding Question: How does gratitude effect the brain?

Strategies/Activity
Create gratitude journals as we write three things we are grateful for in our morning meeting. We will then each take five notecards and write a positive affirmation on these and share them throughout the day with other staff, students, and teachers!

Resources
Gratitude
https://www.youtube.com/watch?v=aT-r3-I6eY0

How Gratitude makes us happy?
https://www.youtube.com/watch?v=U5lZBjWDR_c

Kid President
https://www.youtube.com/watch?v=yA5QptlJRE4

• • • • • • • • • • • • • •
DAY 82
Our Train of Thought

Guiding Question: When do your thoughts become distracted and how do you get back on track?

Strategies/Activity
Lead discussion and have students discuss in small groups. When does your train of thought run smoothly with few stops?When does your train of thought struggle? Why? What can I do in the classroom to help your train run with great speed and accuracy?
What can you do to help your train of thought stay on the tracks and reach its destination? Teaching students about their neuroanatomy is empowering, as well as the foundation of learning and connection.

Resources
Islands of Personality and Trains of Thought
ttps://www.edutopia.org/blog/islands-of-personality-trains-of-thought-lori-desautels

Strategies
Elementary
It is important to have a tangible train of thought in the classroom. This could be a larger model of chairs and cardboard boxes, or students could build individual models of trains. Images of trains posted in an Attention and Focus corner could help to prime the brain for focus and remembering.

Secondary
Creating an analogy or visualization of the train of thought could support goal setting and planning. Where is your train heading right now? Is this where you want to go? What are two changes in planning this journey that you could make today?

• • • • • • • • • • • • • •
DAY 83
Emotional Regulation

Guiding Question: How do we return to our prefrontal cortex (calm) after being triggered (amygdala)?

Strategies/Activity
When we ae angry, anxious, upset in any way, our prefrontal cortex shuts down and it can be hard for us to think clearly and/or rationally. Because of this it is difficult to pause and think before we react. Can you think of a recent time when you felt this way and unintentionally spoke or acted before thinking about the consequence? We learn to pause and regulate at a very young age. If we do not learn to regulate at a young age, it is much more difficult to learn the more we age. Spend time over the next two days to watch videos with students! Discuss our coping strategies again and if we are intentionally using these strategies to emotionally regulate.

Resources

Pause

Young people with ADD often show an inability to create a pause, or a moment of self-restraint between stimulus and reaction while weighing the consequences of their impending reaction. To assist students in creating this pause, give their brains the opportunity to make associations with color, visuals, and concrete objects. Tangible items can be symbolic reminders for students of all ages. Here are examples of signaling an intentional pause:

- Flicking a red rubber band bracelet on our wrists or placing a red ball cap on our heads are two practices that teachers could model and repeatedly share when a pause is needed before making a hurried emotional or academic decision.

- Accompanied with a tangible item, teachers can help students identify words that are analogies to waiting and hesitating. Stop, pause, halt, think, rest, breathe, float, and tread could be posted in specific areas of the room with pictures and images to add meaning.

- Students could bring in an object from home that reminds them to stop, pause, and wait. These personal objects could be placed in a "red corner," a highlighted area in the classroom where they are seen as reminders. Seeing, saying, and experiencing meaningful and personal reminders can effectively create associations and metaphors that the brain desires and needs for personalizing new responses.

The strategies in this section originally appeared on Edutopia in the article: **Strengthening Executive Function Development for Students With ADD** https://www.edutopia.org/blog/executive-function-development-students-add-lori-desautels

22PresenceLearning © 2017. All Rights Reserved.
https://www.youtube.com/watch?v=m4UGDaCgo_s

https://www.youtube.com/watch?v=Zs559guIGDo

https://www.youtube.com/watch?v=pFkRbUKyl9g

• • • • • • • • • • • • • • • •
DAY 84
Emotional Regulation

Guiding Question: How do we return to our prefrontal cortex (calm) after being triggered (amygdala)?

Strategies/Activity
When we ae angry, anxious, upset in any way, our prefrontal cortex shuts down and it can be hard for us to think clearly and/or rationally. Because of this it is difficult to pause and think before we react. Can you think of a recent time when you felt this way and unintentionally spoke or acted before thinking about the consequence? We learn to pause and regulate at a very young age. If we do not learn to regulate at a young age, it is much more difficult to learn the more we age. Spend time over the next two days to watch videos with students! Discuss our coping strategies again and if we are intentionally using these strategies to emotionally regulate.

Resources
Self Regulation Skills
https://www.youtube.com/watch?v=m4UGDaCgo_s

Controlling Emotions: A Lesson From Angry Birds
https://www.youtube.com/watch?v=pFkRbUKyl9g

• • • • • • • • • • • • • • • •
DAY 85
Emotional Regulation

Guiding Question: How do we return to our prefrontal cortex (calm) after being triggered (amygdala)?

Strategies/Activity
The language of the prefrontal cortex is spoken words and the language of the amygdala is feelings. When we are angry, anxious, afraid, sad, hungry or upset in anyway the prefrontal cortex goes offline and we need time to regulate in a safe space to calm the amygdala. We must be proactive in building relationships so we may support co-regulation in times when students become dis-regulated.

Resources
Calm Down and Release the Amygdala
https://www.youtube.com/watch?v=Zs559guIGDo

• • • • • • • • • • • • • •
DAY 86
Coping Strategy: Emotional Freedom Technique—"Tapping"

Guiding Question: What is emotional freedom technique and what happens in the brain when we use this calming strategy?

Strategies/Activity
"Emotional Freedom Techniques, or EFT (often known as Tapping or EFT Tapping), is a universal healing tool that can provide impressive results for physical, emotional, and performance issues. EFT operates on the premise that no matter what part of your life needs improvement, there are unresolved emotional issues in the way. Even for physical issues, chronic pain, or diagnosed conditions, it is common knowledge that any kind of emotional stress can impede the natural healing potential of the human body." Familiarize yourself and students with nine tapping points on the body.

Resources
https://www.emofree.com/eft-tutorial/tapping-basics/what-is-eft.html

https://www.thrivingnow.com/tapping-points-and-instructions/

Teachers
https://www.youtube.com/watch?v=dPqQGsYFsX4

https://www.youtube.com/watch?v=s99M8eJV4sk

https://www.youtube.com/watch?v=uWx_e199k88

• • • • • • • • • • • • • •
DAY 87
Coping Strategy: Emotional Freedom Technique—"Tapping"

Guiding Question: How EFT impacts our emotions and learning?

Strategies/Activity
Use these videos and the resources from the previous day to review and practice EFT practices.

Resources
Elementary
https://www.youtube.com/watch?v=SlefrIBI9BY

Secondary
https://www.youtube.com/watch?v=xtjHUoXYojE

DAY 88
Social Brains

Guiding Question: Why are relationships important?

Strategies/Activity
We cannot live without one another! We are wired for relationship and do not function well without one another. Make a list of everything you can do independently...without anyone. Make a list of everything you do each day that involves other people. Which list brings you the most positive emotions?

DAY 89
Social Brains

Guiding Question: Why are relationships important?

Strategies/Activity
We discussed the important role relationships play in our daily lives. Watch the video *Social Brains* and discuss new takeaways and connect to your lists from yesterday.

Resources
    Social Brains
    https://www.youtube.com/watch?v=J0XmZW6xYSg

DAY 90
Social Brains

Guiding Question: How is technology changing your brain?

Strategies/Activity
Technology plays a large role in many of our lives. Are you aware of how technology is changing your brain (good and bad) each day?

Resources
    From Neurons to Networks!
    https://www.youtube.com/watch?v=zLp-edwiGUU

DAY 91
Social Brains

Guiding Question: In what ways are groups stronger than individuals?

Strategies /Activity
Bring in a thick book like a telephone book! Show how easy it is to tear one page and then grab 50 or 100 pages together and try to tear these! If you have enough pages, they simply will not tear! We are stronger in group and collaboration!

Why do we we sometimes though not get along in groups? Could it be that our survival brain is kicking into action? How could we work to collaborate in better ways working like a thick book that's pages cannot be torn when working together!

Resources
Phone Book

DAY 92
Social Brains

Guiding Question: What are your superpowers?

Strategies /Activity
"Neuroscientist Matthew Lieberman explains that through his studies he's learned that our kryptonite is ignoring the importance of our social superpowers and by building on our social intuition, we can make ourselves smarter, happier, and more productive. In this TEDx Talk, Lieberman explores groundbreaking research in social neuroscience that reveals that our need to connect with other people is even more fundamental than our need for food or shelter and that the social pain and pleasure we experience has just as much impact as physical pain and pleasure."

Resources
The Social Brain and Its Superpowers; Matthew Lieberman, Ph.D.
https://www.youtube.com/watch?v=NNhk3owF7RQ

• • • • • • • • • • • • • •

DAY 93
Social Brains

Guiding Question: What are your superpowers?
Strategies /Activity
Continue watching video and then share reflection in whole group discussion.

Resources
   The Social Brain and Its Superpowers; Matthew Lieberman, Ph.D.
   https://www.youtube.com/watch?v=NNhk3owF7RQ

• • • • • • • • • • • • • •

DAY 94
Empathy

Guiding Question: How can we increase our empathy?

Strategies/Activity
Do you ever feel like you should help someone but you don't when you are in a group of people? Watch this and think of a time when we did or did not! Can animals teach us empathy? Can animals pick up on our emotions?

Resources
   All Students
   https://www.youtube.com/watch?v=UzPMMSKfKZQ
   Teaching Empathy
   https://www.youtube.com/watch?v=aU3QfyqvHk8

• • • • • • • • • • • • • •

DAY 95
Empathy

Guiding Question: How can we increase our empathy?

Strategies/Activity
Empathy is the ability to understand and share the feelings of another. Empathy is a learned trait and must be taught.

Resources
   Elementary
   https://www.youtube.com/watch?v=9_1RtlR4xbM

   Secondary

The Bystander Effect
https://www.youtube.com/watch?v=Wy6eUTLzcU4

The Empathy Gap
https://www.youtube.com/watch?v=bdLOkqMfRJk

• • • • • • • • • • • • • • •
DAY 96
Engagement

Guiding Question: How do we keep our brain engaged?

Strategies/Activity
Have you ever been driving for a long time, and then you realize that several minutes have passed, and you don't remember thinking about driving because you were in such a relaxed state of alertness? That's not how we want our brain to feel at school! We want to keep our brain engaged so our best learning can occur. We need novelty, curiosity, and sometimes even a brief state of confusion because the brain pays close attention to these types of experiences. This is because of our reticular activating system (RAS) in our brain stem.

Resources
    Reticular Activating System
    https://www.youtube.com/watch?v=QCnfAzAIhVw&t=90s

    Unlocking The Screen of Your Mind
    https://www.youtube.com/watch?v=xsrkOSTyWCU

• • • • • • • • • • • • • • •
DAY 97
Multiple Intelligence

Guiding Questions: What are multiple intelligences?

Strategies/Activity
The question we need to begin asking ourselves and our students is: "How are you smart?" Not… "How smart are you?"

Resources
    What is Multiple Intelligence?
    https://www.youtube.com/watch?v=s2EdujrM0vA

    Multiple Intelligence
    https://www.youtube.com/watch?v=cf6lqfNTmaM

    https://www.youtube.com/watch?v=falHoOEUFz0

• • • • • • • • • • • • • •

DAY 98

Guiding Questions: What are multiple intelligences?
Strategies/Activity
There are many ways of being smart. How are you smart? You were born to learn, so then what are you learning?

Resources
Multiple Intelligence
https://www.youtube.com/watch?v=cf6lqfNTmaM

Born to Learn
https://www.youtube.com/watch?v=falHoOEUFz0

• • • • • • • • • • • • • •

DAY 99
Multiple Intelligence

Guiding Question: What are your learning strengths and challenges?

Strategies/Activity
Let's look at our own intelligences! Spend the next couple of days digging into strengths and reflecting.

Resources
Multiple Intelligences Self Assessment
https://www.edutopia.org/multiple-intelligences-assessment

Find Your Strengths
http://literacynet.org/mi/assessment/findyourstrengths.html

Secondary- Multiple Intelligences Inventory
http://kerstens.org/alicia/planning10/Multiple%20Intelligences%20Inventory.pdf

Matching careers to multiple intelligences
http://bestcareermatch.com/career-chart

Thomas Armstrong- Choosing a Career
https://www.teachervision.com/using-multiple-intelligences-theory-choosing-career

• • • • • • • • • • • • • • •

DAY 100
Applied Educational Neuroscience

Guiding Question: What have you learned and how will you use this learning going forward?

Strategies/Activity
So What...Now What? Looking back on what has been covered in these lessons what do you now know about the brain? Maya Angelou is quoted with saying, "When you know better, you do better." How does knowing about your neuroanatomy and the amazing functions of your brain change the way you look at the future? Reflect in groups, write, draw...How will you apply this knowledge moving forward?

Resources
http://faculty.washington.edu/chudler/links.html

https://www.parentingforbrain.com/self-regulation-toddler-temper-tantrums/

https://www.pinterest.com/explore/brain-games/?lp=true

https://www.youtube.com/watch?v=hVy5E2DZkKM&list=PLQwg0Pxp-UPloVUzfl75OuwJTPjCgn8jzM

https://www.youtube.com/watch?v=cgLYkV689s4

https://thecornerstoneforteachers.com/working-memory-games/

http://soulpancake.com/22PresenceLearning © 2017. All Rights Reserved.

NOTES:

"Inside Out" Lesson Plans

Overview

Dear Colleagues,

While making these lesson plans, our main goal was to capture the essence of each article written by Dr. Lori in her "Inside Out" Curriculum and make it accessible through our Indiana Standards for all grades, and for all classrooms in Indiana. You will see that each topic has two lesson plans in each section, one for **ELEMENTARY** Students (K-6) and one designed for **SECONDARY** students (Grades 7-12).

As teachers, you know that lesson plans can never be a one-size-fits-all approach. Keeping that in mind, we tried to leave room to implement classroom traditions and modifications based on your students, while still trying to give enough guidance that you would be able to follow the lesson plan with only having the knowledge that this packet brings.

After the Standards page you will find a "Cheat Sheet" for these lessons. Please know that this is not an exhaustive list of terms, and that the concepts presented here are an extremely simplified version of neuroscience for our purposes in teaching kids about the applicable functions of their brain as it relates to learning and connecting with others.

We hope that these lessons and resources help you to start the conversation of how our brains work with your students.

We are in a critical time of learning how to function in this traumatized society, and it starts with education: it starts with us.

Please feel free to contact either of us at SMidura@IUHealth.org or MIDaniels@avon-schools.org with any questions about these lessons or resources.We look forward to connecting with you.

Mary Kate Daniels and Sara Midura
Licensed Indiana Teachers Certified in Applied Educational
Neuroscience adapted from Dr. Lori Desautels' "Inside Out" Curriculum

DISCLAIMER: THESE ARE SIMPL IFIED EXPLANATIONS OF THE COMPLEX
SYSTEMS IN OUR BRAINS THIS CHEAT SHEET IS SPECIFICAL LY DESIGNED
TO HELP TEACHERS UTILIZING THIS CURRICULUM

TEACHER CHEAT SHEET: NEUROSCIENCE

MAKING APPLIED EDUCATIONAL NEUROSCIENCE EASY TO TEACH

PARTS OF THE BRAIN

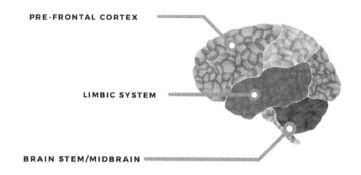

PRE-FRONTAL CORTEX

LIMBIC SYSTEM

BRAIN STEM/MIDBRAIN

PRE-FRONTAL CORTEX

The pre-frontal cortex is the front-most portion of our brain and controls our logic, reasoning, decision making, and social behavior. This is the last portion of our brain to be developed, and many neuroscientists now claim that it continues to develop into our late twenties.

LIMBIC SYSTEM

The limbic system is a complex system made up of multiple parts of the brain. This is the system that is in charge of our basic emotions of fear, anger, and pleasure. This is where our amygdala and hypothalamus are located (which we will talk about later on).

BRAIN STEM/MIDBRAIN

This portion of the brain mainly functions to control our automatic and "primal functions", such as temperature regulation, our senses, heart rate, and breathing.

NEUROPLASTICITY

Our brains have the capacity to be changed at any point in our life due to the amazing concept of Neuroplasticity. This is basically synonymous with malleability, and is perfect to teach our students that we can always learn new things and change the way we think.

MYELIN

Myelin is the insulating sheath around an axon (two neurons that come together to make a neural connection, or a new "idea" we have learned). Every time that we "exercise" that neural connection another layer of myelin is wrapped around it, creating a myelin sheath. The more myelin we have around an axon, the stronger that connection is! This is why "practice makes perfect", because every time we practice something we are making that connection stronger, just like building muscle.

PRUNING

Pruning is another way to say "getting rid of". For these lesson plans, the need-to-know about pruning is that during the adolescent years our brains prune away about half of the neural connections that we have built since birth. There are many connections that our brain recognizes that we don't need anymore, so it gets rid of those to make room for the new ones we will make.

NEUROHORMONES

Neurohormones are quite literally the hormones found in our brains. Two major neurohormones to know for these lessons are Serotonin and Dopamine, They both do a lot for our bodies, but for these lessons it is important to know that Serotonin is a main contributor to our happiness and well-being, while Dopamine is largely responsible for our reward-motivated behaviors as humans.

MIRROR NEURONS

Mirror neurons are exactly as they sound: they are neurons in our brain that literally "mirror" the behaviors and emotions of others. These are responsible for us feeling sad when we see others crying and yawn when we see someone else yawn!

"Inside Out"
TERMINOLOGY

In the film "Inside Out"—that inspired and connected our lessons—there are specific terms that they use to explain functions and phenomenons in the brain. These two are specifically utilized in these lesson plans, so to help here are some definitions. Core Memory: These are memories of extreme importance in one's life that contribute to an aspect of one's personality (i.e. Riley from the film has a core memory of the first time she played hockey, which contributed to her love of hockey). Island of Personality: Stemming from core memories, these "Islands of Personality" are key aspects of one's personality (i.e. Riley has a "Hockey Island")

STRESS RESPONSE SYSTEM

This is what we widely know as the "Fight or Flight" Response. This is a complex response that starts with our eyes and ears- think of an oncoming car. When we see or hear the oncoming car, our eyes and ears send a signal to the amygdala, which processes the information. If it perceives a potential danger (as it would with an oncoming car), it will send a distress signal to the hypothalamus, which is the "command center" for many functions of the body, including our automatic functions (if you remember from the first page, are controlled by the brain stem). This will activate the "fight, flight, or freeze" response, which automatically increases your senses, heart rate, breathing, etc., to give you the best chance for survival. In the example of the oncoming car, this response would allow you to jump out of the way before even really thinking about it - if our body did not do this, our brains would send all of this information to the prefrontal cortex (our "logical brain"), which would take a longer time to process the danger and reach safety.

In shorter terms: when our amygdala perceives a danger it sets the stress response system into motion, which in turn shuts off our pre-frontal cortex and elevates our automatic responses. This happens whether a danger is real or not: it is all about how our amygdala PERCEIVES it. This is why some of us feel the stress response system in situations such as public speaking or large public gatherings.

BRAIN REGULATION STRATEGIES

Since our Stress Response System can be activated without a real danger present, it is important for us and our students to be able to recognize when we are feeling this stress and know how to regulate. These brain regulation strategies can also be known as coping skills or focused attention practices.

Brain Regulation Strategies can be incorporated into daily classroom activities, and we recommend utilizing them in these lessons as you see fit. It is important for students to practice these strategies when they are not experiencing a stressful situation, as they are more likely to be functioning in their pre-frontal cortex and absorb the information. We also know that the more times students can practice these strategies, the more myelin will be coated in those connections so that when their stress response system IS activated they will be more likely to revert to one of the strategies that has a thick myelinated sheath.

Breath and movement are two of the best ways to regulate our brains- as long as you keep those in mind you can get creative with your strategies!

TWO OF OUR FAVORITES

Here are two of our favorite Brain Regulation Strategies to get you started.

Breath: Square Breathing (draw a square with your finger- while drawing left side breathe in for four counts; while drawing the top side hold your breath for four counts; while drawing the right side breathe out for four counts; while drawing the bottom side hold your breath out for four counts. Repeat at least three times).

Movement: Toes and Tense (While standing, slowly lift yourself up on your toes. While on your toes, feel your calves tense up- try to tense them even more and hold for ten seconds. Slowly release the tension and bring yourself down onto flat feet. Repeat at least three times).

LESSON 1

Creating Core Memories
ELEMENTARY

Time 30-45 mins

Objectives:

1. Students will be able to identify the following key terms: core memory, hippocampus, the limbic system.
2. Students will be able to relate to their 5 senses and creating core memories.

Materials:

- Inside Out Core Memories:
    https://www.youtube.com/watch?v=pecha-7QOVo
- Changing Core Memories:
    https://www.youtube.com/watch?v=cYvaQ37EcvU
- 5 Senses Chart
- Post-it notes
- Dry Erase boards and markers
- Celebration materials (sprinkles, candles, streamers, balloons, ornaments, etc.)

Key Terms:

Core Memory
Hippocampus
Limbic System

Why?

Understanding and naming our core memories creates a stronger self and class identity. If teachers provide authentic opportunities for student s to create positive core memories we increase care, concern, and the call to action in our learning communities. Our brains hold the power to recall, recount , and relive some of our most defining moments. On the flipside, we must also note the natural function of pruning, and how it helps the brain prepare for deeper complexity and sophistication. When educators make the effort to listen to these personal core memories it invites stronger dialogue and purpose among the class. The brain learns through stories. It retrieves what is relevant, useful, andinteresting. Make these moments happen in your classroom!

Instructions

Part 1: Hook

a. Have celebration materials (sprinkles, candles, streamers, balloons, ornaments, etc. — know your kids) on the front table "Pick one of these materials in your head. Can you think about a time that you have seen this material?"

b. Engage in a class discussion revolving around when they have seen the different materials. Encourage discussion about different memories, digging deep into the emotions/feelings behind them (does the memory make you happy? Sad?)

Part 2: Discussion and Video

a. Class discussion about specific moments/holidays that students remember related to the materials

Class discussion about Core Memory
  Guiding Questions:
  - Who or what reminds you of this material? Why?
  - What emotions/ feelings arise when you see this item?
  - Where are our memories stored?

b. Watch two "Inside Out" Videos and pay attention to 5 senses

c. Break up into partners and utilize "5 senses materials" to talk about 5 senses in their own core memories
  - Join, share your partner's core memory
  - Talk about how emotions and senses (from hippocampus/limbic system) help create and retain Core Memories

Part 3: Exit Ticket

If time allows:
- Students write the symbol of their Core Memory on a post-it note
- Students gather on the carpet or stand up to willingly share and guess one another's Core Memory. (i.e. Jane volunteers to share her symbol and then Tom guesses what the core memory might be (i.e.) If core memory is watching the Indy 500 then the symbol could be the smell of the gasoline or the opening remarks, "Drivers start your engines!")

Bonus Brain-Aligned Strategies:

"Mingle -Mingle" partner share game

Call on a student to pick the special word. Students can be creative and silly with words like "taco, unicorn, X-Box, etc." After students know the special word they will stand up and sing the chant "mingle, mingle, mingle!" over and over until the special word is said. When the teacher shares the special word, all students will freeze and turn to the person closest to him or her. Partners will share his or her symbol and guess what the core memory is. Students can also act out the symbol and have the partner guess it. Utilize these videos and articles to supplement teacher or student understanding:

MORE RESOURCES:
https://www.edutopia.org/blog/film-festival-brain-learning
http://channel.nationalgeographic.com/brain-games/
http://faculty.washington.edu/chudler/neurok.html
https://video.nationalgeographic.com/video/brain-bank-sci
https://www.youtube.com/user/SentisDigital
https://www.edutopia.org/article/integrating-sel-classroom

5 Senses Chart

Recall your own "core memory" — it could be a birthday party, scoring your first goal in a soccer game, your first vacation, ANYTHING! Work with your partner to share this memory and help each other sort out what sights, smells, feelings, tastes, and sounds you remember.

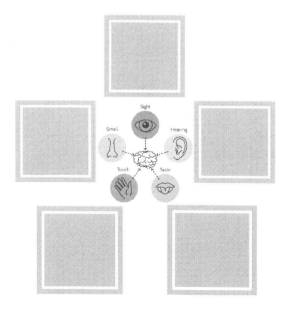

Creating Core Memories
LESSON 1 ~ SECONDARY

Time 30-45 mins

Objectives:

1. Students will be able to identify the following key terms: core memory, hippocampus, limbic system, myelin, and neuroplasticity.
2. Students will be able to relate to their 5 senses and creating core memories.

Materials:

- "Inside Out" Core Memories :
    https://www.youtube.com/watch?v=pecha-7QOVo
- "Inside Out" Changing Core Memories :
    https://www.youtube.com/watch? v =cYvaQ37EcvU
- Sentis Video
    https://www.youtube.com/watch?v =ELpfYCZa87g
- 5 Senses Chart
- Post-it notes
- Dry Erase boards and markers
- Celebration materials (sprinkles, candles, streamers, balloons, ornaments, etc.)

Key Terms :

Core Memory
Limbic System
Myelin
Neuroplasticity

Why?

Understanding and naming our core memories creates a stronger self and class identity. If teachers provide authentic opportunities for students to create positive core memories we increase care, concern, and the call to act ion in our learning communities. Our brains hold the power to recall, re-count, and relive some of our most defining moments. On the flipside, we must also note the natural function of pruning, and how it helps the brain prepare for deeper complexity and sophistication. When educators make the effort to listen to these personal core memories it invites stronger dialogue and purpose among the class. The brain learns through stories. It retrieves what is relevant, useful, and interesting. Make these moments happen in your classroom!

Instructions

Part 1: Hook

a. Have celebration materials (sprinkles, candles, driver's license, keys, pet leash, etc. — know your kids) on front table/tables "Pick one of these materials in your head. Think about a time that you have seen this material."

b. Time students for two minutes to make as many connections to the material as possible (have them record these in a notebook or on scrap paper)

c. Once the two minutes is up, ask student to circle their top three most vivid connections.

d. Launch a discussion setting (inside outside circle, Socratic-seminar, pair share, etc)

   Guiding Questions:
   - Who or what reminds you of this material? Why?
   - What emotions/ feelings arise when you see this item?
   - How does this item define a time or memory in your life?
   - Why are we able to connect to one item in so many different ways?
   -Where are our memories stored?

Part 2: Discussion and Video

a. Class discussion about specific times/holidays/experienced that they remember related to the materials (can be ANY emotion: happy, sad, etc.)

b. Watch two "Inside Out" Videos and pay attention to 5 senses, discuss how memories can be changed

c. Break up into partners and utilize "5 senses materials" to talk about their 5 senses in their own core memories (5 minutes) — ensure understanding that our emotions shape our memories, and emotions are in the limbic system

d. Join together, discuss neuroplasticity – Watch Sentis video

e. Ask for volunteer to come and use dumbbell – while student is doing bicep curls ask kids what is happening to the muscle (building, getting stronger, etc.)- this is what myelin is, basically like you strengthening the muscles in your brain that make memories stronger! (Working out is like neuroplasticity- the ability to change your brain and memories)

f. If time allows:

-Have students write a list poem or haiku using key terms (independent or partners)

Part 3: Exit Ticket:

Write a metaphor, simile or hyperbole for key terms on post-it note (have key terms written on board) Save post it note anchor chart for the classroom community to refer to throughout the year.

Bonus Brain-Aligned Strategies:

"Mingle -Mingle" partner share game

Call on a student to pick the special word. Students can be creative and silly with words like "taco, unicorn, X-Box, etc." After students know the special word they will stand up and sing the chant "mingle, mingle, mingle!" over and over until the special word is said. When the teacher shares the special word, all students will freeze and turn to the person closest to him or her. Partners will share his or her symbol and guess what the core memory is. Students can also act out the symbol and have the partner guess it.

Utilize these videos and articles to supplement teacher or student understanding:

https://www.edutopia.org/blog/film-festival-brain-learning
http://channel.nationalgeographic.com/brain-games/
http://faculty.washington.edu/chudler/neurok.html
https://video.nationalgeographic.com/video/brain-bank-sci
https://www.youtube.com/user/SentisDigital
https://www.edutopia.org/article/integrating-sel-classroom

LESSON 2

Islands of Personality
ELEMENTARY

Time 30-45 mins

Objectives :
1. Students will be able to analyze the main idea and details of a core memory.
2. Students will be able to create his or her own personality island.

Why?
It is important for kids to be able to start to recognize and define their personalities, as well as understand how those aspects of their personalities came to be. This type of language is meant to help foster a strong sense of identity, while al so allowing students to understand different perspectives and personalities of their peers. A better understanding will create a stronger, more trusting learning community. This lesson can also support tolerance, acceptance, and appreciation from other extracurricular activities (sports , theater, clubs, etc.)

Materials:
- Core Memory Chart (see lesson #1)
- Post-it notes
- Paper plates
- Magazines
- Scissors
- Glue
- "Inside Out" Islands of Personality

    https: //www.youtube.com/watch?v=3weU3tST3EM&list=PLg3djftwsUDI yFPYepet525IDOH3lEssQ

Key Terms:
Core Memory
Islands of Personality
Main Idea and Details

Instructions

Part 1: Hook

a. Ask students to refer to core memory lesson (see lesson #1). Students could pull out core memory chart, reference it on the anchor chart, or mentally recall the core memory.

b. Using a piece of scrap paper students will have 30 seconds to write down all and any words that come to mind when thinking about that core memory. Encourage students that there is no right or wrong!

Part 2: Discussion and Video

a. Play clip and ask students to notice how the islands of personality are formed

b. Turn to a partner and discuss what makes an island of personality while standing and mirroring each other's movements (see brain aligned strategies in next section)
   Islands of personality- formed through core memories (ex. "goof-ball island, family island, hockey island, honesty island, and friendship island")

c. Discuss how the main idea of a Core Memory creates an aspect of our personalities Model Riley's hockey island with a visual on the board or anchor chart

d. Show the main idea (hockey) in the center and all other details about this island stemming from the center (ex. images for main idea: sun, flower, table, pizza, etc.)

e. Then have students analyze their words written during hook to generate the main idea of their core memories

f. Draw or write the Core Memory of the same image and model (sun, flower, table, pizza, etc.)

Part 3: Exit Ticket

Students create their own island of personality from the discussion. Students will write the title of this island in the center of their paper plate and use magazine cutouts to display details of their island. Display each island on an ocean like a bulletin board or hang from the ceiling.

Bonus Brain-Aligned Strategies:

Artistic Influence: Make this a long-term art project! Have students create multiple "Islands of Personality" for a character, historical figure, or for themselves out of art materials. Partner with your art teacher to design curricula across disciplines!

Brainiac Word Wall: Create a word wall with student definitions paired next to dictionary definitions. Charge students with the task to bring this word wall to life with hand created pictures, examples, and photographs.

Islands of Personality
LESSON 2 ~ SECONDARY

Time 30-45 mins

Objective:
Students will be able to analyze relevant aspects of personality for a specific character or historical figure being studied.

Materials:
- Core Memory Chart (see lesson #1)
- Post-it notes
- "Inside Out" Islands of Personality

    https://www.youtube.com/watch?v=3weU3tST3EM&list=
    PLg3djftwsUDI yFPYepet525IDOH3lEssQ

Key Terms:
    Core Memory
    Islands of Personality
    Myelin

Why?
It is important for kids to be able to start to recognize and define their personalities, as well as understand how those aspects of their personalities came to be. This type of language is meant to help foster a strong sense of identity, while also allowing students to understand different perspectives and personalities of their peers. A better understanding will create a stronger, more trusting learning community. This lesson can also support tolerance, acceptance, and appreciation from other extracurricular activities (sport s, theater, clubs, etc.)

Instructions

Part 1: Hook

a. Ask students to refer to core memory lesson (see lesson #1). Students could pull out core memory chart, reference it on the anchor chart, or mentally recall the core memory.

b. Using a piece of scrap paper students will have 30 seconds to write down nouns, verbs, and adjectives that come to mind when thinking about that core memory. *Encourage students that there is no right or wrong!

Part 2: Discussion and Video

a. Play clip and ask students to notice how the islands of personality are formed
   Review with students the key terms learned in the "Core Memory" lesson (Myelin, Neuroplasticity).

b. Write the key terms on the board to assist with their memories.

c. Have students turn to a partner and discuss what makes an Island of Personality while standing and mirroring each other's movements (see brain aligned strategies). Ask for volunteers to share what they and their partner discussed.

d. Prompt students if needed to see the connection between Core Memories and Islands of Personality being memories that deeply involve their senses, memories/traits that they use frequently (building a myelin sheath around certain neural connections), and the ability to change these (neuroplasticity).

e. Make a list of characters or historical figures that you are currently studying on the board. Explain to students that they will each be choosing one of these characters/figures to identify one of their Islands of Personalities based on Core Memories and/or traits that they display. They will cite textual evidence and relate it to the key terms to back up their thinking, but can otherwise be creative.

Part 3: Exit Ticket

a. Students create a multimedia work representing the science of emotion behind a historical figure or character's Core Memory/Island of Personality. Examples of technology mediums could include Discover Education Board, PowerPoint, Wordle, etc.

Bonus Brain-Aligned Strategies:

Making this a long-term art project! Have students create multiple "Islands of Personality" for a character, historical figure, or for themselves out of art materials. Partner with your art teacher to design curricula across disciplines! Hang multimedia work around the room and have a gallery walk!

LESSON 3

How Emotions Affect Learning

ELEMENTARY

Time 30-45 mins

Objective:

Students will be able to name their different emotions and analyze the different roles each emotion plays in their lives.

Materials:

- Materials that can be manipulated (i.e. slime, play-doh, silly putty, etc.)
- Materials that cannot be manipulated (i.e. keys, a rock, etc.)
- "Inside Out" Meet Riley's Emotions
    https://www.youtube.com/watch? v = 1SORKRRyqhQ
- Sentis Video: Neuroplasticity
    https://www.youtube.com/watch?v =XSz s I5aGcK4

Key Terms:

Neuroplasticity
Emotions

Why?

"If you can name it, you can tame it" is a common phrase – and for good reason! Many of our children believe that our "negative" emotions such as sadness and anger are inherently bad. This discourages them from sharing their emotions, leaving them vulnerable to isolation, depression, and anxiety. Our students need to know that all emotions are valid and more so all emotions are important ! This lesson will help kids explore that, as well as learn that they can change their thinking about their emotions as we utilize and comprehend the powers of neuroplasticity.

Instructions

Part 1: Hook

a. Have different materials visible, some that are easily changed (i.e. play-doh, slime, putty, etc.), and some that cannot be changed (i.e. a rock, toy car, key, etc.). For extra novelty, hide these items in bags!
   Make sure that the items that can be changed are grouped together and the items that cannot be changed are also grouped together.

b. Ask for two volunteers to come and feel/describe the items. Have two other volunteers be the "recorders" for the two students describing the items.
   The goal is to have them articulate the characteristics of each group of items as other classmates scribe them on the board.

c. Once the items are described, have the class categorize the two groups in one word/phrase.
   The goal is to have them identify that one group is a group of items that is malleable/can change form, and one is not.

Part 2: Model and Video

a. Ask students to STAND if they think that the group that can be changed is like our brains (use the students' language for how they described that group), and tell them to sit on the floor/squat if they think that our brains are like the group that cannot be changed (use the students' language).

b. Students gather in a circle, pass around materials while prompting discussion about how items may relate to our brains. Explain the scientific language of neuroplasticity while discussing that our brains are can change (refer to definition on Teacher Reference Sheet). Write definition on board.

c. Play Sentis Video about Neuroplasticity

d. Students return to seats and pass out a piece paper (or type if technology is available for all students).

e. Play "Inside Out" Meet Riley's Emotions video to introduce our main emotions: Joy, Sadness, Fear, Disgust, and Anger

f. Students get into pairs or groups of three and cite textual evidence of an emotion being shown from text you are currently studying in class (novel, historical figure, article, etc.). Have students explain this scene or part of the text and identify where the emotion is shown.

g. Come back together as a class and have partners/groups share their textual evidence citing the emotions. Discuss as a class how we think about our emotions (i.e. do we always see sadness as a bad thing?). Relate this back to neuroplasticity, discussing the purpose for ALL emotions and trying to change our thinking about them.

Part 3: Exit Ticket

Have students return to their groups. Depending on which emotion the students' group chose to showcase, have them discuss and write down their group's responses to the following discussion questions (If they chose a situation where the character showed sadness, have them answer questions 1-3).

Bonus Brain-Aligned Strategies:

Paths of Neuroplasticity:
To showcase another way of neuroplasticity, utilize Hot Wheels cars/tracks! Discuss the different "roadways" in terms of neuroplasticity.

Use wiki-stix, playdoh, drawing, etc. to model neuroplasticity for the character's situation.

How Emotions Affect Learning
LESSON 3 ~ SECONDARY

Time 30-45 mins

Objective:
Students will be able to name their different emotions and analyze the different roles each emotion plays in their lives.

Materials:
- Materials that can be manipulated (i.e. slime, play-doh, silly putty, etc.)
- Materials that cannot be manipulated (i.e. keys, a rock, etc.)
- Inside Out Meet Riley's Emotions
    https:/ /www. youtube.com/watch? v = 1SORKRRyqhQ

- Sentis Video: Neuroplasticity
  https : / /www. youtube.com/watch?v =XSz s I5aGcK4

Key Terms:

Neuroplasticity
Emotions

Why?

"If you can name it, you can tame it" is a common phrase — and for good reason! Many of our children believe that our "negative" emotions such as sadness and anger are inherently bad. This discourages them from sharing their emotions, leaving them vulnerable to isolation, depression, and anxiety. Our students need to know that all emotions are valid and more so all emotions are important! This lesson will help kids explore that, as well as learn that they can change their thinking about their emotions as we utilize and comprehend the powers of neuroplasticity.

Instructions

Part 1: Hook

a. Have different materials visible, some that are easily changed (i.e. play-doh, slime, putty, etc.), and some that cannot be changed (i.e. a rock, toy car, key, etc.). For extra novelty, hide these items in bags!
   Make sure that the items that can be changed are grouped together and the items that cannot be changed are also grouped together.

b. Ask for two volunteers to come and feel/describe the items. Have two other volunteers be the "recorders" for the two students describing the items.
   The goal is to have them articulate the characteristics of each group of items as other classmates scribe them on the board.

c. Once the items are described, have the class categorize the two groups in one word/phrase.
   The goal is to have them identify that one group is a group of items that is malleable/can change form, and one is not.

Part 2: Model and Video

a. Ask students to STAND if they think that the group that can be changed is like our brains (use the students' language for how they described that group), and tell them to sit on the floor/squat if they think that our brains are like the group that cannot be changed (again, use the students' language).

b. Students gather in a circle, pass around materials while prompting discussion about how items may relate to our brains. Explain the scientific language of neuroplasticity while discussing that our brains are can change (refer to definition on Teacher Reference Sheet). Write definition on board.

c. Play Sentis Video about Neuroplasticity. Assess for understanding by asking for a student to explain neuroplasticity in their own words.

d. Instruct students to return to their seats while you pass out a piece paper to each student.

e. Play "Inside Out" Meet Riley's Emotions video to introduce our main emotions: Joy, Sadness, Fear, Disgust, and Anger. Discuss initial reactions to the information.

f. Then, have students get into pairs (or groups of three). Instruct them that on their pieces of paper they are to cite textual evidence of an emotion being shown from text you are currently studying in class (novel, historical figure, article, etc.).

g. Come back together as a class and have partners/groups share their textual evidence citing the emotions. Discuss as a class how we think about our emotions (i.e. do we always see sadness as a bad thing?). Relate this back to neuroplasticity, discussing that we can purposefully change the way that we think about our emotions. Encourage them to keep thinking about this as you go through future lessons.

Part 3: Exit Ticket

Have students return to their groups. Depending on which emotion the students' group chose to showcase, have them discuss and write down their group's responses to the following discussion questions (If they chose a situation where the character showed sadness, have them answer questions 1-3).

Bonus Brain-Aligned Strategies:

Paths of Neuroplasticity: To showcase another way of neuroplasticity, utilize Hot Wheels cars/tracks! Discuss the different "roadways" in terms of neuroplasticity.

Use wiki-stix, playdoh, drawing, etc. to model neuroplasticity for the character's situation.

LESSON 4

Leaving the Adolescent Brain
ELEMENTARY

Time 30-45 mins

Objectives:
Students will be able to create a tailored list of applicable stress regulation strategies.

Materials:
- Cardstock for bookmarks
- Magazines (try to choose magazines with pictures and words that would be used for "Stress Regulation Strategies" - if magazines are not available, newspapers or online pictures /words can work as well)
- Scissors
- "Inside Out" Mind Workers
    https: / /www. youtube.com/watch?v =E9NMUGhJ7FE

Key Terms:
Neurohormones (Serotonin and Dopamine)
Frontal Lobe
Pruning
Brain Regulation Strategies

Why?
Coming off of our lesson about how all emotions are valid, and how we have the power to change our thinking about them, it is important for our students to learn how we can re-regulate our brains when we are feeling negative emotions such as sadness and anger. It is powerful for kids to learn about the neurohormones responsible for us feeling happy, and that we can do things that help to release those neurohormones, therefore regulating our brains.

It is a crucial time for students to be prepared for the neurological changes that will happen as adolescents, and that their brains will go through a process of getting rid of half of their neural connections! The more that we can normalize the adolescent years and prepare students for the different emotions, the better equipped they will be to face those tough transition years ahead.

Instructions

Part 1: Hook

Bring in something that is meaningful to you that represents your childhood/being a kid. (This could be a blanket, a stuffed animal, and toy, etc.) Pass this around the room and ask students to notice and wonder why you brought this in. Explain to students that this item represents being a kid to you. Then ask students to draw or write some things that represent being a kid to them (this could be playing outside with friends, having a toy, etc.)

Part 2: Discussion and Video

a. Have students gather in a circle. Play the "Inside Out" Mind Workers video. Encourage students to react and share their thoughts on what this video might mean.

b. Use an anchor chart to discuss with students that at some point within the next few years that their brains will go through something called "pruning" (see Teacher Cheat Sheet).
   This means that our brains will start to get rid of connections that they don't need any more and start to "leave" childhood. When this happens, they might experience different emotions because of the neurohormones released.

c. Guiding Questions:

Have students get into pairs (or groups of three) to answer the following discussion questions together. Write discussion questions on the board for whole class OR pass out handouts with discussion questions.

- What are the mind workers doing with the vacuum?

- The female mind worker says, "When Riley doesn't care about a memory it fades." Why would our brain allow for this fading/pruning to occur?

- Can you think of something that you loved as a young child that you no longer remember all the details? (I.e. A favorite toy, a talent, or a phone number?)

- Why does Riley get angry while video chatting her friend? How could her emotions have changed so quickly?

- Can you think of a moment when you felt a negative emotion and did not understand why you felt that way?

d. Come back together as a whole group. Explain to students that this video seemed a bit scary and disheartening, but that there is good news for our brain! Brain regulation strategies are available for us to use at any time we are feeling dysregulated (or that our mind is being "vacuumed"). Use an anchor chart to brainstorm different ways that we can help ourselves cope. See brain regulation strategies list attached for examples.

e. Students return to their seats and pass out cardstock for bookmarks. Have magazines, papers, pens, and other art materials to allow students to create their own "Brain Regulation Strategies Bookmark" with their own personal regulation strategies to use when they feel overwhelmed.

Part 3: Exit Ticket

Have students choose one brain regulation strategy that they can use in the classroom/school if they are feeling overwhelmed and write it down on a notecard to hand to the teacher.

Bonus Brain-Aligned Strategies:

Q & A Search:
Imbed a small brain interval by taping discussion question cards on the bottom of a few students' chairs. After the video, ask students to search for the hidden cards. Students can choose to share the question out loud or pass to a friend. This brain interval offers novelty, movement, and choice for the students to better engage in the discussion questions.

Brain Regulation Strategies *(Examples)*

- Use a fidget
- Listen to music
- Breathing exercises
- Run
- Yoga
- Go for a walk
- Go for a bike ride
- Read a book

- Doodle
- Journal
- Count slowly forward or backward
- Drink water
- Wrap up in a blanket
- Hum or sing
- Diffuse essential oils
- Draw/paint
- Do a craft
- Talk to someone
- Color in a coloring book
- Take a shower or bath
- Ask for a break
- Push against a wall
- Ask for a hug from someone you trust
- Play with an animal
- ROYGBIV I Spy: Look for each color of the rainbow around the room
- Write in your planner
- Paint your nails
- Look at the sky
- Clean/organize something
- Knit or sew
- Meditate
- Bake or cook
- Rip paper into tiny pieces
- Hug a pillow or stuffed animal
- Dance
- Do something that you have been procrastinating
- Create something new
- Go to a friend's house
- Watch a movie or TV show that makes you laugh
- Make a playlist of your favorite songs
- Do something nice for someone else
- Rearrange your room
- Write yourself a positive letter
- Do a puzzle
- Ask your friends to play a game
- Write a poem
- Do a wordsearch or crossword puzzle
- Listen to a podcast or book on tape

Leaving the Adolescent Brain
LESSON 4 ~ SECONDARY

Time 30-45 mins (with optional extension to multiple days)

Objectives:
1. Students will be able to create a tailored list of applicable stress regulation strategies.
2. Students will be able to create and present an argument with research-based claims and transition words.

Materials:
- "Inside Out" Bing Bong: Leaving the Adolescent Brain

  https://www.youtube.com/watch?v=tXj61BXEy2M

- Teen Brain Anatomy

  https://www.pbs.org/wgbh/pages/frontline/shows/teenbrain/work/anatomy.html

- Interview with Jay Giedd

  https://www.pbs.org/wgbh/pages/frontline/shows/teenbrain/interviews/giedd.html

- Teen Brain

  https://www.youtube.com/watch?v=EGdlpaWi3rc

- The Teenage Brain Explained

  https://www.youtube.com/watch?v=hiduiTqlei8

- Web Quest Links:

  Sleep:
  https://www.pbs.org/wgbh/pages/frontline/shows/teenbrain/from/

- More electives/extracurricular activities:

  https://www.pbs.org/wgbh/pages/frontline/shows/teenbrain/work/

- Better nutrition in schools

  https://health.usnews.com/health-news/healthwellness/articles/2016-01-05/teens-your-brain-needs-real-food

Key Terms:
Neurohormones (Serotonin and Dopamine)
Frontal Lobe
Brain Regulation Strategies

Why?
Coming off of our lesson about how all emotions are valid, and how we have the power to change our thinking about them, it is important for our students to learn how we can re-regulate our brains when we are feeling negative emotions such as sadness and anger. It is powerful for kids to learn about the neurohormones responsible for us feeling happy, and that we can do things that help to release those neurohormones, therefore regulating our brains.

This lesson is particular important for this age group, as many are experiencing pruning and the changes in their brains/bodies. The more that we can normalize these adolescent years and prepare them with healthy brain habits and regulation strategies, the better equipped they will be during these transition years.

Instructions

Part 1: Hook

a. Play video: "Inside Out" Bing Bong

Bing Bong Signifies Leaving the Adolescent Brain

Post these questions around the room and give students 90 seconds at each station with a partner to answer the following questions:

- What or who was your Bing Bong?
- Could it be an object (like a blanket or teddy bear) or something abstract?
- What does Bing Bong symbolize?
- Why is it important for Riley to let go of Bing - Bong?
- Why did Bing Bong jump off the wagon?
- What makes it so sad for the audience (especially parents and adults) as we watch this part?
- Do we really ever lose Bing Bong? Explain.

- Do you have a core memory of an experience from your imagination? What is it like?

Part 2: Overview

a. After the students have watched the video and answered the questions around the room, explain to them the process of pruning (see Teacher Cheat Sheet). Engage in a discussion about the fact that their brains are going through a lot of changes, and so they might be experiencing or come to experience many different emotions. Discuss how it is important for us all to always be utilizing brain regulation strategies.

b. Instruct students that they will be partaking in a WebQuest activity that will help them to gather information and research about healthy brain habits and regulation strategies. Have students get into pairs/group of three. (see Bonus Brain- Aligned Strategies for pairing)

c. Students (in their pairs/groups) will research the following topics through the WebQuest links: School Start-Up times, Importance of Sleep, Nutrition, and the Brain, Stress Response System, If you are choosing to do this lesson in one day, please end with step d.
   If you are choosing to stretch this lesson into an argumentative project, please skip step 3 and continue with step e.

d. (If you are choosing to do this lesson in one day) Towards the end of class, have student pairs/groups pick one topic to share out.

e. (If you are choosing to continue this lesson into an argumentative project) Towards the end of class on Day 1, have each student group state their topic/thesis (as their exit ticket) .

f. Day 2 and beyond (time allotted for project up to your discretion): Have students regroup into their pairs/groups and work together to organize an argumentative project to present to the class on their chosen topic Projects can be presented in essay format, a speech, PowerPoint, video, or other means to argue their topic.

Part 3: Exit Ticket

Students will individually write an argumentative piece highlighting the evidence extracted from each source. Students can choose to present essays to the class, another grade level, the administration or parents. While students present, classmates will fill out a feedback form with "two stars and a wish". Stars represent something learned or done well and wishes represents constructive feedback for improvement.

Bonus Brain-Aligned Strategies:

Pairing students — place numbered post it notes underneath each chair before class. Make sure to have two of each number for student to know their partner. Set a timer for 30 seconds for students to find his or her partner in the room. This method is very novel promoting engagement and curiosity. Students will also activate the RAS (reticular activating system) giving a healthy dose of energy and alertness for the activity.

Project presenting — have the students present to a different audience that connects with them! Another class, a principal, etc. Giving students the platform to speak their mind connects them to their learning deeper, as well as forms connections with those they present to!

Brain Regulation Strategies *(Examples)*

- Use a fidget
- Listen to music
- Breathing exercises
- Run
- Yoga
- Go for a walk
- Go for a bike ride
- Read a book
- Doodle
- Journal
- Count slowly forward or backward
- Drink water
- Wrap up in a blanket
- Hum or sing
- Diffuse essential oils
- Draw/paint
- Do a craft
- Talk to someone
- Color in a coloring book
- Take a shower or bath
- Ask for a break
- Push against a wall
- Ask for a hug from someone you trust
- Play with an animal

- ROYGBIV I Spy: Look for each color of the rainbow around the room
- Write in your planner
- Paint your nails
- Look at the sky
- Clean/organize something
- Knit or sew
- Meditate
- Bake or cook
- Rip paper into tiny pieces
- Hug a pillow or stuffed animal
- Dance
- Do something that you have been procrastinating
- Create something new
- Go to a friend's house
- Watch a movie or TV show that makes you laugh
- Make a playlist of your favorite songs
- Do something nice for someone else
- Rearrange your room
- Write yourself a positive letter
- Do a puzzle
- Ask your friends to play a game
- Write a poem
- Do a wordsearch or crossword puzzle
- Listen to a podcast or book on tape

LESSON 5

Contagious Emotions and Stress Response System

ELEMENTARY

Time 30-45 mins

Objectives:

1. Students will be able to describe how mirror neurons affect our mood and brain state.
2. Students will be able to model and educate others about healthy stress response strategies

Materials:

- "Inside Out" Family Dinner Scene

    https : / /www. youtube.com/watch? v =Cjgdi y_SGjA

- Mirror Neurons Part 1

    www. youtube.com/watch? v =XzMqPYfeAs&l i s t =RDQMDz vo_A7NaXY

- Mirror Neurons Part 2

    www. youtube.com/watch?v = xmEsGQ3 JmKg&index =2&l i s t =RDQMDz vo_A7NaXY

- Chocolate/candy (a chocolate chip, Hershey kiss , etc.)

Key Terms:

Mirror Neurons
Stress Response System

Why?

Mirror neurons are a crucial part to understand our interactions with others, which is a foundational aspect of building classroom community. This lesson is meant to build on the previous lessons and teach students another way to recognize how emotions are impacting their learning. The brain regulation strategies created in the previous lesson are something that should not be taught in isolation (as we know the more we utilize something, the stronger that neural connect ion will be!), so you will see that they are incorporated into this crucial lesson.

Instructions

Part 1: Hook

a. Place chocolate/candy on a front table where students can see. You can either demonstrate yourself or ask a student to volunteer in order to slowly and deliberately eat the chocolate/candy piece.

b. While you or the student is eating the piece, ask students to describe what they are seeing/feeling. The goal is to have the students recognize that they can almost "feel" what the volunteer eating the chocolate/candy piece is feeling, so you may prompt students if needed.

c. After students have recognized that they can "feel" what the volunteer is feeling, explain Mirror Neurons (see Teacher Cheat Sheet).

Part 2: Discussion and Video

a. Tell students that you are going to play a humorous scene from "Inside Out." Ask them to pay close attention to how the mom and dad's brain states change based on Riley's mood, and how this might be showing mirror neurons. Play Inside Out Family Dinner Scene.

b. When the video is complete, ask students: "How were Riley's mom and dad feeling at the beginning of dinner, versus when they realized Riley's attitude change?" (Students should recognize that the mom and dad were feeling happy at the beginning of the scene but then their brains "mirrored" Riley's mood when they recognized that she was feeling negative)

c. (optional) Act it out! Create a seemingly organic situation where your mood suddenly changes to angry or sad. You could pretend to spill a drink on your papers or yourself and get angry or sad at the situation, tell the students about the "horrible" day you are having (you could make up flat tire, forgetting lunch, etc. Ensure that the situation you create is benign and not aimed at the class or any specific student, as well as not a trigger for your students). After you do this, ask how your class is feeling. The goal is to have them recognize that once you changed your mood their brain states "mirrored". Tell the students that even though your scenario was made up, their brains mirrored your mood.

d. Brain Regulation Strategies! Discuss with students that the strategies they learned in Lesson #4 (The Adolescent Brain) are important to continuously monitor in order to be able to regulate our brains. Explain that brain regulation strategies help them when they recognize that their brains are mirroring another person's attitude.

e. Have a chalk talk on the board of things students like to do when they are feeling overwhelmed/their brain regulation strategies (i.e. breathing, distraction, reading, doodling, take a break, etc.) Relate this to how we are in control of our brains, and if we can sense that we are mirroring negative emotions we can control what we do.

f. Discuss that we can also do things to help that person, such as validation, take a break, give the person space, etc. Break students off into pairs to practice validation strategies (see Validation scenarios and strategies sheet attached).

Part 3: Exit Ticket

Students will write a short paragraph or draw a short scene describing a time when he or she felt sad or angry from another person (this could also connect to a novel character or historical figure). Next students will write an applicable brain regulation to combat the negative situation. For extra novelty, these brain strategies can be recorded on a popsicle stick to pull out and match each paragraph. You then can the popsicle sticks in a jar and refer to them throughout the year. Display these scenarios in the classroom.

Bonus Brain-Aligned Strategies:

Act it out (continued): Ask another faculty member or parents to step in and model the effects of mirror neurons to the class. Provide this person with a scenario of sadness or anger that the students will believe. After the encounter share your emotions with the class (emotions should match the scenario). Discuss how our mirror neurons were impacted by another person.

Validation

Validation is an important part of co-regulating with someone (helping them regulate their emotions). It is a great way to build connection and relationship with others. The basis of validation is making sure that the person knows their feelings are valid/warranted. Validation offers no judgment, simply listening to learn. On this sheet you will find examples of validating phrases, as well as scenarios to practice using these phrases. You will also find some examples of invalidating phrases - these are phrases that involuntarily make the other person feel as though their feelings are unimportant or unwarranted, and drive disconnection.

Validating Phrases

"That must be really frustrating."

"I can understand why you feel that way."

"I can't imagine what this feels like for you."

"I think I would feel the same way if I were in your shoes."

"I imagine that you are feeling pretty frustrated, right?"

"That feels like that is a really big challenge right now."

"Of course you're scared to do that, new things are scary for everyone!"

Invalidating Phrases

"I think you're overreacting."

"At least _____."

"Don't worry, tomorrow will be better"

"Get over it."

"Look on the bright side..."

"That happened to me, and I got over it."

"This isn't that big of a deal."

"You're tougher than that!"

"Stop complaining, you're being so negative."

"Well maybe that wouldn't have happened if you hadn't been doing _____."

Validation Scenarios

1. A friend's family dog ran away. Your friend is extremely upset and talks to you about it. They say, "I can't believe she ran away, I am so scared for her! I miss her so much, what if something happens to her?"

Validating response: "Of course you're scared, that's such a scary thing! That makes perfect sense to me. I'm here for you."

Invalidating response: "Don't worry about it, worrying doesn't change anything!'

2. Your friend's family had a trip to Kings Island planned this past weekend, but it got rained out and they couldn't go. Your friend tells you "I'm so mad that it rained! I wanted to go to Kings Island and it's the only weekend we could go, it's not fair!"

Validating response: "Oh boy I would be upset too! Those trips don't come up often, and I know how excited you were."

Invalidating response: "It's just an amusement park! At least it wasn't something important!"

Your Turn to Try!

Validating response:
Invalidating response:

Validating response:
Invalidating response:

Contagious Emotions and Stress Response System

LESSON 5 ~ SECONDARY

Time 30-45 mins

Objectives:

1. Students will be able to describe how mirror neurons affect our mood and brain state.
2. Students will be able to model and educate others about healthy stress response strategies

Materials:

- Mirror Neuron Article

  http: / / s i tn.hms .har vard.edu/ f lash/2016/mi r ror -neurons - quar ter -centur y -new- l ight -new-cracks /

- "Inside Out" Family Dinner Scene

  https : / /www. youtube.com/watch? v =Cjgdi y_SGjA

- Mirror Neurons Part 1

  www. youtube.com/watch? v =XzMqPYfeAs& l i s t =RDQMDz vo_A7NaXY

- Mirror Neurons Par t 2

  www. youtube.com/watch?v = xmEsGQ3 JmKg&index =2&l i s t =RDQMDz vo_A7NaXY

- Chocolate/candy (a chocolate chip, Her shey ki s s , etc.)

Key Terms:

Mirror Neurons
Stress Response System

Why?

Mirror neurons are a crucial part to understand our interactions with others, which is a foundational aspect of building classroom community. This lesson is meant to build on the previous lessons and teach students another way to recognize how emotions are impacting their learning. The brain regulation strategies created in the previous lesson are something that should not be taught in isolation (as we know the more we utilize something, the stronger that neural connect ion will be!) , so you will see that they are incorporated into this crucial lesson.

Instructions

Part 1: Hook

a. Place chocolate/candy on a front table where students can see. You can either demonstrate yourself or ask a student to volunteer in order to slowly and deliberately eat the chocolate/candy piece.

b. While you or the student is eating the piece, ask students to describe what they are seeing/feeling. The goal is to have the students recognize that they can almost "feel" what the volunteer eating the chocolate/candy piece is feeling, so you may prompt students if needed.

c. After students have recognized that they can "feel" what the volunteer is feeling, explain Mirror Neurons (see Teacher Cheat Sheet).

Part 2: Discussion and Video

a. Tell students that you are going to play a humorous scene from Inside Out. Ask them to pay close attention to how the mom and dad's brain states change based on Riley's mood, and how this might be showing mirror neurons. Play "Inside Out" Family Dinner Scene.

b. When the video is complete, ask students: "How were Riley's mom and dad feeling at the beginning of dinner, versus when they realized Riley's attitude change?" (Students should recognize that the mom and dad were feeling happy at the beginning of the scene but then their brains "mirrored" Riley's mood when they recognized that she was feeling negative)

c. (optional) Act it out! Create a seemingly organic situation where your mood suddenly changes to angry or sad. You could pretend to spill a drink on your papers or yourself and get angry or sad at the situation, tell the students about the "horrible" day you are having (you could make up flat tire, forgetting lunch, etc. Ensure that the situation you create is benign and not aimed at the class or any specific student, as well as not a trigger for your students). After you do this, ask how your class is feeling. The goal is to have them recognize that once you changed your mood their brain states "mirrored". Tell the students that even though your scenario was made up, their brains mirrored your mood.

d. Brain Regulation Strategies! Discuss with students that the strategies they learned in Lesson #4 (The Adolescent Brain) are important to continuously monitor in order to be able to regulate our brains. Explain that brain regulation strategies help them when they recognize that their brains are mirroring another person's attitude.

e. Have a chalk talk on the board of things students like to do when they are feeling overwhelmed/their brain regulation strategies (i.e. breathing, distraction, reading, doodling, take a break, etc.) Relate this to how we are in control of our brains, and if we can sense that we are mirroring negative emotions we can control what we do.

f. Discuss that we can also do things to help that person, such as validation, take a break, give the person space, etc. Break students off into pairs to practice validation strategies (see Validation scenarios and strategies sheet attached).

Part 3: Exit Ticket

Each pair should write down their validation scenario and the brain regulation strategy that they chose for the situation on a note card to hand into the teacher.

OR

Students will write a short paragraph or draw a short scene describing a time when he or she felt sad or angry from another person (this could also connect to a novel character or historical figure).

Bonus Brain-Aligned Strategies:

Have students make their own notecards, bookmarks, or sheets of paper with brain regulation strategies! Relate this to a historical figure or character that you are studying in class and identify a scenario where they were mirroring another person's emotions, as well as what brain regulation strategy they could have done.

Validation

Validation is an important part of co-regulating with someone (helping them regulate their emotions). It is a great way to build connection and relationship with others. The basis of validation is making sure that the person knows their feelings are valid/warranted. Validation offers no judgment, simply listening to learn. On this sheet you will find examples of validating phrases, as well as scenarios to practice using these phrases. You will also find some examples of invalidating phrases - these are phrases that involuntarily make the other person feel as though their feelings are unimportant or unwarranted, and drive disconnection.

Validating Phrases

"That must be really frustrating."

"I can understand why you feel that way."

"I can't imagine what this feels like for you."

"I think I would feel the same way if I were in your shoes."

"I imagine that you are feeling pretty frustrated, right?"

"That feels like that is a really big challenge right now."

"Of course you're scared to do that, new things are scary for everyone!"

Invalidating Phrases

"I think you're overreacting."

"At least _____."

"Don't worry, tomorrow will be better"

"Get over it."

"Look on the bright side..."

"That happened to me, and I got over it."

"This isn't that big of a deal."

"You're tougher than that!"

"Stop complaining, you're being so negative."

"Well maybe that wouldn't have happened if you hadn't been doing _____."

Validation Scenarios

1. A friend has failed a test, and comes up to you. They say "I studied so hard for this test, I cannot believe that I failed! I'm never going to do well!"

Validating response: "Wow, I would be upset too if I put that much effort in! It makes sense that you're frustrated."

Invalidating response: "Whatever, I'm sure you'll do fine on the next one."

2. One of your friends just found out that they didn't make it onto the school basketball team. They say to you, "I can't believe that I didn't make the team - this is so stupid!!!"

Validating response: "Man, of course you're upset, I know how hard you've been working for this! I'd be really hurt."

Invalidating response: "Just practice more next time, I bet that will help!"

Your Turn to Try!

Validating response:
Invalidating response:

Validating response:
Invalidating response:

NOTES:

CORE Standards

"Creating Core Memories"

Elementary:
1.RV.3.1 Identify words and phrases in stories, poems, or songs that suggest feelings or appeal to
the senses (touch, hearing, sight, taste, smell).

6.RL.3.2: Explain how an author develops the point of view of the narrator or speaker in a work of literature, and how the narrator or speaker impacts the mood, tone, and meaning of a text.
(Health & Wellness)

2.1.2 Recognize that there are multiple dimensions of health. (emotional, intellectual, physical, and social health)

5.1.2 Identify examples of emotional, intellectual, physical, and social health

Secondary:
9-10.SL.2.1 Initiate and participate effectively in a range of collaborative discussions (one-on-one, in groups, and teacher-led) on grade-appropriate topics, texts, and issues, building on others' ideas and expressing personal ideas clearly and persuasively.
(Health & Wellness)

8.1.2 Describe the interrelationships of emotional, intellectual, physical, and social health in adolescence.

12.1.2 Cite evidence that demonstrates the interrelationships of emotional, intellectual, physical, and social health across the lifespan.

"Islands of Personality"

Elementary:
(Health & Wellness)

2.1.2 Recognize that there are multiple dimensions of health. (emotional, intellectual, physical, and social health)

3.RN.2.2 Determine the main idea of a text; recount the key details and explain how they support the main idea.

Secondary:
9-10.SL.2.1 Initiate and participate effectively in a range of collaborative discussions (one-on-one, in groups, and teacher-led) on grade-appropriate

topics, texts, and issues, building on others' ideas and expressing personal ideas clearly and persuasively.

9-10.SL.4.1 Present information, findings, and supporting evidence clearly, concisely, and logically such that listeners can follow the line of reasoning and the organization, development, substance, and style are appropriate to purpose, audience, and task.

11-12.RN.2.2 Compare and contrast the development of similar central ideas across two or more texts and analyze how they emerge and are shaped and refined by specific details

"How Emotions Affect Learning"

Elementary:
1.SL.1 Listen actively and adjust the use of spoken language (e.g., vocabulary) to communicate effectively with a variety of audiences and for different purposes.
1.SL. 4.2 Add drawings or other visual displays, such as pictures and objects, when sharing information to clarify ideas, thoughts, and feelings.

Secondary:
9-10.SL.2.1 Initiate and participate effectively in a range of collaborative discussions (one-on-one, in groups, and teacher-led) on grade-appropriate topics, texts, and issues, building on others' ideas and expressing personal ideas clearly and persuasively.

"Leaving the Adolescent Brain"

Elementary:
6.SL.3.1 Interpret information presented in diverse media and formats (e.g., visually, quantitatively, orally) and explain how it contributes to a topic, text, or issue under study.

Secondary:
9-10.RN.2.1 Cite strong and thorough textual evidence to support analysis of what a text says explicitly as well as inferences and interpretations drawn from the text.

9-10.W.3.1 Write arguments in a variety of forms that – Introduce precise claim(s), distinguish the claim(s) from alternate or opposing claims, and create an organization that establishes clear relationships among claim(s), counterclaims, reasons, and evidence.

11-12.SL.4.1 Present information, findings, and supporting evidence, conveying a clear and distinct perspective, such that listeners can follow the line of reasoning, alternative or opposing perspectives are addressed, and the organization, development, substance, and style are appropriate to purpose, audience, and a range of formal and informal tasks.

"Contagious Emotions and Responding to Stress"

Elementary:

2.W.3.1 Write a logically connected paragraph or paragraphs that introduce an opinion, with a concluding statement or section and multiple reasons to explain why a certain course of action should be followed.

5.S.L.2.2 Reflect on and contribute to ideas under discussion by drawing on readings and other resources.

Secondary:

9-10. SL. 4.3 Present information, findings, and supporting evidence clearly, concisely, and logically such that listeners can follow the line of reasoning and the organization, development, substance, and style are appropriate to purpose, audience, and task.

11-12. RV-2.1 Use context to determine or clarify the meaning of words and phrases.

"Inside Out" Curriculum Resources

Creating Core Memories:
https://www.edutopia.org/blog/creating-core-memories-in-classroom-lori-desautels

Islands of Personality and Trains of Thought:
https://www.edutopia.org/blog/islands-of-personality-trains-ofthought-lori-desautels

How Emotions Affect Learning, Behavior, and Relationships:
https://www.edutopia.org/blog/emotions-affectlearning-behavior-relation-ships-lori-desautels

Leaving the Adolescent Brain:
https://www.edutopia.org/blog/adolescent-brain-leaving-childhood-be-hind-loridesautels

Contagious Emotions and Responding to Stress:
https://www.edutopia.org/blog/contagious-emotionsresponding-to-stress-lori-desautels

NOTES:

Adversity Surveys
for Educators and Students

Adversity/ Trauma and Brain Aligned School Assessment

An adversity sensitive and educational neuroscience informed school/district is a safe and cohesive environment that embraces attachment and emotional regulation brain aligned strategies in all classrooms. The school deeply considers the brain state of all educators and staff who serve the students. This district, school, and/or classroom embrace the emotional, social, and academic health and challenges of all students. The adversity and brain aligned environment prepares students to understand their own neuro-anatomy along with brain aligned strategies implemented as procedures, routines, and structure, dampening the stress response systems when activated. In this environment, the language of applied educational neuroscience and adversity is implemented schoolwide.

Please use the following scale when rating your school/district in the different components involved in creating an adversity and brain aligned informed and responsive school.

1. **Not yet** (no evidence within school/district)
2. **Emerging** (little evidence within school/district)
3. **Developing** (some evidence within school/district)
4. **Established** (evident throughout school/district)

Schoolwide Policies and Practices

1. To what extent do schools/districts contain predictable and safe environments (classrooms, hallways, playgrounds, lunchrooms, bathrooms, bus) and are attentive to the sensory, emotional, and present moment needs of students as they transition through their days.

`1  2  3  4`

2. To what extent does your school have a strategy or plan in place for a student who may present harm to staff or another student? In other words, do you have backup systems that are created for

`1  2  3  4`

co-regulation if the removal of a student is necessary within a safe and connected environment?

3. To what extent has your staff been trained in
regulation and attachment brain aligned practices which make up the prevention strategies
that provide predictability, routine, and connection?

`1 2 3 4`

4. To what extent do your discipline policies balance accountability with sensitivity to students
who have been exposed to significant adversity?

`1 2 3 4`

5. To what extent have teachers been trained to
provide emotional support to students following
a traumatic event?

`1 2 3 4`

6. To what extent is the healthy brain state of all
staff and teachers addressed in this school? In
other words, is the emotional and social well-
being of staff a priority?

`1 2 3 4`

7. To what extent has the staff been trained in
identifying ACE's and stress response systems of
both staff and students?

`1 2 3 4`

8. To what extent has the staff been trained on
how adversity and trauma impact brain development, behavior, learning, and life perceptions?

`1 2 3 4`

9. To what extent does your school/district train
all staff in brain aligned strategies for attachment
and regulation?

`1 2 3 4`

10. To what extent do these educator preparation
trainings enhance the culture and climate in
every classroom?

`1 2 3 4`

11. To what extent has school staff been trained in
identifying potential triggers of students and ways
to effectively de-escalate and regulate emotions
when a child or adolescent has been triggered?

`1 2 3 4`

12. To what extent are classroom guidelines procedures, routines, and discipline procedures implemented in cohesive brain aligned systemic ways?

1 2 3 4

13. To what extent do teachers consistently provide and model positive behaviors and coping strategies that can replace negative actions?

1 2 3 4

14. To what extent does the school utilize morning meetings, bell work, and times of transition to consistently implement brain aligned strategies THAT REGULATE AND USE ATTACHMENT?

1 2 3 4

15. To what extent are classrooms implementing organic consequences that are aligned to how the brain feels, learns, and behaves? (Organic consequences are designed to teach rather than punish, focusing solely on supporting positive behaviors and providing opportunities and situations where the only outcome or behavior is the positive one.)

1 2 3 4

16. To what extent are schools including parent involvement in adversity and brain aligned learning?

1 2 3 4

17. To what extent are there positive supports, resources, and procedures for staff and students who need regulation and some time to repair and make a new plan of action?

1 2 3 4

18. To what extent has your school created a team of staff Educational Neuroscience Adversity Teams (ENAT) to be prepared and called upon during growing emotional crises?

1 2 3 4

19. To what extent is the leadership in the building and district informed and responsive to adversity/educational neuroscience?

1 2 3 4

20. To what extent does your school/ district engage community partners, organizations and

1 2 3 4

families in the preparation of applied educational neuroscience/brain and adversity?

21. To what extent has the school/district developed "touch points" for students who carry in pain-based behaviors/trauma? These touchpoints are dyadic conversations and check-ins by a variety of educators and staff each day connecting with students.

| 1 | 2 | 3 | 4 |

22. To what extent have students been given a voice and choice in sharing their emotional, social, and academic needs?

| 1 | 2 | 3 | 4 |

23. To what extent have office and discipline referrals decreased because of these adversity/trauma and brain aligned practices and instruction?

| 1 | 2 | 3 | 4 |

Assessment Results

Directions: Circle the score given to each survey question (bolded). Add the scores together for each section to determine a total. Sections averaging a total of 8 or less indicate areas for growth.

Professional Development						District/School Planning & Preparation							School-wide Practices					Teacher Practice				
3	**5**	**7**	**8**	**9**	**11**	**2**	**4**	**6**	**16**	**18**	**19**	**20**	**1**	**6**	**10**	**17**	**23**	**12**	**13**	**14**	**15**	**22**
1	1	1	1	1	1	1	1	1	1	1	1	1	1	1	1	1	1	1	1	1	1	1
2	2	2	2	2	2	2	2	2	2	2	2	2	2	2	2	2	2	2	2	2	2	2
3	3	3	3	3	3	3	3	3	3	3	3	3	3	3	3	3	3	3	3	3	3	3
4	4	4	4	4	4	4	4	4	4	4	4	4	4	4	4	4	4	4	4	4	4	4
Section Total:						Section Total:							Section Total:					Section Total:				

Is Our School Brain and Adversity Aligned?

We need your help! As we work to make our school more brain friendly we have been asking for feedback from the many members of our school community. Students are the most important part of that community, so we want to hear directly from you!

Our brains are incredible! They weigh about three pounds, feel a little like jello, and have enough storage space to store three million television shows! Pretty impressive right? Scientists have discovered that this amazing organ is not fully developed when we are born but continues to grow until we are in our late twenties. Even more crazy, the brain may reach full development in our twenties, but it never stops learning and rewiring. Looks like you really can teach an old dog, or human, new tricks!

With all that we know about the human brain there are still many things that remain a mystery. One thing WE know for sure is how important YOUR developing brain is, so we want to work together to make our school brain friendly. To help us do this we have some questions we would like you to honestly answer. We cannot do this without you! Your answers will be anonymous so do not be afraid to speak your mind!

So... What do you think? (circle your answer)

1. Does your school help you to understand your brain better? How about your emotions?

> Never   Sometimes   Most of the time   All the time

2. Do your teachers talk about how the brain grows and develops?

> Never   Sometimes   Most of the time   All the time

3. Do you understand how the brain learns? If so, do you think your school teaches in a way that supports your brain?

> Never   Sometimes   Most of the time   All the time

4. Do you feel safe in your school environment (classrooms, hallways, playgrounds, lunchrooms, bathrooms, bus) and are these environments predictable/consistent?

> Never   Sometimes   Most of the time   All the time

5. Do you think the adults in your school want to get to know you? Do you feel like they care about who you are as a person?

     Never   Sometimes   Most of the time   All the time

6. Do you feel like there is at least one adult at school that cares about you? That really knows you?

     Never   Sometimes   Most of the time   All the time

7. Do you have opportunities throughout the school day to spend positive time with the adults you connect with?

     Never   Sometimes   Most of the time   All the time

8. Do you feel like you can share your emotional, social, and academic needs with those at your school?

     Never   Sometimes   Most of the time   All the time

9. Do you feel like you have choices throughout the school day?

     Never   Sometimes   Most of the time   All the time

10. Do you have a voice at school? Do adults and other students at your school listen to your voice?

     Never   Sometimes   Most of the time   All the time

11. Would you say the beginning of the day at your school is calm, welcoming, and friendly?

     Never   Sometimes   Most of the time   All the time

12. Does the way you begin your school day help you feel supported and prepared for the day ahead?

     Never   Sometimes   Most of the time   All the time

13. Do you know how your brain responds to stress, fear, or danger? If so, do you feel like your teachers help you to understand this response?

       Never   Sometimes   Most of the time   All the time

14. Do you feel like your school supports your emotional needs and present moment needs?

       Never   Sometimes   Most of the time   All the time

15. Do you feel confident in your abilities to calm yourself, to self-regulate your brain and emotions?

       Never   Sometimes   Most of the time   All the time

16. Do you feel like the adults in your school would help you if you were to lose your cool or "flip your lid"?

       Never   Sometimes   Most of the time   All the time

17. Do your teachers support your emotions? Especially when you are angry, scared, or sad?

       Never   Sometimes   Most of the time   All the time

18. Do the adults at your school teach and show you ways to self-regulate?

       Never   Sometimes   Most of the time   All the time

19. Can you identify the things that trigger you?

       Never   Sometimes   Most of the time   All the time

20. Do you think the adults in your school can help students when they are triggered?

       Never   Sometimes   Most of the time   All the time

21. Do you think your school/classroom's rules or guidelines are fair? Do they make sense to you?

       Never   Sometimes   Most of the time   All the time

22. Do you think most students follow these rules or guidelines?

       Never   Sometimes   Most of the time   All the time

23. If you do not follow these rules or guidelines do you know what the consequences would be, what would happen?

       Never   Sometimes   Most of the time   All the time

24. Do you think these consequences are fair?

       Never   Sometimes   Most of the time   All the time

25. Do they help you to follow the rules or guidelines better next time?

       Never   Sometimes   Most of the time   All the time

26. Do the adults in your school offer or show you ways to follow these rules or guidelines?

       Never   Sometimes   Most of the time   All the time

27. Do you think your school supports the emotions of the teachers?

       Never   Sometimes   Most of the time   All the time

28. Do you think your teachers are happy? Do you think they enjoy teaching?

       Never   Sometimes   Most of the time   All the time

29. Do you think the adults in your school know how to self-regulate their own emotions and brain states?

Never   Sometimes   Most of the time   All the time

30. Does your school use parents to help support students and teachers?

Never   Sometimes   Most of the time   All the time

31. Do you think your school values (cares about) parents?

Never   Sometimes   Most of the time   All the time

32. Do you think your school values (cares about) students?

Never   Sometimes   Most of the time   All the time

33. Do you think your school values (cares about) you?

Never   Sometimes   Most of the time   All the time

Is there anything else you would like to share? (write response below)

_____

Created by Courtney Boyle, Elementary Education & Special Education, Graduate Candidate, Masters in Effective Teaching and Leadership, Butler University

Trauma and Tension Releasing Exercises

Tension and Trauma Releasing Exercises known as TRE are ways to regulate our nervous system. TRE is a simple series of exercises that assist the body in releasing deep muscular patterns of stress, tension and trauma. Created by Dr. David Berceli, PhD, TRE safely activates a natural reflex mechanism of shaking or vibrating that releases muscular tension, calming down the nervous system.

When conducting a group TRE class, I'm teaching a self-regulation technique that can assist the body to release stress. When a group of people come together and do any positive activity together, it can be quite special.

Below are a few exercises for students that attune to body awareness, dampening down the stress response systems while priming the brain for learning.

Amygdala Reset / "Update Your App"

If we were hungry, and were to eat a hot dog, our digestive system could handle this amount of food and we would feel somewhat full, yet ready to move on to the next task. But if we were to feel hungry and we were forced to eat four, then five hot dogs, our digestive system and bodies would have a really hard time digesting all of this food at once and we would have to rest sensing our fullness, discomfort, and lack of energy. This is how stress affects our brains and bodies. If we encounter unpredictable and chronic stressors in our lives as youth, these adverse experiences affect the developing brain and nervous system. When there is too much stress and adversity, our bodies do not have the awareness and time to recover and then to reset and repair.

Too much food is stored in the body as fat. Too many negative experiences are stored in the body as stress or chronic adversities.

The exercises below are helpful for students who need to regulate their stress response systems using rhythm, breath, and movement.

A. Relaxation/Reset the Amygdala or Fight/ Flight / Freeze Response

1. Take a deep breath and stretch arms and hands in the air, drop hands to your side as you exhale. Shake the body out.

2. Place hands on head and inhale as you squeeze your scalp. Exhale while you drop hands to your side. Shake the body out.

3. Place your hands on your forehead and gently squeeze the skin on your forehead while inhaling. Drop hands to your side as you exhale. Shake the body out.

4. Do the same to your cheeks and shake the body out.

5. Cross your arms over your chest and squeeze your upper arms as you inhale. Exhale and drop your hands to your side. Shake the body out.

6. Inhale and squeeze your left forearm with your right hand. Exhale and let go of your arm. Do the same to your right forearm with your left hand. Shake the body out.

7. Clasp your hands together, inhale and allow each hand to squeeze the other at the same time. Let go and exhale. Shake the body out.

8. Continue this format with the rest of the body including the front and back of thighs, the shins, the calves and the feet (if shoes can be removed). Both hands can be used to squeeze each leg area and each foot. Remember to inhale when squeezing and exhale when releasing.

B. Invigorating/ Alert My Brain Stem

1. Using the same format, start with the feet and move up the body. Tap 10 - 20 times each area with the palm of the hand that coordinates with the same side of the body. Tap, with rhythm, the left and right foot, calf, shin and front and back of each thigh. You can add hips and stomach to this variation. Continue with the rest of the areas mentioned in the relaxation version of this exercise, including the top of your head and ending with the same reaching stretch that the first exercise started with, inhaling up and exhaling down. Shake the body out.

C. Match My Rhythm!

This exercise should be done standing. It is a full body rhythmic movement exercise.

1. Stand with arms relaxed to the side. Simply start rocking left and right, placing more weight on the foot you're rocking towards. Do this 10 - 20 times. Take a deep breath and shake the body out.

2. Stand with arms relaxed to the side. Twist the body left and right from the torso, in a rhythmic fashion. Let the arms swing where they want to go. Do this 10 -20 times. Take a deep breath and shake the body out.

3. Combine the two exercises, twisting your body from the torso, towards the direction you're swaying. To increase difficulty, twist your body from the torso in the opposite direction from the direction you're swaying. Do this 10 - 20 times. Take a deep breath and shake the body out.

Have fun creating your own variations of this exercise. See how many similar rhythmic movements your students can do individually or layered together. Some ideas could be various head movements, lifting or kicking out the legs, or various arm movements.

1. How do you feel?

2. What do you notice about your body?

3. Do you sense anything different about how you feel?

4. What are two ways you can change these exercises?

5. Where and when could you use these exercises for calming the brain or alerting the brain to what it needs to do?

Created by: Chad Brown, Certified TRE Trainer

Bridging Education and Neuroscience:
An Integrative Model of Applied Educational Neuroscience Practices

Educational neuroscience (EN) is a transdisciplinary convergence of neurosciences, education, and psychology that has gained international momentum throughout the last decade. Its purpose is to advance the application of neurosciences in P-12 education as a way to improve the design of instructional environments and practices that support the multidimensional social, affective, and cognitive learning needs of students. The potential integration of EN practices into school settings affects educators who promote positive school climates and address barriers to learning. Despite the ascension of scholarly and professional discourse proposing the integration of neuroscience knowledge with education practices, a shared conceptual framework remains elusive for the emergent discipline, and the translation of the social and affective dimensions of EN into education practices has not been systematically and empirically examined. A constructivist grounded theory study was conducted to begin the bridging of that gap. This summary explains The Integrative Applied Educational Neuroscience Model that emerged from a study that was conducted to investigate the conceptualization of EN practices and the implications for promoting a positive classroom climate.

Rationale and Study Impetus

There is a growing call from scholars and educators to translate the expanding scientific knowledge on neurobiological development into educational practice as a way to evolve outmoded theories and methodologies (Center on the Developing Child at Harvard University, 2016). Philosophies currently governing education delivery do not reflect the robust scientific knowledge that highlight the non-linearity of child development and students' learning processes (Stafford-Brizard, Cantor, & Rose, 2017). Furthermore, education systems are designed to facilitate academic development but oftentimes lack the necessary resources and structures to adequately support the interrelated cognitive, social-emotional, and physical developmental domains inextricably linked within learning processes (Durlak, Weissberg, Dymnicki, Taylor, & Schellinger, 2011). Addressing this dissonance, EN provides a more complete and rigorous scope of students' developmental domains that support learning processes (Cantor, Osher, Berg, Steyer, & Rose, 2018; Osher, Cantor, Berg, Steyer, & Rose, 2018).

The Centrality of Classroom Climate. Researchers have acknowledged the importance of school climate for over a century (Perry, 1908) and have studied the social phenomena of school climate since the 1950s (Cohen, McCabe, Michelli, & Pickeral, 2009). School climate is characterized by the quality of relationships in the school context and comprised of patterns of perceived social experiences within the life of the school (Cohen et al., 2009). Systematic reviews of the climate literature (Cohen et al., 2009; Thapa, Cohen, Guffey, & Higgins-D'Alessandro, 2013) indicate that school climate has a substantive impact on students' mental, emotional, and physical health. There is a positive correlation between school climate and students' self-concept, and climate influences students' motivation to engage in learning. Importantly, a positive school climate has been shown to be especially beneficial for vulnerable students, including minority, economically disadvantaged, gender diverse, and urban youth. Consequently, understanding how applied EN practices contribute to a positive classroom climate is of central importance for educators.

Educational Neuroscience Practices: Interpreting the Data

Data collection included semi-structured interviews with two administrators, three teachers, and 48 students as well as four classroom observations from three different fourth and fifth grade general education classrooms in a US Midwest city. The data analyses generated an integrative conceptual model that revealed how EN practices unfolded in these classrooms to facilitate the co-creation of a positive classroom climate and illuminate a potential vehicle for transmuting educational neuroscience knowledge into a new system of intersubjective meaning for the classroom climate and culture. Aligning with specific research questions, five distinct analytic categories were present in the findings. These categories threaded together to create a synthesized depiction of the social and affective dimensions of applied EN practices in the classroom.

Conceptualizing Applied Educational Neuroscience

Study participants emphasized the centrality of connected relationships as part of the pivot toward educational neuroscience principles. This perspective corresponds with scientific knowledge grounded in interpersonal neurobiology, a field that fuses biological and social sciences with modern attachment theory (Siegel, 2012). Interpersonal neurobiology provides insight into how the developing child relies on collaborative communication and relationships for regulatory functions that are critical to attention, cognition and memory (Cozolino, 2013; Siegel, 2012). It also draws from the deepening human development knowledge that spotlights the manner in which the brain develops through reciprocal exchanges between the individuals and their culturally-situated contexts, with relationships driving the developmental processes (Osher et al., 2018).

The integrative model also provides a compass for supporting students who present with exceptional life stressors. Espousing EN principles provides a lens for interpreting behavior based upon causes rooted in pain and dysregulation versus the predominant focus of behaviorism, which assumes a system of mandated and managed behaviors (Siegel & Payne-Bryson, 2014). Applied EN approaches include strategies for social-emotional scaffolding and opportunities for buffering relationships to provide co-regulation to address triggers and dysregulation. These practices align with a trauma-sensitive approach, giving attention to the neurobiological effects of chronic stress that affect brain architecture and diminish neural connections involved in the learning process (Blair & Raver, 2016; Center on the Developing Child, 2016; Osher et al., 2018).

Humanizing the Supportive Structures

Hopson and Lawson (2011) stress that "climate is a sociopsychological feature of organizational life in each school district " (p. 107). Consequently, a focus on classroom climate is inextricably associated with organizational features shaping classroom functioning and the relationships that comprise the classroom. The school's organizational culture is central to the teacher's ability to effectively incorporate EN practices into the classroom setting. The key features of the humanistic organizational culture present in the integrative model include flexible administrative structures, holistic perspectives, differentiated support, and autonomous decision-making. Contrasting a more traditional philosophy informing school administration, a humanistic paradigm supports students' and teachers' differentiated emotional, behavioral, and cognitive needs. Teachers are allowed autonomy to interpret the social-emotional needs of individual students, which oftentimes entails a departure from standardized approaches that typically characterize classroom functioning.

Aligning with a humanistic philosophy, the teacher's regulatory state becomes central to the EN application process. The teacher's presence is like the nucleus of a cell, whose symbiotic connection with the students generates the tenor and overall health of the classroom context. Corresponding with what Rodriguez (2012) terms *the teaching brain*, the model incorporates a view of learning as a social, biologic, and cognitive interaction between learner and teacher (Battro, 2010). As teachers are living organisms, sensitive to life stressors and contextual stimuli, synchrony with the classroom members is dynamic and rooted in the intricacies of implicit and explicit interactions occurring throughout the classroom ecology (Kent, 2013).

Infusing Educational Neuroscience Practices

Five themes characterizes EN practices: (1) Teaching Neuroanatomy, (2) Taming the Mind and Body, (3) Giving Voice to Emotions, (4) Letting Classroom Boundaries Breathe, and (5) Honoring the Whole Student. These EN practices converge to create in the students core skills to regulate thoughts, actions, and emotional responses in a way that enhances goal-oriented behavior conducive for learning. Collectively, these core skills comprise executive functioning and self-regulation (Blakemore & Bunge, 2012). Students develop social-emotional competencies in ways similar to academic skills, including instruction, modeling, scaffolding, and application (Jones & Bouffard, 2012). EN practices, incorporating a neurobiological perspective, merge with academic skill development to provide an integrative approach to educating students. This approach is based upon the scholarly assumption that teachers using EN practices are creating experiences that build neural structures in students' brains that support pro-social behaviors (Dubinsky, Roehrig, & Varma, 2013; Willis, 2009). The following breakdown provides specific insight into the application of each of the five identified practices.

(1) **Teaching Neuroantomy** involves intentionally teaching students about their neurobiology. Using knowledge of their neurobiology, students are taught a variety of self-regulation strategies to increase their attention in preparation for learning and to identify and apply what works best for their unique needs.

(2) **Taming the Mind and Body** includes a repertoire of multi-sensory strategies that teachers use to facilitate the students' self-regulation, calming them physically, socially, and emotionally. Teachers link these strategies with students' neuroanatomy and help them use the strategies to transition to instructional time. A common example of this strategy is mindfulness exercises.

(3) **Giving Voice to Emotions** entails attending to and validating emotions throughout the learning process and teaching students how to emotionally regulate. Teachers are routinely attuned to their own and students' emotional states. Teachers instruct students to recognize and reflect on their emotions and emphasize how this intentional engagement with emotions is integral to the learning process.

(4) **Letting Classroom Boundaries Breathe** is an approach that allows for boundaries that are adaptive to individual student needs in the classroom. Students are given the opportunity to apply a variety of self-regulation strategies at the times when they need to regulate. The physical and social structures of the learning environment are flexible and learner-centered. Adaptive learning allows for co-regulation and shared regulation strategies to occur at times needed to facilitate students' self and emotional regulation.

(5) **Honoring the Whole Student** is an EN practice where the human relationship is central to learning and unconditional regard toward students shapes social and academic interactions in the classroom. A holistic perspective is applied where students are treated as whole persons who are entwined with complex historical, family, and sociocultural contexts that shape their interpretive reality.

Co-Creating the Classroom Climate

The classroom climate is comprised of four main dimensions (1) safety, (2) relationships, (3) teaching and learning, and (4) structure of the learning environment (Gerlach & Hopson, 2013).

Safety: The neurobiology of learning and memory is intertwined with the primitive survival circuitry that attends to stress, arousal, and fear (Hohnen & Murphy, 2016). Stress activates emotional processing in the limbic regions, reducing activity in the frontal lobes, the part of the brain that facilitates thinking and developing higher order circuits (Willis, 2009). Providing emotional scaffolding, co-regulation, and nurturing relationships in the classroom calms students' limbic systems and contributes to their sense of safety.

Relationships: The teaching and learning enterprise is profoundly relational. The relationship dimension of school climate is comprised of the patterns of norms, goals, values, and interactions and the level of quality connection people feel toward one another and with themselves (Thapa et al., 2013). Drawing from attachment theory (Bowlby, 1969; 1988; Schore & Schore, 2008), learning, human development, and regulated behavior occur within a web of relationships (Cozolino, 2013), and developing children and adolescents depend on secure connections and relationships for co-regulation and support when they become dysregulated (Osher et al., 2018; Siegel, 2012).

Teaching and Learning: According to Gerlach and Hopson (2013), the norms, goals, and values of a school community inform the pedagogical methods that are used. Teachers intentionally integrate curricular content on students' neurobiology and self-regulation related to students' specific social, emotional, and physiological needs. This curricular approach is encouraged by administrators who embrace the philosophical shift associated with the way they conceptualize EN practices. The curriculum is not only academic but also addresses the social, emotional, and physiological aspects of development.

Structure of the Learning Environment: EN principles and practice focus on the individual needs of students, giving them choice and a degree of freedom to apply the practices at the times they identify the need to self-regulate. The physical space in the classroom is flexible and meets the variance of students' learning and self-regulation needs.

Building Students' Resiliency

Students respond to the EN practices with adaptive response that contribute to their ability to do the following (1) reflect on their emotions, (2) identify when they need to regulate, and (3) choose regulatory strategies that correspond with their unique neurobiological states. The interactions resulting from applied EN practices contribute to the process of co-creating a positive classroom climate that yield psychosocial outcomes related to reduced discipline referrals, readiness to learn, empowered decision-making, greater empathy, and enhanced social connectedness. The co-created climate emerging from the application of EN practices aligns with the body of research that suggests positive school climate is an integral component for effectively fostering protective factors and mitigating risk factors for students (Catalano, Berglund, Ryan, Lonczak, & Hawkins, 2002; Centers for Disease Control, 2009; Gerlach & Hopson, 2013; Greenberg, et al., 2003).

Conclusion

Youth development is embodied, socially and culturally-situated, and contextualized within a physical ecology (Bronfenbrenner, 1979; Osher et al., 2018). The reciprocal interactions between a youth's neurobiology, her/his/their physical and social environments, and these multi-system contexts have the ability to provide a "constructive web" through which complex executive functioning skills are constructed and positive adaptation to life stressors is promoted (Fischer & Bidell, 2006). The Integrative Model of Applied Educational Neuroscience is a visual depiction showing how schools that foster developmentally-rich social and organizational structures can mediate the effects of stress and trauma and foster all students' resilience by attending to the social and affective domains of educational neuroscience. The Integrative Model of Applied Educational Neuroscience is grounded in the data analyses from three elementary general education classrooms which are socially and culturally-situated. Consequently, there are limitations to be considered with interpreting and applying the model to other classrooms. Still, the model provides a seminal opening into a research-informed practice pathway and begins the translational journey of bridging education and neuroscience and expanding education theory to include a more complete depiction of human development.

REFERENCES

Battro, A. M. (2010). The teaching brain. *Mind, Brain, and Education, 4*(1), 28-33. doi: 10.1111/j.1751-228X.2009.01080.x

Blair, C., & Raver, C. (2016). Poverty, stress, and brain development: New directions for prevention and intervention. *Academic Pediatrics, 16*(3), 30-36.

Blakemore, S. J., & Bunge, S. A. (2012). At the nexus of neuroscience and education. *Developmental Cognitive Neuroscience, 2*(Supplement 1), S1-S5. doi:10.1016/j.dcn.2012.01.001

Bowlby, J. (1969). *Attachment and loss. Vol. 1: Attachment.* New York, NY: Basic Books.

Bowlby, J. (1988). *A secure base* (2nd ed.). New York, NY: Basic Books.
Bronfenbrenner, U. (1979). *The ecology of human development.* Cambridge, MA: Harvard University Press.

Cantor, P., Osher, D., Berg, J., Steyer, L., & Rose, T. (2018). Malleability, plasticity, and individuality: How children learn and develop in context. *Applied Developmental Science.* 1-31. doi:10.1080/10888691.2017.1398649

Catalano, R. F., Berglund, M. L., Ryan, J. A. M., Lonczak, H. S., & Hawkins, J. D. (2002). Positive youth development in the United States: Research findings on evaluations of positive youth development programs. *Prevention & Treatment, 5*(15), 1-11. doi: 10.1037//1522-3736.5.1.515a

Center on the Developing Child at Harvard University. (2016). *From best practices to breakthrough impacts: A science-based approach to building a more promising future for young children and families.* Retrieved from www.developingchild. harvard.edu

Centers for Disease Control and Prevention. (2009). *School connectedness: Strategies for increasing protective factors among youth.* Retrieved from http://www.cdc.gov/HealthyYouth/AdolescentHealth/pdf/connectedness.pdf

Cohen, J., McCabe, E. M., Michelli, N. M., & Pickeral, T. (2009). School climate: Research, policy, practice, and teacher education. *Teachers College Record, 111,* 180–213.

Cozolino, L. (2013). *The social neuroscience of education: Optimizing attachment & learning in the classroom.* New York, NY: W. W. Norton.

Dubinsky, J. M., Roehrig, G., & Varma, S. (2013). Infusing neuroscience into teacher professional development. *Educational Researcher, 42*(6), 317-329.

Durlak, J. A., Weissberg, R. P., Dymnicki, A. B., Taylor, R. D., & Schellinger, K. B. (2011). The impact of enhancing students' social and emotional learning: A meta-analysis of school-based universal interventions. *Child Development, 82,* 405-432. doi:10.1111/j.1467-8624.2010.01564.x
Fischer, K. W. & Bidell, T. R. (2006). Dynamic development of action, thought, and emotion. In R. M. Lerner (Ed.), *Handbook of child psychology: Vol. 1. Theoretical models of human development* (6th ed., pp. 3130399). New York, NY: Wiley.

Gerlach, B., & Hopson, L. M. (2013). Effective methods for improving school climate. In C. Franklin, M. B. Harris, & P. Allen-Meares (Eds.), *The school services sourcebook: A guide for school-based professionals.* (pp. 13-23). New York, NY: Oxford University Press.

Greenberg, M. T., Weissberg, R. P., O'Brien, M. U., Zins, J. E., Fredericks, L., Resnik, H., & Elias, M. J. (2003). Enhancing school-based prevention and youth development through coordinated social, emotional, and academic learning. *American Psychologist, 58*, 466-474. doi: 10.1016/j.tate.2007.06.005

Hohnen, B. & Murphy, T. (2016). The optimum context for learning: Drawing on neuroscience to inform best practice in the classroom. *Educational & Child Psychology, 33*(1), 75-90.

Hopson, L. & Lawson, H. (2011). Social workers' leadership for positive school climates via data-informed decision-making. *Children & Schools, 33*(2), 106-11.

Jones, S. M. & Bouffard, S. (2012). Social and emotional learning in schools: From programs to strategies. *Social Policy Report, 26*(4), 1-33.

Kent, A. (2013). Synchronization as a classroom dynamic: A practitioner's perspective. *Mind, Brain, and Education, 7*(1), 13-18.

Osher, D., Cantor, P., Berg, J., Steyer, L., & Rose, T. (2018). Drivers of human development: How relationships and context shape learning and development. *Applied Developmental Science*, 1-31. doi: 10.1080/10888691.2017.1398650

Perry, A. (1908). *The management of a city school*. New York, NY: MacMillan.

Rodriguez, V. (2012). The teaching brain and the end of the empty vessel. *Mind, Brain, and Education, 6*(4), 177-185.

Schore, J. R. & Schore, A. N. (2008). Modern attachment theory: The central role of affect regulation in development and treatment. *Clinical Social Work Journal, 36*, 9-20. doi: 10.1007/s10615-007-0111-7

Siegel, D. J. (2012). *The developing mind: How relationships and the brain interact to shape who we are* (2nd ed.). New York, NY: Guildford Press.

Siegel, D. J. & Payne-Bryson, T. (2014). *No-drama discipline: The whole-brain way to calm the chaos and nurture your child's developing mind*. New York, NY: Bantam Books.
Stafford-Brizard, K. B., Cantor, P., & Rose, T. (2017). Building the bridge between science and practice: Essential characteristics of a translational framework. *Mind, Brain, and Education, 11*(4), 155-165. doi:10.1111/mbe.12153

Thapa, A., Cohen, J., Guffey, S., & Higgins-D'Alessandro, A. (2013). A review of school climate research. *Review of Educational Research, 83*(3), 357-385.

Willis, J. (2009). How to teach students about the brain. *Educational Leadership, 67*(4). Retrieved from http://www.ascd.org/publications/educational-leadership/dec09/vol67/num04/How-to-Teach-Students-About-the-Brain.aspx

Snapshot

RTi/ MTSS Supports for Children and Adolescents with Significant Adversity and Trauma

Created by Students, Teachers, and Parents.

This template is created collaboratively to support all students who come to school with significant Adverse Childhood Experiences. These supports and resources are for our children and youth who carry in pain based behaviors, needing accommodations and possible modifications during the school day with regard to their environments and school work. These supports will address the critical needs of attachment and regulation. This document specifically lays out adjustments, alternative options and interventions that support the developing brain and stress response systems of all students. This document is shared with all those who interface with students each day in hopes of creating touchpoints throughout the school day so that consistency and emotional availability are key components.

This document of accommodations and supports are reviewed weekly or as often as needed in the initial phases of this support plan.

Why

If our social and emotional learning outcomes, programs and competencies are to be reflective of the current brain research addressing the severe life disruptions/ trauma that are occurring in our student populations across the country, we need to address specific areas of brain development with regard to acquiring these competencies. Brain development is complex, and even today, we know very little about how individual regions of the brain work collectively through neuronal connections and projections. We do know, however, that human brains are not complete at birth, but, by design, continue to develop throughout a person's life. This development is intimately impacted by experiences. Because our students spend over 13,000 hours in school during their K-12 span, educators have the opportunity and the obligation to address the social and emotional skills, competencies, through creating the modifications and adjustments needed for emotional, social and cognitive well-being.

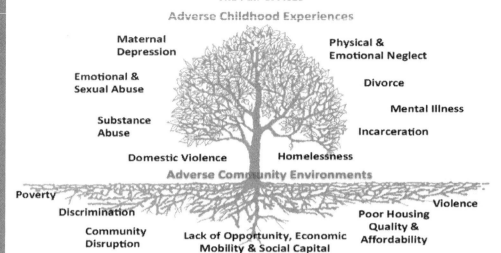

The Pair of ACEs

Adverse Childhood Experiences

Maternal
Depression

Physical &
Emotional Neglect

Emotional &
Sexual Abuse

Divorce

Mental Illness

Substance
Abuse

Incarceration

Domestic Violence

Homelessness

Adverse Community Environments

Poverty

Violence

Discrimination

Poor Housing
Quality &
Affordability

Community
Disruption

Lack of Opportunity, Economic
Mobility & Social Capital

Used with permission of Milken Institute School of Public Health
https://publichealth.gwu.edu/sites/default/files/downloads/Redstone-Center/Pair%20of%20ACEs%20Tree.png

A Comparison of Traditional Accommodations and Accommodations using the lens of Adverse Childhood Experiences (ACE's) as well as Adverse Community Environments

School Accommodations:

Traditional Accommodations	*Accommodations using ACE's Lens*
1. Seating at the front of the class	1. NEED A SEAT WHERE I FEEL SAFE & SECURE
2. Graph paper to line up math problems	2. TWO ADULTS IN THE BUILDING I CAN TRUST AND A PLACE TO WALK WHEN I BEGIN TO FEEL TRIGGERED
3. Multiplication table or use of calculator	3. A PERSONALIZED ROUTINE OF THREE INTERVENTIONS THAT I CAN IMPLEMENT WHEN I BEGIN TO FEEL ANXIOUS, ANGRY, OR NEGATIVE IN ANY WAY

4. Repetition and explanation of directions when needed

4. ACCESS TO SENSORY AREA OR TABLE IN OUR CLASSROOM FOR PATTERNED REPETITIVE ACTIVITIES USED TO CALM ME DOWN

5. Pre-printed classroom notes from the teachers

5. A PERSONALIZED SET OF MY ACCOMADATIONS GIVEN TO ALL WHO WORK WITH ME TO ALLOW ME TO DE-ESCALATE AND CALM DOWN AND BECOME READY TO LEARN.

6. Occupational therapy every Wednesday

6. MEETING WITH MY ADVERSITY TEAM EACH WEEK

7. Math one on one tutoring twice a week during study hall

7. ONE ON ONE SCHEDULED TIME WITH MY PRE-ARRANGED MENTOR WHOM I MEET WITH REGULARILY AS A CHECK IN AND WHO I CAN GO SEE TO HELP ME CO-REGULATE AS NEEDED

Test Accommodations:

Traditional Accommodations

Accommodations using ACE's Lens

1. Extended time on tests and quizzes

1. EXTENDED TIME TO REGULATE IF I NEED THIS AND ACADEMIC MODIFICATIONS OF MY ASSIGNMENTS WHEN I AM DYSREGUATED

2. Quiet testing room with small group setting

2. QUIET AREA FOR ME TO USE WHEN I NEED TO REGULATE MY NERVOUS SYSTEM

My Goals:

Traditional:

ACE's Lens Goals:

Improve my mental math skills

Get better at asking for help when needed

Join a school club or activity

TO LEARN TO REGULATE WITH AN ADULT BEFORE I REACH THE TIPPING POINT
LESSEN THE NUMBER OF TIMES I NEED TO USE THE ADVERSITY TEAM AND THE AMYGDALA RESET AREA
CREATE A JOURNAL OF MY UPS AND DOWNS TO TRACK MY PROGRESS

I. *Strengths to Help Me with My Goals*

I love to learn. I'm seen as a leader and good friend by others.
I have a great imagination
I know how I feel and learn best!
I work quickly
I notice everything
I am good at sensing others and all nonverbal communication

II. *Interests/ Areas of Expertise*

III. *Triggers*

What are the experiences, events, sights, sounds, smells, relationships, and people who can unexpectedly trigger you producing anxiety or negative emotion?

IV. *Members of this student's adversity team*

V. Key Adult Mentor assigned to this student:

RESEARCH

Bruce Perry and Maia Szalavitz, The Boy Who Was Raised As a Dog (New York: Basic Books, 2006), 92.

Bessel van der Kolk, The Body Keeps the Score (New York: Penguin Books, 2014), 81.

Peter Levine and Maggie Kline, Trauma Through a Child's Eyes (California: North Atlantic Books, 2007), 27.

Center on the Developing Child, Harvard University, "InBrief: The Impact of Early Adversity on Children's Development," last accessed August 26, 2018, https://developingchild.harvard.edu/resources/inbrief-the-impact-of-early-adversity-on-childrens-development/.

Center on the Developing Child, Harvard University, "InBrief."

Perry and Szalavitz, The Boy, 232-233.

Raymond Wlodkowski, Motivational Opportunities for Successful Teaching [Leader's Guide], (Phoenix, AZ: Universal Dimensions, 1983).

Nicholas J. Long, Frank A. Fecser, and Mary M. Wood, Life Space Crisis Intervention, Talking with Students in Conflict, (Austin: PRO-ED, Inc., 2001), 87-94.

Lori Desautels, "Navigating Confrontations with Parents," Edutopia, May 21, 2018,

https://www.edutopia.org/article/navigating-confrontations-parents.

Perry and Szalavitz, The Boy, 80.

Christine R. Ludy-Dobson and Bruce D. Perry, "The Role of Healthy Relational

Interactions in Buffering the Impact of Childhood Trauma," Working with Children to Heal Interpersonal Trauma: The Power of Play, ed. Eliana Gil (New York, NY: The Guilford Press, 2010), 26-43.

Made in the USA
Lexington, KY
11 November 2019

56860125R00187